BRITISH RAILWAYS Locomotives
1955

BRITISH RAILWAYS Locomotives

1955

Chris Banks

Oxford Publishing Co

Half title page: Originally built by Johnson for the Midland Railway in December 1899 as No 2431, No 40513 was rebuilt by Fowler with a new G7 boiler in December 1912. This view was recorded on Derby shed on 15 April 1955 after a works visit, the locomotive looking resplendent repainted and lined out. Withdrawal came during the week ended 17 October 1959 from Nottingham Midland shed, and after storage at Derby Works until September 1961 it was sold for scrap. *Initial Photographics/R. J. Buckley*

Title page: BP&GVR power in the shape of Hudswell Clarke-built 0-6-0T No 2198, dating back to 1919. Llanelly shed in 1953 is the venue. No 2198 outlasted the other members of the class, which had all gone by the end of 1956, and was withdrawn in March 1959. *R. H. G. Simpson*

This page: The ubiquitous Stanier 'Black Five' with a total of 842 produced was certain to have variations in the class members. Willesden shed in May 1955 has an example in No 44686. Built at Horwich and entering traffic during the week ended 7 April 1951, it was fitted with a double-chimney, Caprotti valve gear, Skefko roller bearings and high running plate and went new to Manchester Longsight shed with the only other one so treated, No 44687, joining it during the week ended 26 May 1951. The first transfer was to Llandudno Junction in May 1960, and then on to Southport in October 1963. Withdrawal came during the week ended 16 October 1965. *R. H. G. Simpson*

Contents page: A fine study of 'Modified Hall' No 6977 *Grundisburgh Hall* and an unidentified 'Castle' hammering away on Hemerdon Bank in July 1955 bound for Bristol. No 6977 lasted until December 1963, its last allocation being Westbury, having gone new to Old Oak Common in November 1947. *G. W. Sharpe*

Front cover, left: Ex-works Stanier 2-8-0 No 48064 cautiously descends the Lickey incline with a freight with wagon brakes pinned down in June 1955. *Author's Collection*

Front cover, top right: Beattie Well Tank No 30586 at Wadebridge station May 1955. *Author's Collection*

Front cover, centre right: Drummond '0P' 0-4-4T No 55053, recently outshopped from St Rollox Works, at Dornoch in July 1955. *Author's Collection*

Front cover, bottom right: D20/2 No 62360 at Northallerton on Sunday 4 September 1955 on the SLS 'Northern Dales' railtour. *Author's Collection*

Back cover, top: 'E1' class 4-4-0 No 31497 at Stewarts Lane shed in November 1955. *Author's collection*

Back cover, centre: Standard 5MT 4-6-0 No 73007 at Gleneagles on the 'Granite City' express in July 1955. *Author's Collection*

Back cover, bottom: 'Castle' class 4-6-0 No 7017 *G.J. Churchward* at Bournville on Saturday 16 April 1955 coming off the Ian Allan *Trains Illustrated* 'Lickey Limited' excursion, to be replaced by Stanier 4-6-0 No 44842. *Author's Collection*

First published 2001

ISBN 0 86093 560 4

Published by Oxford Publishing Co

an imprint of Ian Allan Publishing Ltd, Hersham, Surrey KT12 4RG.
Printed by Ian Allan Printing Ltd, Hersham, Surrey KT12 4RG.

Code: 0111/A2

Contents

Above: 'B4' class 0-4-0T No 30096 takes time out from shunting duties at Eastleigh shed in 1955. An Adams design for dock shunting, this example was built in November 1893 and was the last of the class to be withdrawn on 6 October 1963, still at Eastleigh. Sold to a local firm, Corralls at Southampton, she survived until July 1968 and was then secured for preservation, being now at the Bluebell Railway. *G. W. Sharpe*

Below: Eastleigh Works in August 1955 shows an interesting view of 'Q' class 0-6-0 No 30535 without its tender. This was a Maunsell design dating from 1938, this engine being put to traffic in September and lasting until 25 April 1965. The last allocation was at Salisbury. *R. H. G. Simpson*

Introduction

The year 1955 was unique in the history of British Railways, dominated by the Modernisation Plan announced by the British Transport Commission's Chairman Sir Brian Robertson on Tuesday 25 January. The aim was to develop the railways as the nation's bulk transporter of goods and passengers, and to revolutionise and improve the service. The total cost was estimated at £1,240 million, with the prospect of improving annual turnover by £85 million. It was also the first year that examples of every class of Standard steam locomotive were operating alongside numerous older types dating, in some instances, to the 19th century. This was a time never to be repeated for the locomotive enthusiast. Some types did disappear such as the ex-Rhymney Railway 'A' and 'P' class 0-6-2Ts; the ex-Taff Vale Railway '04' class; the last Alexandra Docks Railway and Cardiff Railway 0-6-0PTs; the '2181' 0-6-0PTs; the '4400' 2-6-2Ts; Southern 'E' and 'L12' 4-4-0s; 'D3' and 'R' class 0-4-4Ts; Webb 2-4-2Ts; LNWR 'G1' 0-8-0s; Webb 18in Goods 0-6-0s; LNER 'D10' 4-4-0s; 'J5' 0-6-0s; 'J66' 0-6-0Ts; the 'J70' Tram Engines; 'L3' 2-6-4Ts, 'N9' 0-6-2Ts and the 'U1' Beyer-Garratt. Conversely, the last 'new' type of steam locomotive appeared in the shape of the Crosti-boilered 2-10-0, as well as 136 new diesel shunters and the prototype *Deltic*.

Derby Carriage Works' first diesel multiple-units had appeared in 1954 and were working from Bradford Hammerton Street Depot. Further sets were introduced during 1955 and took over services radiating from Carlisle, Norwich, Lincoln, Newcastle and Bury, with trial runs also from Birmingham. As well as Derby, Metropolitan Cammell produced the stock. The St Albans to Watford line also had a diesel service provided by BUT lightweight four-wheel units.

The year was notable for many other events, and a review in chronological order must start with a return to the Modernisation document. Looking at the motive power situation, it was proposed that the building of new steam locomotives would cease, although no firm date was fixed. The report stated that the steam locomotive had a useful life in service of some 40 years and careful planning would be required to ensure that, as the existing stock was gradually replaced by diesel or electric power, it could be used to best advantage. There would be careful selection of types for the condemnation programme to eliminate as quickly as possible the less efficient types and small classes for which it would not be economical to maintain spares. With regard to steam motive power depots, it was recognised that many needed to be rebuilt or substantially modernised. However, in the light of the phasing out of steam, careful consideration into how this would be achieved would be given and it was estimated that £10 million should be set aside to cover the cost.

The future choice of motive power would be in the form of electric and diesel units, with the report stressing the advantage of both but leaning towards diesel. This offered the advantage of not having to spend large amounts on civil engineering for electrification work. Suburban electrification was to be extended, with further lines from London and Glasgow being highlighted. The intention to electrify two major trunk routes — King's Cross to York and Euston to Birmingham, Crewe, Liverpool and Manchester — was also stated. It was also accepted that where traffic was within their capacity, a considerable improvement in net revenue could be secured by the introduction of diesel multiple-units. Three principal types of service would be targeted: city-to-city express services, secondary and cross-country routes, and branch lines. The total number of vehicles needed was estimated at 4,600 which included the 300 already in use or on order. The cost of the new units was expected to be £230 million. The first electrification scheme was completed on 3 January with the energisation of the short section from Sheffield Victoria to Rotherwood sidings of the Manchester to Sheffield Woodhead route.

1955 Chronology

The year started on a sombre note with a rail crash at Sutton Coldfield on Sunday 23 January which killed 17 people, including three enginemen.

The 12.15pm York to Bristol express, headed by Class 5MT 4-6-0 No 45274 of Bristol Barrow Road shed, had been diverted via Lichfield and Aston because of engineering work at Tamworth. The conductor driver, who was actually driving as the rostered driver was travelling in the train (which was a breach of the rules), ran round the sharp curve into the station at 60mph instead of the 30mph allowed. The engine and first five carriages piled up in the station. No 45274 was rerailed two days later and towed to Aston shed where a new bogie was fitted before leaving for Crewe Works.

During January ex-LMS Fowler 2-6-4Ts were working into King's Cross on outer suburban services. No 42328 had been transferred from Neasden to Hitchin to join sister engine No 42374 which had gone there earlier. A regular working was the 8.54am Hatfield into the capital. Also on the Eastern Region, diesel No 10800 was on loan to Plaistow in January working test trains from Fenchurch Street to Shoeburyness.

Unusual visitors to Bristol Bath Road shed on Saturday 8 January were three Bulleid Pacifics – Nos 34020, 34051 and 34093 – which had worked in on specials for the Bristol Rovers-Portsmouth FA cup-tie.

On the evening of Saturday 22 January the 6.30pm Weymouth to Waterloo headed by 'H15' class 4-6-0 No 30485 collided at Bournemouth station with a light engine, 'N15' class 4-6-0 No 30783 *Sir Gillemere*, which had reversed out of the station against adverse signals. The 'H15' was partially overturned and one of its cylinders sheared off, being thrown a considerable distance. As a result, the engine was subsequently withdrawn on 9 April.

Bad weather at the end of January had a serious effect on the operating of diesel trains in the Leeds/Bradford area, frosty conditions causing radiators and piping to burst, and the sanding gear not working effectively. Steam had to come to the rescue, working certain services and having to push at least two units into Bradford station. Atrocious weather conditions also affected the north of Scotland with snowdrifts as high as 25ft on the Helmsdale to Wick and Thurso line. It was no better in February when on the 16th and 17th the Highland line was closed at Slochd, and working between Inverness and Perth and again to Wick was impossible. Northeast England also got its fair share of weather problems, for on 21 February the Darlington to Penrith line was submerged in snow and a freight train powered by 2MT 2-6-0 No 78018, the Darlington snowploughs with 'J21' No 65061 and 'J25' No 65696, and two more engines on banking duty, 2-6-2T No 82027 and 2-6-0 No 77004, were all stranded. Kirkby Stephen shed sent out three 2MT 2-6-0s between its two largest snowploughs, but even then double-track working was not restored until the second week in March.

On two Sundays in March trials were carried out on the Lickey incline with unbanked trains of a considerable heavier weight than previously allowed up the notorious 1 in 37 incline. On 6 March Stanier 4-6-0 No 44776 from Saltley shed made three ascents with a seven-coach load, including a dynamometer car. One of the runs required three stops and restarts, which were successfully achieved. The following weekend, Nottingham's 'Jubilee' No 45554 *Ontario* had a try with one coach extra, but after four vain attempts at a restart had to back down to Bromsgrove. Another attempt was tried and proved successful. During the tests all trailing and trap points were locked, guards were stationed at the front, rear and centre of the trains to assist in hand-braking if necessary, and 0-10-0 No 58100 was available in the loop beyond Bromsgrove station for assistance.

Heavy snow once again caused difficulties in Scotland blocking the West Coast main line between Ecclefechan and Lockerbie on Monday 21 March; seven northbound night expresses were diverted over the Waverley route, bringing the rare sight of LMR Pacifics and 'Royal Scots' to the line, including Nos 46123 (8A), 46145 (20A), 46203 (5A), 46221 (66A) and 46230 (66A).

7

On Monday 4 April soon after 11pm, Salisbury-allocated 'Battle of Britain' 4-6-2 No 34050 *Royal Observer Corps* hauling the 7.45pm goods from Yeovil Junction collided with the Exmouth Junction yard shunter, 'Z' class 0-8-0T No 30954. Both engines sustained considerable damage to their cylinders and valve gear and were not rerailed until late the following day.

On Tuesday 12 April Standard 2-6-4T No 80011 on the 1.5pm from Redhill to Tonbridge collided with goods wagons just outside Redhill station. Luckily, there were no serious casualties, despite considerable damage being caused to the coaches.

An unusual excursion ran on Saturday 16 April for Ian Allan *Trains Illustrated* readers, the 'Lickey Limited'. It brought 'Castle' class 4-6-0 No 7017 *G. J. Churchward* to the Lickey incline on a triangular Paddington-Bristol-Birmingham-Paddington itinerary. At Bournville the 'Castle' was replaced by 5MT 4-6-0 No 44842, No 7017 returning to Worcester light engine. No 44842 ran to Bordesley Junction via Birmingham New Street because of clearance problems barring the 'Castle' class from the station. At Bordesley another 'Castle', No 7007 *Great Western* returned the train to London. This was almost certainly a 'first' for a 'Castle' up the Lickey and at Bournville. The cost of the trip was 30s (£1.50) for adults and 18s (90p) for juveniles, with light lunch and full dinner for 12s 6d (62p).

On Tuesday 19 April Stanier Pacific No 46237 *City of Bristol* was transferred from Camden to the Western Region for a series of trials that lasted four weeks. The following day it was at Old Oak Common for inspection and on 21 and 22 April worked the 11.15am 'Merchant Venturer' to Bristol. The aim of the trials was to compare another type of Class 8 locomotive against the GWR 'Kings' which were going through a phase of inconsistent and poor performance. No 46237 was tried on all three main routes and even powered the 'Cornish Riviera'. However, nothing conclusive came from the trials, although the locomotive did put up one magnificent performance, lifting 420 tons over Whiteball Summit at over 46mph. The only major change to the 'Kings' after these tests was to equip them with double-chimneys.

At about 8.40am on Wednesday 20 April on the line between Luton and Leighton Buzzard, the 8.30am push-pull train from Luton, headed by Bletchley-based Ivatt 2-6-2T No 41222 running bunker-first, was travelling between Luton Bute Street and Dunstable Town stations when a fierce blow-back took place soon after the engine had passed the line's summit. Both enginemen were forced off the footplate, the fireman being fatally injured. The train of two coaches and a fish van ran on down the gradient for nearly two miles through Dunstable Town and North stations, where it should have stopped, until finally being brought under control and stopped by the guard.

May brought the first rumblings of discontent between the railway management and ASLEF (the footplatemen's union) with a dispute over wage differentials. A wage claim for a maximum driver's weekly wage of 200s 6d (£10.02) and a fireman's of 166s 6d (£8.32) had been rejected. A call for strike action on 1 May was averted at the 11th hour after lengthy discussions, with the promise of further talks.

What was believed to be the first passenger train to be hauled by a Standard '9F' 2-10-0 occurred on Saturday 7 May when No 92031 arrived at Hitchin shortly before 5pm with the 14-coach 11.50am Harrogate and Hull express, due into King's Cross at 4.50pm. It had taken over from 'A1' class 4-6-2 No 60154 *Bon Accord* which had expired at Biggleswade. The 2-10-0 was banned from working into King's Cross, so Hitchin 'B1' 4-6-0 No 61093 had to take the train on.

During April two Class Q6 0-8-0s had been allocated to Kirkby Stephen shed for heavy mineral traffic workings, the first to be based there for over 30 years. However, on Friday 20 May disaster struck as they hauled the return 12.00 noon Kirkby to Tebay minerals running double-headed and tender-first, when the leading engine, No 63355, broke part of a tender spring and left the rails. It plunged down a 20ft embankment at Smardale, dragging its companion No 63373 off the track, although it fortunately remained on the trackbed. Luckily both crews escaped with bruises. After

the incident both locomotives were transferred to Middlesbrough, never to return again.

Saturday 28 May was the date of a serious derailment at Wormit, Fife. The 6.35pm return Sunday School Special from Tayport to Dundee, hauled by Perth-allocated Class 5 4-6-0 No 45458 running tender-first, entered Wormit station where the tender derailed, causing the engine to overturn and severely damage the first four coaches. The accident was caused by excessive speed, the engine taking the sharply curved approach to the Tay Bridge at 45mph instead of the maximum 10mph. Evidence at the enquiry showed the driver to have been drinking between the outward and homebound run, and that an unauthorised adult and child had been on the footplate, both of whom as well as the fireman were killed.

At midnight on 28 May strike action was taken by ASLEF union members following a breakdown in talks with the British Transport Commission concerning the earlier problems with a differential wage structure. ASLEF claimed that its members had a higher degree of responsibility than other grades of railway employees and this should be reflected in the pay scales. The National Union of Railwaymen was not involved and continued to work. The effects were varied throughout the country, with some services still operating to a much reduced timetable, but everywhere there were difficulties in travelling. On the Southern and Scottish Regions the effects were particularly noticeable, with only 4% of Southern motormen reporting for duty, and very few other services running. In Scotland all the large sheds in the Glasgow area were virtually closed and the main termini almost completely deserted. The West Highland line was completely closed, except for the Fort William to Mallaig section which managed to put on two daily trains. The strike was called off at 6pm on 14 June when parties to the dispute agreed to a referee appointed by the Minister of Labour, and Lord Justice Morris was selected. He later announced rises varying from 1s to 3s per week for certain grades of drivers, but no increases for firemen. The cost to British Railways in lost revenue for the 17-day strike was at least £10 million.

July saw the Crosti-boilered Standard 2-10-0s enter service, the first arriving at Wellingborough on the 5th followed by others over the next few days. On receipt they were immediately put to work on coal trains to Cricklewood. As a consequence of the planned introduction of the new locomotives, the first two Beyer-Garratts were withdrawn on 11 June (No 47985) and on 28 May (No 47990), and a further two, Nos 47970 and 47975, on 2 July.

August was marred by a derailment at Barby, south of Rugby, on the Great Central main line. On Sunday 7 August the 10.35am Manchester to Marylebone was running more an hour late and had been reversed on to the down line at Rugby due to engineering work. It was powered by 'V2' 2-6-2 No 60828, which Neasden had on loan from Kings Cross, and driven by Driver C. Simpson, a man of experience and excellent record. For reasons never really explained, he accelerated up to a speed in excess of 50mph and hit the crossing that was to return the train to its proper road. The engine and a number of coaches left the track and plunged down an embankment, the driver being the only fatality.

In early September two of the USA Southern Region dock tanks, Nos 30061 and 30066, were transferred to the LMR for trials on shunting duties. Diesels were expected to replace steam in Southampton Docks and the LMR was invited to try out the tank engines as possible replacements for its own elderly dock shunting engines. No 30061 was stationed at Kentish Town and No 30066 at Liverpool Bank Hall. They returned to the Southern in October, presumably being not quite what the LMR wanted.

On Thursday 1 September 'W1' class 4-6-4 No 60700, working its usual turn of the 3.50pm King's Cross to Doncaster, became derailed at Westwood Junction, Peterborough, and overturned. Speed was only 20mph so casualties were not serious. The cause was a broken right-hand bogie frame, and as a result other Pacifics had their bogie frames whitewashed to see if any cracks could be detected.

The Crosti-boiler 2-10-0s strayed away from the Midland main line on occasions and on Saturday 24 September No 92029 was recorded at Coventry after working in on the 1.56am freight from Crewe. After

unsuccessful attempts to turn it on the 60ft turntable, it worked tender-first to Nuneaton for use of the turntable there. It was borrowed by Nuneaton to work the 6.6pm Saturdays-only Hawkesbury Lane to Banbury goods, returning in the early hours of Sunday morning. It was still in the district the following week, being noted under repair at Nuneaton shed on Sunday 2 October. The unusual appearance of the engine caused much local comment, including a press report and photograph in the local newspaper! Earlier in the month, on the 7th, No 92028 ran light to Brighton from Wellingborough for inspection by Brighton Works staff and officials. It returned home on the 9th and turned on the Preston Park-Hove triangle as it was not permitted to enter Brighton shed. Commencing on 11 October, another Crosti, No 92023, had a period away from coal trains when it began a series of test runs between Carlisle Durran Hill and Hurlford which lasted for three weeks.

On Sunday 20 November a 10-coach excursion from Treherbert to Paddington derailed at Milton, between Steventon and Didcot. A diversion from the main line on to the goods loop was taken at speed and the locomotive, 'Britannia' 4-6-2 No 70026 *Polar Star*, based at Cardiff Canton, rolled down a 20ft embankment, taking the first four coaches with it. Ten passengers were killed and 96 taken to hospital. This was the first fatal accident on the Western since 1942. The driver admitted overlooking the special notice advising of the diversion and failing to observe two signals at the approach to the loop. A contributory factor was that the locomotive, with left-hand drive, was a type with which the driver was unfamiliar.

At the end of November the British Transport Commission announced that orders worth £10 million had been placed for 141 complete main line diesel locomotives and for 30 power units to be used in diesel locomotives, all to be built in BR workshops. This was for pilot scheme engines, and English Electric, Birmingham C&W, Brush Traction, Metropolitan-Vickers and North British Loco Co were the companies named, plus Sulzer and BTH for the power units.

On 29 November the prototype English Electric *Deltic* diesel made its first visit to London, working the 8.30pm Liverpool Edge Hill to Camden freight. It made its first appearance on an express passenger working on Tuesday 13 December on the 10.10am 'Merseyside Express' from Liverpool Lime Street to Euston, returning on 'The Shamrock', the 4.55pm departure, the same day.

Three rear-end collisions – at Hellifield, Luton and Woking – occurred in less than two days later in December. On Thursday 22nd at 4.45am the 9.15pm express from St Pancras to Glasgow, hauled by 'Royal Scot' 4-6-0 No 46109 *Royal Engineer*, ran into the rear of the 9.5pm express from St Pancras to Edinburgh, which was standing in Hellifield station. The estimated speed of No 46109 was around 25mph and only one person was injured, even though the rearmost van of the Edinburgh train was lifted into the air and the second coach from the rear was lifted off the rails and wedged against the station roof. The cause was later established as an infringement of signalling rules. On the same day at Luton Midland Road station, at 7.57pm, the 7.10pm express from St Pancras to Derby, headed by a Class 5MT 4-6-0, ran into the back of the 6.45pm St Pancras to Leicester as it was stationary, derailing three of its coaches, killing one passenger and injuring 24. This was a result of the driver missing the Luton distant signal which was warning of the home signal at danger, and passing this signal too late to stop a collision.

On 23 December the driver of Southern 'N15X' class 4-6-0 No 32327 *Trevithick*, on the 7.54pm Waterloo to Basingstoke, misread the Maybury intermediate signals between West Byfleet and Woking and collided at low speed with the 7.50pm Waterloo to Portsmouth electric at 8.29pm. Nine passengers were taken to hospital, none seriously hurt.

So 1955 was a year of difficulties and tragedy, yet with an exciting look to the future and a strategy that was to have far-reaching effects on Britain's railways for many years to come.

Following is the complete listing of locomotives and their allocations in service on 1 January 1955, with named locomotives denoted by an asterisk against the number. The majority of photographs are previously unpublished and cover, in the main, the 1954 to 1956 period.

Chris Banks
April 2001

A real old lady, 'O1' class 0-6-0 No 31425 is seen on shunting duties at Dover on Thursday 4 August 1955. This was a Stirling design for the SE&CR and originally 122 were built between 1878 and 1899 with domeless boilers and rounded cabs. Later, 58 were rebuilt with domed boilers and new cabs. This example had been built in August 1897 and rebuilt in May 1914. Withdrawal came on 29 August 1959 while still based at Dover. *L. Hanson*

Locomotive Depots and Sub Sheds at 1 January 1955

London Midland Region

1A	**London Willesden**	9F	Heaton Mersey	**20A**	**Leeds Holbeck**
1B	London Camden	9G	Northwich	20B	Leeds Stourton
1C	Watford			20C	Royston
1D	London Devons Road	**10A**	**Wigan Springs Branch**	20D	Normanton
1E	Bletchley	10B	Preston	20E	Bradford Manningham
	Leighton Buzzard	10C	Manchester Patricroft		Ilkley
	Newport Pagnell	10E	Sutton Oak, St Helens	20F	Skipton
					Keighley
2A	**Rugby**	**11A**	**Carnforth**	20G	Hellifield
	Market Harborough	11B	Barrow		
	Seaton		Coniston	**21A**	**Birmingham Saltley**
2B	Nuneaton	11C	Oxenholme		Stratford-on-Avon
2C	Warwick Milverton	11D	Tebay	21B	Birmingham Bournville
2D	Coventry	11E	Lancaster Green Ayre		Redditch
2E	Northampton			21C	Bromsgrove
		12A	**Carlisle Upperby**		
3A	**Bescot**	12C	Penrith	**22A**	**Bristol Barrow Road**
3B	Wolverhampton Bushbury	12D	Workington	22B	Gloucester Barnwood
3C	Walsall				Tewkesbury
3D	Birmingham Aston	**14A**	**London Cricklewood**		Dursley
3E	Birmingham Monument Lane	14B	London Kentish Town		
		14C	St Albans	**24A**	**Accrington**
5A	**Crewe North**			24B	Rose Grove
	Whitchurch	**15A**	**Wellingborough**	24C	Lostock Hall
5B	Crewe South	15B	Kettering	24D	Lower Darwen
5C	Stafford	15C	Leicester Midland	24E	Blackpool Central
5D	Stoke-on-Trent	15D	Bedford		Blackpool North
5E	Alsager			24F	Fleetwood
5F	Uttoxeter	**16A**	**Nottingham Midland**		
			Southwell	**25A**	**Wakefield**
6A	**Chester LMS**	16C	Kirkby-in-Ashfield	25B	Huddersfield
6B	Mold Junction	16D	Mansfield	25C	Goole
6C	Birkenhead			25D	Mirfield
6D	Chester Northgate	**17A**	**Derby**	25E	Sowerby Bridge
6E	Wrexham Rhosddu	17B	Burton-on-Trent	25F	Bradford Low Moor
6F	Bidston		Horninglow	25G	Leeds Farnley Junction
6G	Llandudno Junction		Overseal		
6H	Bangor	17C	Coalville	**26A**	**Manchester Newton Heath**
6J	Holyhead	17D	Rowsley	26B	Manchester Agecroft
6K	Rhyl		Cromford	26C	Bolton
	Denbigh		Middleton	26D	Bury
			Sheep Pasture	26F	Lees, Oldham
8A	**Liverpool Edge Hill**			26G	Manchester Belle Vue
8B	Warrington Dallam	**18A**	**Toton**		
	Warrington Arpley	18B	Westhouses	**27A**	**Liverpool Bank Hall**
8C	Liverpool Speke Junction	18C	Hasland	27B	Liverpool Aintree
8D	Widnes		Clay Cross	27C	Southport
8E	Liverpool Brunswick	18D	Staveley Barrow Hill	27D	Wigan L&Y
			Sheepbridge	27E	Liverpool Walton-on-the-Hill
9A	**Manchester Longsight**				
9B	Stockport Edgeley	**19A**	**Sheffield Grimesthorpe**	CW	Crewe Works
9C	Macclesfield	19B	Sheffield Millhouses	HW	Horwich Works
9D	Buxton	19C	Canklow		
9E	Manchester Trafford Park				

Eastern Region

30A	**London Stratford**		Wells-on-Sea	**36A**	**Doncaster**	
	Brentwood		Dereham	36B	Mexborough	
	Chelmsford		Swaffham		Wath	
	Enfield Town		Wymondham	36C	Frodingham	
	Epping	**32B**	Ipswich	36D	Barnsley	
	Palace Gates		Felixstowe Beach	36E	Retford GC & GN	
	Ware		Aldeburgh		Newark	
	Wood Street		Stowmarket			
30B	Hertford East	**32C**	Lowestoft	**37A**	**Ardsley**	
	Buntingford	**32D**	Yarmouth South Town	37B	Leeds Copley Hill	
30C	Bishops Stortford	**32E**	Yarmouth Vauxhall	37C	Bradford Hammerton Street	
30D	Southend Victoria	**32F**	Yarmouth Beach			
	Southminster	**32G**	Melton Constable	**38A**	**Nottingham Colwick**	
30E	Colchester		Norwich City		Derby Friargate	
	Clacton		Cromer Beach	38B	Annesley	
	Walton-on Naze			38C	Leicester Central	
	Kelvedon	**33A**	**London Plaistow**		Leicester GN	
	Maldon		Upminster	38D	Staveley Great Central	
	Braintree	**33B**	Tilbury	38E	Woodford Halse	
30F	Parkeston	**33C**	Shoeburyness			
				39A	**Manchester Gorton**	
31A	**Cambridge**	**34A**	**London Kings Cross**		Dinting	
	Ely	**34B**	London Hornsey		Hayfield	
	Huntingdon East	**34C**	Hatfield		Macclesfield	
	Saffron Walden	**34D**	Hitchin		Reddish	
31B	March	**34E**	London Neasden	**39B**	Sheffield Darnall	
	Wisbech		Aylesbury			
31C	Kings Lynn		Chesham	**40A**	**Lincoln**	
	Hunstanton				Lincoln St Marks	
31D	South Lynn	**35A**	**Peterborough New England**	40B	Immingham	
31E	Bury St Edmunds		Spalding	40C	Louth	
	Sudbury		Bourne	40D	Tuxford	
			Stamford	40E	Langwith Junction	
32A	**Norwich**	**35B**	Grantham	40F	Boston	
	Cromer	**35C**	Peterborough Spital Bridge			

North Eastern Region

50A	**York**	**51F**	West Auckland	**52E**	Percy Main	
50B	Leeds Neville Hill		Wearhead	**52F**	North Blyth	
	Ilkley	**51G**	Haverton Hill		South Blyth	
50C	Selby	**51H**	Kirkby Stephen			
50D	Starbeck	**51J**	Northallerton	**53A**	**Hull Dairycoates**	
50E	Scarborough		Leyburn	**53B**	Hull Botanic Gardens	
50F	Malton	**51K**	Saltburn	**53C**	Hull Springhead	
	Pickering				Hull Alexandra Dock	
50G	Whitby	**52A**	**Gateshead**	**53D**	Bridlington	
			Bowes Bridge			
51A	**Darlington**	**52B**	Heaton	**54A**	**Sunderland**	
	Middleton-in-Teesdale	**52C**	Blaydon		Durham	
51B	Newport		Hexham	**54B**	Tyne Dock	
51C	West Hartlepool		Alston		Pelton Level	
51D	Middlesbrough		Reedsmouth	**54C**	Borough Gardens	
	Guisborough	**52D**	Tweedmouth	**54D**	Consett	
51E	Stockton		Alnmouth			

Scottish Region

60A	**Inverness**		Alloa	**65A**	**Glasgow Eastfield**
	Dingwall			65B	Glasgow St Rollox
	Fortrose	**63A**	**Perth**	65C	Glasgow Parkhead
	Kyle of Lochalsh		Aberfeldy	65D	Glasgow Dawsholm
60B	Aviemore		Blair Atholl		Dumbarton
	Boat of Garten		Crieff	65E	Glasgow Kipps
60C	Helmsdale	**63B**	Stirling	65F	Grangemouth
	Dornoch		Stirling Shore Road	65G	Glasgow Yoker
	Tain		Killin	65H	Helensburgh
60D	Wick	**63C**	Forfar		Arrochar
	Thurso		Brechin	65I	Balloch
60E	Forres	**63D**	Fort William		
			Mallaig	**66A**	**Glasgow Polmadie**
61A	**Aberdeen Kittybrewster**	**63E**	Oban	66B	Motherwell
	Ballater		Ballachulish	66C	Hamilton
	Fraserburgh			66D	Greenock Ladyburn
	Peterhead	**64A**	**Edinburgh St Margarets**		Greenock Princes Pier
61B	Aberdeen Ferryhill		Dunbar		
61C	Keith Junction		Galashiels	**67A**	**Glasgow Corkerhill**
	Banff		Longniddry	67B	Hurlford
	Elgin		North Berwick		Beith
			Peebles		Muirkirk
62A	**Thornton Junction**		Seafield	67C	Ayr
	Anstruther	**64B**	Edinburgh Haymarket	67D	Ardrossan
	Burntisland	**64C**	Edinburgh Dalry Road		
	Ladybank	**64D**	Carstairs	**68A**	**Carlisle Kingmoor**
62B	Dundee Tay Bridge	**64E**	Polmont	68B	Dumfries
	Dundee West	**64F**	Bathgate		Kirkcudbright
	Arbroath	**64G**	Hawick	68C	Stranraer
	Montrose		Kelso		Newton Stewart
	St Andrews		Riccarton	68D	Beattock
62C	Dunfermline		St Boswells	68E	Carlisle Canal

Southern Region

70A	**London Nine Elms**	71I	Southampton Docks	73C	London Hither Green
70B	London Feltham	71J	Highbridge	73D	Gillingham
70C	Guildford			73E	Faversham
70D	Basingstoke	**72A**	**Exmouth Junction**		
70E	Reading		Bude	**74A**	**Ashford**
70F	Fratton		Exmouth		Canterbury West
70G	Newport, Isle of Wight		Lyme Regis	74B	Ramsgate
70H	Ryde, Isle of Wight		Okehampton	74C	Dover
			Seaton		Folkestone Junction
71A	**Eastleigh**	**72B**	Salisbury	74D	Tonbridge
	Andover Junction	**72C**	Yeovil Town	74E	St Leonards
	Lymington	**72D**	Plymouth Friary		
	Winchester		Callington	**75A**	**Brighton**
71B	Bournemouth	**72E**	Barnstaple Junction		Newhaven
	Branksome		Ilfracombe	75B	Redhill
	Swanage		Torrington	75C	London Norwood Junction
71C	Dorchester	**72F**	Wadebridge	75D	Horsham
71G	Bath Green Park			75E	Three Bridges
	Radstock	**73A**	**London Stewarts Lane**	75F	Tunbridge Wells West
71H	Templecombe	73B	London Bricklayers Arms		

Western Region

81A	**London Old Oak Common**
81B	Slough
	Marlow
	Watlington
81C	Southall
81D	Reading
	Henley-on Thames
81E	Didcot
	Wallingford
81F	Oxford
	Fairford

82A	**Bristol Bath Road**
	Bath
	Wells
	Weston-super-Mare
	Yatton
82B	Bristol St Philip's Marsh
82C	Swindon
	Andover Junction
	Chippenham
82D	Westbury
	Frome
82E	Yeovil Pen Mill
82F	Weymouth
	Bridport

83A	**Newton Abbot**
	Ashburton
	Kingsbridge
83B	Taunton
	Bridgwater
	Minehead
83C	Exeter
	Tiverton Junction
83D	Plymouth Laira
	Launceston
	Princetown
83E	St Blazey
	Bodmin
	Moorswater
83F	Truro
83G	Penzance
	Helston
	St Ives

84A	**Wolverhampton Stafford Road**
84B	Wolverhampton Oxley
84C	Banbury
84D	Leamington Spa
84E	Birmingham Tyseley
	Stratford-on-Avon
84F	Stourbridge Junction
84G	Shrewsbury
	Builth Road
	Clee Hill
	Craven Arms
	Knighton
84H	Wellington
	Crewe Gresty Lane

84J	Wrexham Croes Newydd
	Bala
	Penmaenpool
	Trawsfynydd
84K	Chester GWR

85A	**Worcester**
	Evesham
	Kingham
85B	Gloucester Horton Road
	Brimscombe
	Cheltenham
	Cirencester
	Lydney
	Tetbury
85C	Hereford
	Ledbury
	Leominster
	Ross-on-Wye
85D	Kidderminster

86A	**Newport Ebbw Junction**
86B	Newport Pill
86C	Cardiff Canton
86D	Llantrisant
86E	Severn Tunnel Junction
86F	Tondu
86G	Pontypool Road
86H	Aberbeeg
86J	Aberdare
86K	Abergavenny
	Tredegar

87A	**Neath**
	Glyn Neath
	Neath N&B
87B	Duffryn Yard
87C	Swansea Danygraig
87D	Swansea East Dock
87E	Swansea Landore
87F	Llanelly
	Burry Port
	Pantyffynon
87G	Carmarthen
87H	Neyland
	Cardigan
	Milford Haven
	Pembroke Dock
	Whitland
87J	Goodwick
87K	Swansea Victoria
	Gurnos
	Llandovery
	Upper Bank

88A	**Cardiff Cathays**
	Cardiff Radyr
88B	Cardiff East Dock
88C	Barry

88D	Merthyr
	Cae Harris
	Dowlais Central
	Rhymney
88E	Abercynon
88F	Treherbert
	Ferndale

89A	**Oswestry**
	Llandiloes
	Moat Lane
	Welshpool
89B	Brecon
	Builth Wells
89C	Machynlleth
	Aberayron
	Aberystwyth
	Portmadoc
	Pwllheli

NOTE:

During 1955 there were changes to certain shed codes as detailed below.

With effect from 28 February:

Fort William recoded 65J from 63D;

Oban recoded 63D from 63E.

With effect from 8 October:

Market Harborough coded 2F from a sub-shed to Rugby;

Sutton Oak recoded 10D from 10E;

Penrith recoded 12B from 12C;

Workington recoded 12C from 12D;

Kirkby-in-Ashfield recoded 16B from 16C;

Mansfield recoded 16C from 16D;

Lees, Oldham, recoded 26E from 26F;

Manchester Belle Vue recoded 26F from 26G;

Sheffield Darnall recoded 41A from 39B.

Ex-Rhymney Railway 0-6-2T 4F

35	88B
36	88B
37	88B
38	88B
39	88B
41	88B
42	88B
43	88A
44	88A

Ex-Rhymney Railway 'A' class 0-6-2T 4P

59	88B
66	88B
69	87B
70	87B

Ex-Rhymney Railway 'P' class 0-6-2T 3P

78	88B
79	88A
83	88B

Ex-Taff Vale Railway 'O4' class 0-6-2T 4MT

204	88B
208	88B
210	88B
211	88B
215	88B
216	88B
290	88B

Ex-Taff Vale Railway 'A' class 0-6-2T 4P

303	88C
304	88E
305	88A
306	88C
307	88A
308	88B
312	88C
316	88E
343	88A
345	88A
346	88A
347	88A
348	88A
349	88C
351	88E
352	88F
356	88E
357	88C
360	88A
361	88C
362	88A
364	88A
365	88F
366	88F
367	88A
368	88F
370	88E
371	88B
372	88C
373	88C
374	88B
376	88C
377	88F
378	88B
379	88E
380	88E
381	88F
382	88C
383	88A
384	88F
385	88F
386	88E
387	88C
388	88C
389	88C
390	88C
391	88A
393	88C
394	88C
397	88E
398	88E
399	88E

Ex-Alexandra Docks Railway 0-6-0T 3F

666	86B

Ex-Cardiff Railway 0-6-0PT 4F

681	88B

1000 'County' class 4-6-0 6MT

1000*	82A
1001*	87H
1002*	83G
1003*	84G
1004*	82C
1005*	82A
1006*	83G
1007*	83F
1008*	84K
1009*	87H
1010*	83D
1011*	82A
1012*	83D
1013*	84G
1014*	82A
1015*	83D
1016*	84G
1017*	84G
1018*	83G
1019*	82C
1020*	87H
1021*	83D
1022*	84K
1023*	83F
1024*	84K
1025*	84G
1026*	84K
1027*	87H
1028*	82A
1029*	87H

1101 class 0-4-0T 3F

1101	87C
1102	87C
1103	87C
1104	87C
1105	87C
1106	87C

Ex-Swansea Harbour Trust 0-4-0ST 1F

1140	87D
1142	87C
1143	87C
1144	87D
1145	87C

Ex-Powlesland & Mason 0-4-0ST OF

1151	87C
1152	87D
1153	87K

Ex-Alexandra Docks Railway 2-6-2T 4MT

1205	86C

Ex-Cardiff Railway 0-4-0ST OF

1338	83B

1361 class 0-6-0ST OF

1361	83D
1362	83B
1363	83D
1364	83D
1365	83D

1366 class 0-6-0PT 1F

1366	83B
1367	82F
1368	82F
1369	82C
1370	82F
1371	82C

1400 class 0-4-2T 1P

1400	82C
1401	85B
1402	85B
1403	82F
1404	85B
1405	83C
1406	85B
1407	81D
1408	85A
1409	85B
1410	81C
1411	81B
1412	89A
1413	85B
1414	84F
1415	82A
1416	84J
1417	6C
1418	85A
1419	83E
1420	81F
1421	86A
1422	86G
1423	87J
1424	85B
1425	81F
1426	81C
1427	83A
1428	87E
1429	83C
1430	86A
1431	87J
1432	89A
1433	82C
1434	84J
1435	83C
1436	82C
1437	81F
1438	84F
1439	83A
1440	83C
1441	85B
1442	81F
1443	81C
1444	81D
1445	85C
1446	82C
1447	81D
1448	81B
1449	83C
1450	81B
1451	83C
1452	87J
1453	82F
1454	82A
1455	85C
1456	81C
1457	6C
1458	84F
1459	89A
1460	85C
1461	85A
1462	81C
1463	82A
1464	85B
1465	89C
1466	83A
1467	82F
1468	83C
1469	83C
1470	83A
1471	86D
1472	87G
1473	34E
1474	81C

1500 class 0-6-0PT 4F

1500	81A
1501	81C
1502	81E
1503	81A
1504	81A
1505	81A
1506	86B
1507	86B
1508	86E
1509	86A

1600 class 0-6-0PT 2F

1600	88C
1601	87H
1602	87H
1603	89A
1604	89A
1605	85A
1606	87H
1607	87F
1608	83A
1609	87F
1610	88E
1611	87H
1612	85B
1613	87F
1614	87F
1615	88C
1616	85B
1617	85C
1618	87F
1619	84F
1620	88E
1621	84F
1622	87F
1623	85B
1624	83E
1625	85B
1626	83E
1627	85B
1628	87F
1629	85A
1630	85B
1631	85B
1632	85B
1633	87F
1634	87C
1635	84J
1636	89C
1637	87H
1638	87F

Above: **Ex-Rhymney Railway 'R1' class 0-6-2T with its GWR and BR number 41 at its home shed, Cardiff East Dock in 1955. Built in December 1921 by Beyer Peacock to a design by Riches, it was withdrawn in May 1956 still at 88B.**

G. W. Sharpe

Below: **Ex-Taff Vale Railway '04' class 0-6-2T No 208 at Cardiff East Dock shed in 1954. Another Beyer Peacock build, this time in October 1910, it was withdrawn in July 1955.**

G. W. Sharpe

Above: Another ex-Taff Vale Railway engine – an 'A' class 0-6-2T No 380. Built in July 1919 to a Cameron design, it acquired a GWR superheated taper boiler in September 1930. It is seen here at its home shed of Abercynon in 1955 where it remained allocated until withdrawn in October 1956.　　　*R. H. G. Simpson*

Below: Hawksworth 1945 design 'County' class 4-6-0 No 1003 *County of Wilts* on Shrewsbury shed in 1955. It remained based here until January 1961 when transfer took place to Plymouth Laira from where withdrawal was actioned in October 1962. Cashmore's at Newport reduced the engine to scrap metal in 1964 after storage at Plymouth.　　　*G. W. Sharpe*

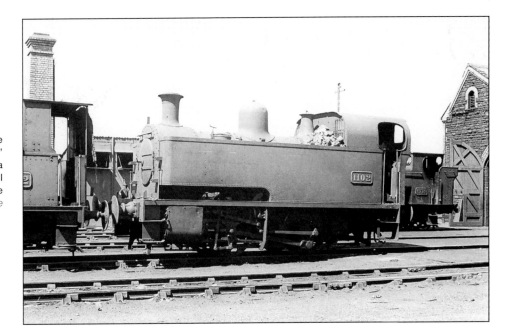

Introduced in 1926 and built by Avonside Engine Co to a GWR design for dock shunting, '1101' class 0-4-0T No 1102 takes a rest at Swansea Danygraig shed in 1954. Remaining here until withdrawal in January 1960, scrapping took place at Ward's yard at Briton Ferry. *G. W. Sharpe*

Built by Andrew Barclay in 1905 for the Swansea Harbour Trust, this 0-4-0ST No 1140 spent most of its life at Swansea East Dock, where it was photographed in May 1955. In November 1955 it was sent to Swansea Victoria shed, but in March 1956 returned to East Dock. Withdrawal came in May 1958 and cutting up took place at Swindon Works the following July. *G. W. Sharpe*

The unique Kitson-built 0-4-0ST No 1338, dating from 1898, seen at Swindon Works in May 1956. For many years it was based at Taunton for work on the short radius curves in the docks at Bridgwater, but in June 1960 moved to Swansea East Dock from where it was withdrawn in September 1963. Saved from the scrapyard, it can now be seen at Didcot Railway Centre. *G. W. Sharpe*

A 1910 Churchward design for dock shunting, No 1363 is seen at Swindon Works in 1952 after works attention. Behind is '2021' class 0-6-0PT No 2148 which was not so lucky, being withdrawn and awaiting scrapping. No 1363 remained at Plymouth Laira until withdrawn in December 1962 and was put into storage for nearly two years before being rescued for preservation, and is another resident at Didcot. *R. H. G. Simpson*

The Collett development of the '1361' class was the '1366' class, introduced in 1934. This 1956 view has No 1369 alongside the coaling stage at Swindon shed. Moving in March 1960 to Weymouth and then in August 1962 to Wadebridge, withdrawal came in November 1964. This is the only member of this class that survived into preservation and it is now at the South Devon Railway at Buckfastleigh. *R. H. G. Simpson*

Kennington Junction, Oxford, is the setting for this view of '1400' 0-4-2T No 1442 on a local freight working in 1954. Built to a Collett design and put to traffic in April 1935, its first allocation was at Staines, a sub-shed to Southall. Allocated to Oxford in February 1951 from Slough, it remained at Oxford until 1962, apart from a three-month period in 1953 when based at Reading. In October 1962 Westbury became its home, and then Exeter, St Blazey, Taunton and finally Exmouth Junction, from where it was withdrawn in May 1965. Regularly used on the Tiverton to Tiverton Junction auto train and known affectionately as the 'Tivvy Bumper', thanks to the generosity of Lord Amory it escaped the torch and is preserved at Tiverton Museum. *R. H. G. Simpson*

Above: New from Swindon Works in August 1949, '1500' class 0-6-0PT No 1504, seen leaving Paddington in 1955, went new to Old Oak Common and remained there throughout its short career. Withdrawal came in May 1963 and its final journey was to Ward's at Briton Ferry for scrap in May 1964.

R. H. G. Simpson

Below: Another short-lived class was the '1600' 0-6-0PT, the first appearing from Swindon Works in October 1949. This is No 1664 at St Blazey in April 1956 and had been added to traffic in March 1955. Its only move was to Swindon shed in December 1961 from where it was withdrawn in November 1964. *G. W. Sharpe*

1639	85B
1640	87C
1641	87D
1642	85B
1643	87F
1644	87F
1645	87A
1646	84J
1647	87C
1648	87C
1649	82B
1650	83D
1651	87K
1652	87D
1653	86A
1654	87F

1901 class 0-6-0PT 2F

2008	6C
2011	6C
2012	87F

2021 class 0-6-0PT 2F

2027	87F
2034	85C
2035	86A
2040	6C
2043	6C
2061	84H
2069	87G
2070	82B
2072	6C
2082	6C
2088	83B
2090	86A
2092	6C
2097	83D
2101	6C
2107	6C
2134	6C
2136	6C
2138	85C
2144	85A
2160	85C

Ex-Burry Port & Gwendraeth Valley Railway 0-6-0T 2F

2162	87F
2165	87F
2166	87D
2168	87F
2176	87F

2181 class 0-6-0PT 2F

2182	83E
2183	84J
2186	84J

Ex-Burry Port & Gwendraeth Valley Railway 0-6-0T 1F

2196*	87F
2198	87F

2251 class 0-6-0 3MT

2200	89C
2201	82B
2202	84C
2203	82B
2204	89C
2205	85A
2206	84G
2207	85D
2208	83B
2209	84C
2210	89A
2211	83C
2212	83B
2213	83B
2214	81E
2215	82B
2216	87G
2217	89C
2218	86A
2219	89A
2220	87H
2221	81E
2222	81A
2223	87J
2224	87G
2225	85C
2226	87H
2227	86A
2228	87H
2229	87H
2230	83C
2231	86E
2232	84G
2233	89A
2234	84G
2235	89B
2236	81F
2237	85A
2238	84E
2239	86A
2240	81E
2241	85A
2242	85A
2243	81A
2244	84G
2245	81D
2246	84C
2247	85A
2248	85B
2249	85C
2250	82B
2251	82B
2252	81E
2253	85A
2254	85B
2255	89A
2256	84C
2257	84E
2258	85A
2259	84C
2260	89C
2261	82B
2262	82C
2263	85A
2264	81D
2265	82B
2266	85C
2267	83B
2268	83B
2269	82B
2270	84C
2271	89C
2272	87G
2273	87G
2274	85C
2275	83B
2276	81A
2277	85A
2278	85A
2279	84E
2280	86A
2281	85C
2282	81A
2283	87H
2284	87E
2285	81C
2286	89A
2287	89B
2288	87H
2289	81F
2290	85A
2291	85B
2292	86E
2293	82B
2294	85A
2295	85A
2296	84E
2297	84C
2298	89C
2299	81D

2301 'Dean Goods' class 0-6-0 2MT

2474	81D
2513	89B
2516	89A
2538	89A

2800 class 2-8-0 8F

2800	87B
2801	86G
2802	86G
2803	86E
2804	84F
2805	86C
2806	86E
2807	85A
2808	86E
2809	83A
2810	86J
2811	86E
2812	84C
2813	86E
2814	83B
2815	86E
2816	84C
2817	84C
2818	82C
2819	84B
2820	81D
2821	86G
2822	84C
2823	84C
2824	81D
2825	85A
2826	84G
2827	84C
2828	86J
2829	86E
2830	84B
2831	86J
2832	84G
2833	84B
2834	84C
2835	84C
2836	86J
2837	86C
2838	86E
2839	86E
2840	84J
2841	84B
2842	86A
2843	83D
2844	86E
2845	82B
2846	83A
2847	84C
2848	84E
2849	84E
2850	84C
2851	86A
2852	82C
2853	84J
2854	84B
2855	85A
2856	84E
2857	84C
2858	86A
2859	86E
2860	86E
2861	86A
2862	86E
2863	86J
2864	86E
2865	82C
2866	86E
2867	84C
2868	82B
2869	83A
2870	86J
2871	84J
2872	86E
2873	86C
2874	84F
2875	83A
2876	86J
2877	86C
2878	84J
2879	82B
2880	81C
2881	83A
2882	84B
2883	86E

2884 class 2-8-0 8F

2884	86G
2885	84F
2886	84C
2887	86E
2888	86E
2889	82B
2890	84K
2891	86C
2892	86C
2893	86E
2894	87B
2895	86E
2896	86C
2897	84C
2898	82B
2899	81C

R.O.D. class 2-8-0 7F

3010	87G
3011	87G
3012	84E
3014	87G
3015	87G
3016	84B
3017	82B
3018	87G
3022	85B
3023	84E
3024	86G
3028	84B
3029	84B
3031	84B
3032	82B
3036	86G
3038	86G
3040	86G
3041	84G
3042	86G
3043	86G
3044	86G
3048	85B

3100 class 2-6-2T 4MT

3100	86F
3101	84E
3102	84A
3103	86A
3104	84A

3150 class 2-6-2T 4MT

3150	86E
3163	85B
3164	85B
3170	86A
3171	85B
3172	86E
3174	86E
3176	86E
3177	86E
3180	85B
3183	86E
3185	86E
3186	83D

Above: Much older than the '1600' class was the '1901' class of 0-6-0PT. This example, No 2012, dated back to November 1894 and started life as a Dean saddletank, later being rebuilt as a pannier. Photographed at Birkenhead shed in May 1955 after its transfer from Llanelly the previous month, it remained on the active list until June 1958.

G. W. Sharpe

Below: The '2021' class was another Dean saddletank design rebuilt to panniers with a higher tractive effort than the '1901' type. This example, No 2027, dated from 1897 and is here inside Llanelly shed in 1953. It was withdrawn in February 1957 still at 87F and dismantled at Swindon.

R. H. G. Simpson

Another look inside Llanelly shed in 1953 sees 0-6-0T No 2168. Built for the BP&GVR in 1912 by Hudswell Clarke and later rebuilt by the GWR, withdrawal came in May 1956 as the last active member of the class. *R. H. G. Simpson*

Another BP&GVR engine, this time 0-6-0ST No 2196 *Gwendraeth*, is seen at Llanelly in 1953. Built by Avonside in 1906, it remained substantially in original condition and was the last of its type when withdrawn in January 1956. *R. H. G. Simpson*

Entering traffic in November 1918, the powerful lines of the Churchward 2-8-0 are shown on Shrewsbury shed in 1955 in the shape of No 2874. This first batch did not have the provision of side-window cabs. Its BR days were spent at Banbury until May 1948 when it transferred to Stourbridge Junction, and on to Newport Ebbw Junction in October 1955. It stayed in South Wales, operating from a number of depots, until withdrawn from Neath in May 1963. Storage at Barry Docks then occurred, with No 2874 eventually being rescued; it is now based at the Pontypool & Blaenavon Railway. *G. W. Sharpe*

Birmingham Snow Hill on Saturday 21 May 1955 and Dean Goods 0-6-0 No 2516 is preparing to depart at 1.25pm on an SLS special. Based at Oswestry and specially prepared for the trip, this veteran engine, dating from 1897, shared the working with pannier tank No 2144. The itinerary took in Oldbury, Old Hill, Dudley, Wolverhampton, the Wombourne Branch, Kidderminster, Cleobury Mortimer and the Ditton Priors line, and return to Snow Hill for 9.30pm. Tickets cost 12s (60p). No 2516 was withdrawn in May 1956 and stored at Swindon for later preservation in the Great Western Museum. *Michael Mensing*

Running into Shrewsbury from Wolverhampton in 1955 is 2-8-0 No 3031. Purchased from the Government by the GWR between 1919 and 1921, these engines were Robinson's design for the Great Central Railway and constructed for the War Department. This engine was withdrawn in May 1956 from Oxley, and the last, No 3024, went in October 1958. *G. W. Sharpe*

The '3100' class with 5ft 3in wheels had been reconstructed in 1938-9 from the Churchward '3150' class with 5ft 8in wheels. Here we have No 3100, formerly No 3173, at Swindon Works in April 1957 awaiting the decision for withdrawal. Its last operating base had been Tondu. *G. W. Sharpe*

3187 — 83D
3190 — 86E

2251 class 0-6-0 3MT

No.	Shed	No.	Shed
3200	89A	3210	81E
3201	89C	3211	81E
3202	89C	3212	81E
3203	85B	3213	85A
3204	85A	3214	85A
3205	85B	3215	82B
3206	81E	3216	87G
3207	89C	3217	81F
3208	89A	3218	85A
3209	85C	3219	81D

5700 class 0-6-0PT 3F

No.	Shed	No.	Shed	No.	Shed	No.	Shed
3600	83A	3650	88B	3700	86B	3750	81C
3601	85D	3651	86G	3701	87E	3751	84F
3602	84G	3652	86C	3702	84G	3752	87F
3603	83C	3653	81E	3703	86G	3753	86J
3604	82B	3654	87H	3704	81C	3754	81A
3605	86J	3655	86J	3705	83E	3755	86C
3606	83C	3656	86D	3706	89B	3756	84A
3607	85A	3657	87H	3707	88B	3757	87A
3608	81F	3658	84F	3708	86G	3758	82B
3609	85B	3659	83A	3709	81E	3759	82A
3610	86J	3660	84E	3710	84F	3760	84H
3611	87A	3661	87F	3711	86H	3761	87F
3612	86D	3662	86A	3712	86A	3762	84K
3613	84H	3663	86B	3713	87E	3763	82F
3614	82B	3664	84A	3714	86A	3764	82B
3615	84A	3665	82C	3715	87A	3765	82B
3616	86F	3666	84F	3716	86H	3766	87A
3617	86D	3667	84F	3717	86G	3767	89B
3618	81C	3668	86F	3718	87B	3768	87E
3619	84D	3669	83B	3719	87F		
3620	81C	3670	86C	3720	82B		
3621	87A	3671	82E	3721	81E		
3622	81E	3672	88A	3722	81F		
3623	82B	3673	84E	3723	81D		
3624	84D	3674	86F	3724	82C		
3625	84E	3675	83D	3725	85A		
3626	6C	3676	82B	3726	86A		
3627	86F	3677	83C	3727	81C		
3628	86G	3678	87E	3728	85C		
3629	83D	3679	87D	3729	84F		
3630	84K	3680	86D	3730	86G		
3631	84D	3681	88B	3731	82B		
3632	82B	3682	82C	3732	84H		
3633	87D	3683	86G	3733	82E		
3634	86A	3684	82C	3734	88B		
3635	83E	3685	86G	3735	82D		
3636	86A	3686	83D	3736	83B		
3637	87J	3687	87A	3737	82C		
3638	89B	3688	81A	3738	81D		
3639	83D	3689	84E	3739	82C		
3640	86G	3690	86F	3740	81B		
3641	87D	3691	86A	3741	87A		
3642	87F	3692	82F	3742	6C		
3643	82B	3693	84E	3743	84F		
3644	86D	3694	84C	3744	84H		
3645	82C	3695	86J	3745	84F		
3646	84E	3696	82D	3746	82C		
3647	86J	3697	81B	3747	86H		
3648	81A	3698	87F	3748	82B		
3649	84F	3699	86J	3749	84H		

No.	Shed
3769	84E
3770	89B
3771	87F
3772	86F
3773	82B
3774	87A
3775	85A
3776	86D
3777	87F
3778	84A
3779	86G
3780	82C
3781	87C
3782	84G
3783	88B
3784	82A
3785	87E
3786	84K
3787	83D
3788	84G
3789	85C
3790	83D
3791	87B
3792	84A
3793	84A
3794	83C
3795	82A
3796	83A
3797	87E
3798	86A
3799	81C

2884 class 2-8-0 8F

No.	Shed	No.	Shed
3800	86A	3834	83A
3801	86C	3835	84C
3802	84B	3836	86C
3803	86C	3837	81E
3804	86A	3838	86E
3805	86A	3839	84E
3806	86E	3840	83A
3807	86A	3841	83A
3808	86E	3842	86C
3809	86C	3843	86E
3810	86C	3844	86E
3811	87F	3845	81E
3812	86C	3846	86C
3813	84B	3847	86E
3814	86C	3848	85A
3815	86E	3849	86E
3816	86C	3850	86E
3817	86C	3851	87F
3818	86E	3852	86E
3819	84C	3853	86E
3820	84K	3854	82B
3821	84F	3855	86G
3822	86G	3856	81C
3823	82B	3857	81C
3824	86A	3858	84K
3825	84B	3859	84C
3826	86G	3860	84B
3827	84F	3861	84B
3828	86G	3862	83D
3829	84C	3863	84B
3830	86A	3864	83A
3831	84C	3865	84B
3832	86E	3866	86E
3833	86A		

4000 'Star' class 4-6-0 5P

No.	Shed
4056*	82A
4061*	84A
4062*	82C

4073 'Castle' class 4-6-0 7P

No.	Shed
4000*	84A
4037*	81A
4073*	82A
4074*	87E
4075*	82A
4076*	83A
4077*	83D
4078*	87E
4079*	84A
4080*	82A
4081*	87E
4082*	81A
4083*	84A
4084*	82A
4085*	81D
4086*	83D
4087*	83D
4088*	81A
4089*	84A
4090*	82A
4091*	84A
4092*	82A
4093*	87E

Shrewsbury shed in 1956 plays host to '2251' class 0-6-0 No 3208, a Collett design dating from 1930. This was one of the later batch constructed in October 1946 and first allocated to Oswestry where it remained until January 1963 when Machynlleth received it on allocation. Withdrawal came in May 1965. *G. W. Sharpe*

'5700' class 0-6-0PT No 3706 at home at Brecon shed in 1955. Built in October 1936, this engine had been delivered new to Brecon. In BR days it moved to Newport Ebbw Junction in October 1959 where it remained until withdrawal in November 1963.

R. H. G. Simpson

The '2884' class 2-8-0 differed from the earlier '2800' type by having a more substantial cab with side-windows. This is shown in this example, No 3802, at Stourbridge shed in July 1954. Entering traffic in December 1938, it was first allocated to Leamington Spa. After spending time at sheds in the Wolverhampton Division, in March 1963 it was moved to Severn Tunnel Junction, then on to Taunton in May 1964 and finally the ex-Midland shed at Bristol Barrow Road. From here it was withdrawn in August 1965 and placed in store awaiting scrapping at Barry Docks. Saved from destruction, it is now in the safe hands of the Bodmin & Wenford Railway group. *G. W. Sharpe*

4094*	84A
4095*	87E
4096*	82A
4097*	81A
4098*	83A
4099*	83A

5101 class 2-6-2T 4MT

4100	85D
4101	88D
4102	84C
4103	84A
4104	84F
4105	84G
4106	87E
4107	87E
4108	84A
4109	83A
4110	84E
4111	84E
4112	84D
4113	85A
4114	85D
4115	84K
4116	84E
4117	83B
4118	84D
4119	86E
4120	6C
4121	86E
4122	6C
4123	6C
4124	6C
4125	6C
4126	6C
4127	6C
4128	6C
4129	6C
4130	86A
4131	87H
4132	87H
4133	82D
4134	87G
4135	86G
4136	83B
4137	86E
4138	86G
4139	82A
4140	84A
4141	85B
4142	86E
4143	88D
4144	86E
4145	83A
4146	84F
4147	81F
4148	85B
4149	84C
4150	82F
4151	86E
4152	88D
4153	85D
4154	85A
4155	84H
4156	86E
4157	82A
4158	84H
4159	82A
4160	88D
4161	88D
4162	88D
4163	88D
4164	88D
4165	84K
4166	82D
4167	83E
4168	86A
4169	87A
4170	84E
4171	84D
4172	84E
4173	84F
4174	85B
4175	85D
4176	83B
4177	88C
4178	84E
4179	83A

4200 class 2-8-0T 7F

4200	86E
4201	86B
4203	86A
4206	83E
4207	86C
4208	86D
4211	86A
4212	87B
4213	87F
4214	86B
4215	86H
4217	86F
4218	86F
4221	87A
4222	86F
4223	87F
4224	88C
4225	86C
4226	86C
4227	86H
4228	86J
4229	86G
4230	86G
4231	86C
4232	87A
4233	86B
4235	86B
4236	86F
4237	86B
4238	86H
4241	86F
4242	86A
4243	87A
4246	86A
4247	83E
4248	86A
4250	86H
4251	86F
4252	87A
4253	86B
4254	86C
4255	86A
4256	87B
4257	86J
4258	86B
4259	86A
4260	87F
4261	86D
4262	82B
4263	86B
4264	86J
4265	87B
4266	86C
4267	88C
4268	86D
4269	86H
4270	86C
4271	86A
4272	86J
4273	86F
4274	87A
4275	86E
4276	86F
4277	86A
4278	87F
4279	87A
4280	86B
4281	87A
4282	87A
4283	86A
4284	87A
4285	86B
4286	86A
4287	86H
4288	87A
4289	86E
4290	86A
4291	86B
4292	87B
4293	87A
4294	86A
4295	87A
4296	87B
4297	86J
4298	86E
4299	87C

4300 class 2-6-0 4MT

4326	84F
4358	87H
4375	84F
4377	82D

4400 class 2-6-2T 3MT

4405	83A
4406	83D
4410	83D

4500 class 2-6-2T 4MT

4505	83E
4506	87H
4507	82E
4508	83E
4519	87H
4521	85B
4522	86H
4523	83E
4524	83D
4526	83E
4530	83D
4532	82A
4533	86G
4534	83D
4535	82A
4536	82D
4537	83G
4538	82C
4539	82A
4540	83G
4541	87H
4542	83D
4545	83G
4546	89A
4547	83A
4548	83G
4549	89C
4550	82C
4551	82D
4552	83E
4553	87H
4554	83F
4555	89C
4556	87H
4557	87H
4558	82A
4559	83E
4560	89C
4561	83F
4562	82A
4563	83G
4564	85B
4565	83E
4566	83G
4567	85A
4568	83E
4569	83E
4570	83G
4571	85A
4572	82D
4573	82C
4574	83G

4575 class 2-6-2T 4MT

4575	89C
4576	87H
4577	82A
4578	88C
4579	87H
4580	88A
4581	88A
4582	82A
4583	83D
4584	83E
4585	83E
4586	85B
4587	83F
4588	83F
4589	88A
4590	83D
4591	83D
4592	82A
4593	86H
4594	85A
4595	82A
4596	85D
4597	82A
4598	83F
4599	89C

5700 class 0-6-0PT 3F

4600	85C
4601	88C
4602	84K
4603	82B
4604	83B
4605	84H
4606	81D
4607	82D
4608	81C
4609	81D
4610	81C
4611	86A
4612	82C
4613	85A
4614	85D
4615	81A
4616	88D
4617	84J
4618	88A
4619	82B
4620	86D
4621	87A
4622	86C
4623	84G
4624	82F
4625	85A
4626	88B
4627	85B
4628	85B
4629	85A
4630	88D
4631	84C
4632	88D
4633	86C
4634	86F
4635	88D
4636	82D
4637	86D
4638	81B
4639	86G
4640	87B
4641	85D
4642	86G
4643	86H
4644	81A
4645	84J
4646	84F
4647	82D
4648	84E
4649	81E
4650	81B
4651	82C
4652	86H
4653	83D
4654	87H

Churchward four-cylinder 'Star' class 4-6-0 No 4056 *Princess Margaret*, looking in need of care and attention but still capable of useful work, is seen at Plymouth Laira shed in July 1957. Built in July 1914, withdrawal came in October 1957 from Bristol Bath Road, No 4056 being the last survivor of this famous class.   *G. W. Sharpe*

The Collett-designed 'Castle' class was a development of the 'Star' class. Entering Dawlish on an 'up' express in May 1958 is No 4083 *Abbotsbury Castle*, recently transferred from Wolverhampton to Newton Abbot. Added to stock in May 1925, withdrawal came in September 1961 when the engine was allocated to Cardiff Canton.

G. W. Sharpe

Exeter St Davids station in August 1956 and '5101' class 2-6-2T No 4117 is in charge of a local from Taunton. Added to stock in November 1936 and first allocated to Newton Abbot, this Collett-designed engine, based on an earlier Churchward design, spent all its time in the West Country and was withdrawn in September 1961 when based at Taunton.   *P. H. Groom*

Churchward-designed 2-8-0T No 4225, with inside steam-pipes, at its home shed Cardiff Canton in April 1956. This powerful engine had entered service in November 1913 and lasted until January 1963, when based at Llanelly. *P. H. Groom*

One of the first batch of Churchward Moguls, No 4326, at Shrewsbury in 1955 on a goods for Chester. Introduced in 1913, withdrawal came in March 1957 after operating from Stourbridge shed since April 1953. *G. W. Sharpe*

'4500' class 2-6-2T No 4573 takes water at Gloucester Central station in July 1956 after a run to Charlford. Entering traffic in November 1924, this was a Churchward design ideal for branch line work. No 4573 was a new arrival on Gloucester's allocation, arriving the month before from Swindon. It stayed until October 1960 when it was sent to Neyland to work out its final days until withdrawal in August 1961. *G. W. Sharpe*

(continued) — 2251 class numbers

No.	Shed	No.	Shed
4655	82B	4678	85C
4656	83D	4679	83D
4657	85C	4680	81B
4658	83D	4681	87B
4659	85B	4682	86H
4660	82B	4683	84J
4661	81D	4684	87B
4662	86C	4685	86H
4663	83B	4686	88B
4664	85A	4687	84F
4665	81D	4688	82B
4666	87C	4689	82E
4667	88A	4690	88D
4668	86G	4691	81B
4669	86F	4692	88C
4670	81D	4693	83D
4671	86A	4694	87C
4672	84G	4695	81C
4673	81C	4696	84F
4674	86D	4697	82C
4675	86F	4698	88B
4676	81F	4699	87H
4677	87J		

4700 class 2-8-0 7F

No.	Shed
4700	81A
4701	81A
4702	81A
4703	82B
4704	81A
4705	81A
4706	82B
4707	81A
4708	81A

4900 'Hall' class 4-6-0 5MT

No.	Shed	No.	Shed	No.	Shed
4900*	85A	4934*	86C	4968*	86C
4901*	86G	4935*	81E	4969*	81F
4902*	81F	4936*	83D	4970*	83B
4903*	81F	4937*	84G	4971*	83B
4904*	84E	4938*	81F	4972*	82C
4905*	85C	4939*	81D	4973*	82C
4906*	83F	4940*	83B	4974*	86C
4907*	85C	4941*	87F	4975*	85C
4908*	83G	4942*	82A	4976*	85C
4909*	82A	4943*	81A	4977*	84C
4910*	87G	4944*	81C	4978*	83D
4912*	84A	4945*	81E	4979*	81C
4913*	86C	4946*	86C	4980*	84C
4914*	82A	4947*	82B	4981*	87E
4915*	84G	4948*	83C	4982*	86A
4916*	86A	4949*	83B	4983*	82B
4917*	82D	4950*	83D	4984*	87G
4918*	84B	4951*	86A	4985*	83B
4919*	84B	4952*	87F	4986*	81A
4920*	83B	4953*	86C	4987*	84C
4921*	81F	4954*	81E	4988*	82F
4922*	87G	4955*	84B	4989*	81D
4923*	81A	4956*	81C	4990*	86G
4924*	84B	4957*	86A	4991*	86G
4925*	82C	4958*	82B	4992*	83D
4926*	84A	4959*	84B	4993*	81D
4927*	82D	4960*	81D	4994*	81E
4928*	82C	4961*	82A	4995*	81D
4929*	85B	4962*	81D	4996*	85B
4930*	82D	4963*	84B	4997*	84A
4931*	83G	4964*	84E	4998*	81D
4932*	83B	4965*	83D	4999*	82B
4933*	81F	4966*	84B		
		4967*	81A		

4073 'Castle' class 4-6-0 7P

No.	Shed	No.	Shed	No.	Shed
5000*	82A	5034*	81A	5068*	87E
5001*	86C	5035*	81A	5069*	84G
5002*	87E	5036*	81D	5070*	86C
5003*	83C	5037*	85A	5071*	84K
5004*	81A	5038*	81A	5072*	82A
5005*	86C	5039*	87G	5073*	82A
5006*	81A	5040*	81A	5074*	83A
5007*	86C	5041*	83A	5075*	83A
5008*	84A	5042*	85B	5076*	86C
5009*	82C	5043*	87G	5077*	85A
5010*	84A	5044*	81A	5078*	81A
5011*	83A	5045*	84A	5079*	82C
5012*	81F	5046*	86C	5080*	82C
5013*	87E	5047*	84A	5081*	82A
5014*	81A	5048*	82A	5082*	85A
5015*	84A	5049*	86C	5083*	81A
5016*	87E	5050*	84G	5084*	84A
5017*	85B	5051*	87E	5085*	87E
5018*	85B	5052*	86C	5086*	85A
5019*	82A	5053*	83D	5087*	84G
5020*	86C	5054*	86C	5088*	85A
5021*	83C	5055*	81A	5089*	81A
5022*	84A	5056*	81A	5090*	82A
5023*	83D	5057*	82A	5091*	81A
5024*	83A	5058*	82C	5092*	82A
5025*	82A	5059*	82A	5093*	84G
5026*	81F	5060*	82A	5094*	83D
5027*	82A	5061*	81A	5095*	86C
5028*	83A	5062*	81A	5096*	84G
5029*	81A	5063*	82A	5097*	83D
5030*	86C	5064*	82C	5098*	86C
5031*	84K	5065*	83D	5099*	86C
5032*	84A	5066*	84A		
5033*	84K	5067*	83A		

5101 class 2-6-2T 4MT

No.	Shed	No.	Shed
5101	84F	5176	6C
5102	87A	5177	84K
5103	84K	5178	84H
5104	84D	5179	84K
5105	84F	5180	84F
5106	84A	5181	84E
5107	84F	5182	82A
5108	83A	5183	88C
5109	84H	5184	84D
5110	85D	5185	84D
5112	84A	5186	84K
5113	83A	5187	84A
5148	83D	5188	84A
5150	83A	5189	84F
5151	84A	5190	82F
5152	84E	5191	84F
5153	83A	5192	84E
5154	84G	5193	83D
5155	86E	5194	84D
5156	84E	5195	88F
5157	83B	5196	83A
5158	83A	5197	82A
5159	88F	5198	84E
5160	84F	5199	84F
5161	84D		
5162	88F		
5163	84E		
5164	84E		
5165	84F		
5166	84E		
5167	84F		
5168	84G		
5169	86E		
5170	84C		
5171	87G		
5172	83B		
5173	86A		
5174	84K		
5175	83D		

Passing Winson Green in Birmingham in 1955 is '4700' class 2-8-0 No 4708 on a freight. Dating from April 1923, this engine spent its days allocated to Wolverhampton Oxley and Old Oak Common from where it was withdrawn in October 1962. Stored in London until March 1963, it then went into further storage at Tyseley before being broken up at Cashmore's, Great Bridge.

G. W. Sharpe

Hereford's 'Hall' class 4-6-0 No 4975 *Umberslade Hall* pays a visit to Shrewsbury depot in 1955. Dating from January 1930, and here paired with a high-sided tender, it moved on to the West Country in 1958 for a time at Laira and Newton Abbot, then to Reading in 1962 and finally Oxford in June 1963, working from there until withdrawn three months later.

G. W. Sharpe

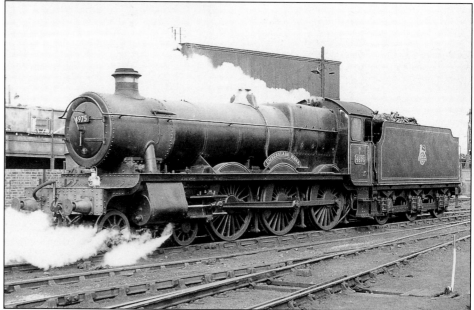

'Castle' class 4-6-0 No 5017 at Gloucester in May 1956. Completed in July 1932 and first allocated to Newton Abbot, it was named *St Donats Castle*. A renaming ceremony took place at Gloucester station on 24 April I954, the engine becoming *The Gloucestershire Regiment 28th, 61st*. Appropriately it remained based at Gloucester Horton Road until withdrawal in September 1962. *G. W. Sharpe*

'5101' class 2-6-2T No 5104 at Tyseley station on a local in August 1956. Built in November 1929, this was a Leamington-based engine for many years until transfer to Bristol St Philip's Marsh in February 1958, where it remained on allocation until withdrawn in November 1960.

G. W. Sharpe

4200 class 2-8-0T 7F		5230	87F	5263	86J	5339	83A	5390	84B
5200		5231	86B	5264	86A	5341	84B	5391	84A
5201	86A	5232	87D			5344	84K	5392	87F
5202	86C	5233	86A	**4300 class 2-6-0 4MT**		5345	85B	5393	6C
5203	87F	5234	86A	5306	82A	5347	85B	5394	85B
5204	87F	5235	86B	5307	82B	5350	82B	5395	89C
		5236	86A	5310	87G	5351	82C	5396	82C
5205 class 2-8-0T 8F		5237	86J	5311	84K	5353	87G	5397	81E
5205	86E	5238	86A	5312	84B	5355	85B	5398	85B
5206	86A	5239	87A	5313	84F	5356	83D	5399	84C
5207	86C	5240	82C	5314	82F	5357	87H		
5208	86F	5241	86H	5315	84K	5358	82D	**5400 class 0-6-0PT 1P**	
5209	87F	5242	87A	5316	6C	5360	83A	5400	87G
5210	87D	5243	86A	5317	84C	5361	84C	5401	89A
5211	87D	5244	86B	5318	86A	5362	83A	5402	82D
5212	86E	5245	86J	5319	84J	5367	82B	5403	82D
5213	87F	5246	87D	5321	83B	5368	81D	5404	84C
5214	86E	5247	87F	5322	81F	5369	84E	5405	89A
5215	87F	5248	87F	5323	82B	5370	84E	5406	82D
5216	87B	5249	87F	5324	87H	5371	84F	5407	84C
5217	86A	5250	86B	5325	83B	5372	87H	5408	85B
5218	86C	5251	86A	5326	81D	5375	84B	5409	34E
5219	87F	5252	86B	5327	82D	5376	83D	5410	81C
5220	87B	5253	86E	5328	84G	5377	85C	5411	83B
5221	87D	5254	87B	5330	81D	5378	84B	5412	83C
5222	86A	5255	86A	5331	84G	5379	84F	5413	81F
5223	87F	5256	86A	5332	84C	5380	81E	5414	86A
5224	86E	5257	87B	5333	84E	5381	84B	5415	81C
5225	87A	5258	86J	5334	86C	5382	86A	5416	84J
5226	82C	5259	86A	5335	87F	5384	82F	5417	85B
5227	86A	5260	86A	5336	84B	5385	82D	5418	81C
5228	86A	5261	87F	5337	82F	5386	84E	5419	82D
5229	86A	5262	86E	5338	82D	5388	86C	5420	81C

Ex-works at Swindon in 1954 is '5205' class 2-8-0T No 5260. Leaving Swindon Works new in February 1940, the first base was Duffryn Yard, Port Talbot. Designed for South Wales coal traffic haulage, No 5260 spent its career based in this part of the world, finally being declared redundant in March 1963 from its Aberbeeg home.

R. H. G. Simpson

The second batch of '4300' class 2-6-0s are represented by No 5317, seen beginning the descent of Hatton Bank on the Birmingham-Leamington line with a mixed goods train on Tuesday 25 October 1955. A 1917 build, No 5317 survived until November 1956 after transfer from Banbury to Tyseley during the previous June.

Michael Mensing

Banbury shed in June 1955 has on show its own Collett 0-6-0PT No 5404. Motor-fitted and with 5ft 2in wheels for passenger work, No 5404 had been built in 1931. Based at Banbury throughout its BR ownership, withdrawal came in December 1957.

R. H. G. Simpson

5421	83B	5525	82A	5556	89C	5610	88A	5641	88E
5422	82D	5526	83F	5557	83A	5611	88F	5642	88B
5423	82D	5527	88C	5558	83B	5612	87F	5643	88E
5424	84C	5528	82A	5559	82A	5613	88F	5644	86J
		5529	88C	5560	86F	5614	88C	5645	86H
4575 class 2-6-2T 4MT		5530	85B	5561	82A	5615	88D	5646	87H
5500	83F	5531	83D	5562	83F	5616	87D	5647	84K
5501	83B	5532	82A	5563	82E	5617	88E	5648	88C
5502	83E	5533	83B	5564	82C	5618	88E	5649	86J
5503	83B	5534	88A	5565	82A	5619	88C	5650	88A
5504	83B	5535	82A	5566	82C	5620	86C	5651	84F
5505	83F	5536	82C	5567	83D	5621	88C	5652	88D
5506	82A	5537	83F	5568	88A	5622	88D	5653	88A
5507	89C	5538	85B	5569	83D	5623	88E	5654	88A
5508	82D	5539	83A	5570	89C	5624	86F	5655	88D
5509	82C	5540	82C	5571	83B	5625	86G	5656	87E
5510	82C	5541	89C	5572	88A	5626	87B	5657	87F
5511	88A	5542	83A	5573	86G	5627	88C	5658	84F
5512	82A	5543	83A	5574	86F	5628	87D	5659	88A
5513	87H	5544	83A			5629	81E	5660	88D
5514	82A	5545	86F	**5600 class 0-6-2T 5MT**		5630	88A	5661	88D
5515	83F	5546	82A	5600	88A	5631	87E	5662	88D
5516	86G	5547	82A	5601	88A	5632	88C	5663	88A
5517	89C	5548	82A	5602	86C	5633	86C	5664	88C
5518	85B	5549	87H	5603	88D	5634	84A	5665	88C
5519	83E	5550	87H	5604	87E	5635	88D	5666	88D
5520	86H	5551	83A	5605	88D	5636	88A	5667	88C
5521	83E	5552	83A	5606	84F	5637	88E	5668	88F
5522	83B	5553	82A	5607	88F	5638	86G	5669	88A
5523	82A	5554	82D	5608	88A	5639	81E	5670	88A
5524	86F	5555	86F	5609	88C	5640	88D	5671	88D

The '4575' class of 2-6-2Ts was a modified version of the '4500' type with increased water capacity. No 5510 sits in the bay platform at Swindon in July 1954 on station pilot duties. Dating from November 1927, this was a long-time resident at Swindon, spending its entire BR allocation at 82C. Withdrawn in October 1960, instead of being scrapped at Swindon, it went to Barry Docks, not seeing the cutter's torch until April 1965.

R. H. G. Simpson

No.	Shed		No.	Shed
5672	88D		5735	81E
5673	87E		5736	84E
5674	88D		5737	81E
5675	82B		5738	84E
5676	88F		5739	84K
5677	88A		5740	86B
5678	88A		5741	86J
5679	86C		5742	84J
5680	88E		5743	87D
5681	88D		5744	81E
5682	88E		5745	84H
5683	88A		5746	87A
5684	84B		5747	86B
5685	86C		5748	87H
5686	88E		5749	86C
5687	88A		5750	86H
5688	88F		5751	83B
5689	82D		5752	81E
5690	84G		5753	81C
5691	88F		5754	84F
5692	88A		5755	81C
5693	88F		5756	86G
5694	88D		5757	82D
5695	88F		5758	84H
5696	88D		5759	87E
5697	81E		5760	83B
5698	86J		5761	87K
5699	88E		5762	81D
			5763	81D

5700 class 0-6-0PT 3F

No.	Shed		No.	Shed
5700	89A		5764	81A
5701	82D		5765	85C
5702	87F		5766	81D
5703	87C		5767	82D
5704	87D		5768	86G
5705	87F		5769	88D
5706	86B		5770	87B
5707	86F		5771	82D
5708	86D		5772	81D
5709	86A		5773	87K
5710	88B		5774	84J
5711	88D		5775	87G
5712	84H		5776	86C
5713	87B		5777	86B
5714	86B		5778	87A
5715	81B		5779	83B
5716	87J		5780	84A
5717	81A		5781	82F
5718	82D		5782	87F
5719	84F		5783	81E
5720	87A		5784	82C
5721	83B		5785	86H
5722	87F		5786	86C
5723	84K		5787	87B
5724	84C		5788	86D
5725	84K		5789	87B
5726	89A		5790	84E
5727	81C		5791	84K
5728	86G		5792	86G
5729	86E		5793	88A
5730	87C		5794	86C
5731	87D		5795	84F
5732	86A		5796	83A
5733	86B		5797	86J
5734	87B		5798	83B
			5799	81C

5800 class 0-4-2T 1P

No.	Shed
5800	82C
5801	89B
5802	82C
5803	81F
5804	82C
5805	82C
5806	89A
5807	85C
5808	81F
5809	82A
5810	84J
5811	84J
5812	89A
5813	82A
5814	85C
5815	85A
5816	85A
5817	85C
5818	85C
5819	87G

4900 'Hall' class 4-6-0 5MT

No.	Shed		No.	Shed
5900*	84E		5941*	81A
5901*	81D		5942*	81D
5902*	87F		5943*	85A
5903*	87H		5944*	84B
5904*	82A		5945*	84B
5905*	87J		5946*	86C
5906*	81D		5947*	84C
5907*	85B		5948*	86G
5908*	87J		5949*	82B
5909*	83D		5950*	84C
5910*	86C		5951*	85B
5911*	86C		5952*	83G
5912*	84E		5953*	81C
5913*	87F		5954*	84C
5914*	85A		5955*	87E
5915*	83G		5956*	81D
5916*	86G		5957*	81D
5917*	85A		5958*	87E
5918*	81C		5959*	83G
5919*	82A		5960*	81F
5920*	83A		5961*	87F
5921*	86A		5962*	84K
5922*	82C		5963*	87G
5923*	86C		5964*	83D
5924*	82B		5965*	81F
5925*	86C		5966*	84B
5926*	83E		5967*	84C
5927*	84E		5968*	84K
5928*	87J		5969*	83G
5929*	87E		5970*	86C
5930*	84C		5971*	85A
5931*	81A		5972*	83F
5932*	81A		5973*	81D
5933*	81D		5974*	82D
5934*	83D		5975*	82C
5935*	81E		5976*	83C
5936*	81A		5977*	86C
5937*	87G		5978*	82F
5938*	87G		5979*	81D
5939*	81A		5980*	85B
5940*	81A		5981*	84G
			5982*	82B
			5983*	81C
			5984*	87G
			5985*	83F
			5986*	84G
			5987*	81A
			5988*	87E
			5989*	81C
			5990*	85B
			5991*	84B
			5992*	83B
			5993*	81D
			5994*	82C
			5995*	84B
			5996*	81A
			5997*	82F
			5998*	83D
			5999*	83B

6000 'King' class 4-6-0 8P

No.	Shed		No.	Shed
6000*	81A		6004*	83D
6001*	84A		6005*	84A
6002*	81A		6006*	84A
6003*	81A		6007*	81A
			6008*	83D
			6009*	81A
			6010*	83D
			6011*	84A
			6012*	81A
			6013*	81A
			6014*	84A
			6015*	81A
			6016*	81A
			6017*	83D
			6018*	81A
			6019*	81A
			6020*	84A
			6021*	81A
			6022*	83D
			6023*	83D
			6024*	81A
			6025*	83D
			6026*	83D
			6027*	83D
			6028*	81A
			6029*	83D

6100 class 2-6-2T 4MT

No.	Shed
6100	81D
6101	81D
6102	86A
6103	81D
6104	81D
6105	84E
6106	81F
6107	82A
6108	81B
6109	81A
6110	81A
6111	81F
6112	81F
6113	81F
6114	86A
6115	81B
6116	84E
6117	81D
6118	84E
6119	81B
6120	81A
6121	81A
6122	81F
6123	81B
6124	81B
6125	81C
6126	81D
6127	81B
6128	81C
6129	81D
6130	81D
6131	81B
6132	81B
6133	81B
6134	84E
6135	81A
6136	81B

A '5700' class 0-6-0PT with a difference: No 5744 is shown at Didcot shed in July 1957 with a spark-arresting chimney. This was one of the April 1929 batch and moved to Truro in July 1960 and on to Westbury in March 1962, to be withdrawn the next month. Cutting up was undertaken at the Central Wagon Co at Wigan. *G. W. Sharpe*

Shunting at Swindon in 1954 is '5800' class 0-4-2T No 5800. Built in 1933 and first allocated to Bristol St Philip's Marsh, this was a later version of the '1400' class, but not motor-fitted. All but one had been withdrawn by the end of 1959, No 5800 going in July 1958. *R. H. G. Simpson*

Solihull on a sunny Sunday 30 October 1955 finds 'Hall' class 4-6-0 No 5900 *Hinderton Hall* on a southbound freight. Built in March 1931, it was withdrawn from St Philip's Marsh in December 1963, languished at Barry Docks until 1971, and was then removed for preservation. It is now at Didcot Railway Centre. *Michael Mensing*

Above: A 'King' in action, No 6015 *King Richard III* on the down 'Inter-City' approaching the summit of Hatton Bank on Tuesday 25 October 1955. Built in June 1928, it was fitted with a double-chimney in September 1955. Wolverhampton Stafford Road was its last operating base when withdrawn in September 1962.

Michael Mensing

Below: Appleford Halt on the Oxford to Didcot line receives '6100' class 2-6-2T No 6122 on a local in 1954. Similar to the '5101' class, it had a higher boiler pressure and tractive effort for fast London suburban traffic. This example moved on, after a lengthy stay at Oxford, to Slough in September 1956, to Didcot in May 1959, to Swindon in August 1964 and was taken out of traffic the next month.

R. H. G. Simpson

No.	Shed
6137	81A
6138	81F
6139	84E
6140	81B
6141	81A
6142	81A
6143	81B
6144	81A
6145	81D
6146	81B
6147	81C
6148	81C
6149	81A
6150	81B
6151	81B
6152	81B
6153	81B
6154	81B
6155	81A
6156	81C
6157	81B
6158	81A
6159	81A
6160	81B
6161	81D
6162	81D
6163	81D
6164	81B
6165	81C
6166	84E
6167	81B
6168	81A
6169	81C

4300 class 2-6-0 4MT

No.	Shed
6300	83E
6301	83C
6302	81D
6303	84J
6304	81E
6305	83E
6306	82B
6307	84E
6308	85C
6309	82C
6310	87G
6311	84J
6312	81D
6313	81E
6314	85C
6316	84J
6317	84G
6318	86A
6319	83D
6320	82C
6321	84E
6322	83C
6323	83B
6324	84B
6325	87F
6326	85C
6327	84E
6328	83B
6329	87G
6330	85B

No.	Shed
6331	84K
6332	84F
6333	86C
6334	85A
6335	84B
6336	81F
6337	84K
6338	84J
6339	84J
6340	81E
6341	85B
6342	84E
6343	83B
6344	84K
6345	84K
6346	6C
6347	87H
6348	85A
6349	85B
6350	6C
6351	82B
6352	86C
6353	86C
6354	85A
6355	84B
6356	83A
6357	85A
6358	82D
6359	85A
6360	82C
6361	86G
6362	84J
6363	82B
6364	83B
6365	85B
6366	81D
6367	84K
6368	85B
6369	86E
6370	86A
6371	89C
6372	83B
6373	85B
6374	82B
6375	86E
6376	6C
6377	83B
6378	85A
6379	81F
6380	84K
6381	85B
6382	85A
6383	89C
6384	82C
6385	83C
6386	86E
6387	82C
6388	85A
6389	85A
6390	83B
6391	84F
6392	84K
6393	86G
6394	84E
6395	85C
6396	85A
6397	83E
6398	83B
6399	82D

6400 class 0-6-0PT 2P

No.	Shed
6400	86G
6401	88E
6402	88A
6403	86G
6404	84A
6405	84J
6406	83D
6407	83D
6408	88D
6409	86A
6410	86J
6411	88E
6412	87E
6413	86J
6414	83D
6415	86A
6416	88A
6417	86J
6418	84A
6419	83D
6420	83D
6421	83D
6422	84A
6423	88A
6424	86G
6425	87E
6426	86A
6427	88D
6428	86A
6429	86G
6430	86A
6431	87E
6432	86G
6433	88D
6434	88D
6435	88D
6436	88D
6437	86J
6438	88E
6439	86A

5600 class 0-6-2T 5MT

No.	Shed
6600	86C
6601	82B
6602	86C
6603	88A
6604	87E
6605	86J
6606	84G
6607	88A
6608	88A
6609	84F
6610	84B
6611	84J
6612	88A
6613	87D
6614	84E
6615	88C
6616	87B
6617	84J
6618	88A
6619	88C
6620	84E
6621	86H
6622	86J
6623	87B
6624	84D
6625	82D
6626	88A
6627	81D
6628	86J
6629	87B
6630	81E
6631	85B
6632	84J
6633	84G
6634	86G
6635	88A
6636	86G
6637	88C
6638	88A
6639	86E
6640	84B
6641	88C
6642	86A
6643	88C
6644	87D
6645	84B
6646	84F
6647	88A
6648	88F
6649	86J
6650	87B
6651	86J
6652	86J
6653	86G
6654	81C
6655	81C
6656	82B
6657	84D
6658	88C
6659	88A
6660	88A
6661	86J
6662	87D
6663	
6664	81B
6665	88A
6666	86E
6667	84F
6668	84E
6669	84E
6670	82B
6671	82B
6672	86E
6673	86E
6674	84F
6675	86G
6676	86F
6677	84F
6678	84F
6679	86F
6680	87E
6681	84F
6682	88A
6683	84F
6684	88A
6685	86G
6686	87B
6687	86J
6688	87E
6689	86E
6690	85B
6691	87B
6692	84F
6693	86G
6694	84J
6695	87E
6696	84J
6697	84D
6698	84F
6699	82D

6700 class 0-6-0PT 3F

No.	Shed
6700	88B
6701	88B
6702	88B
6703	88B
6704	88B
6705	88B
6706	88B
6707	88B
6708	88B
6709	88B
6710	86B
6711	86B
6712	88C
6713	87K
6714	87C
6715	87B
6716	82C
6717	87B
6718	87B
6719	87B
6720	87K
6721	88B
6722	88C
6723	88C
6724	88C
6725	86B
6726	86B
6727	86B
6728	86B
6729	86B
6730	86B
6731	86B
6732	86B
6733	88C
6734	87K
6735	86B
6736	88B
6737	82C
6738	88C
6739	82C
6740	88C
6741	82C
6742	86B
6743	86B
6744	88B

6745	88C	6774	88C	6820*	86A	6849*	84K	6878*	6C
6746	88C	6775	88C	6821*	83D	6850*	82C	6879*	84B
6747	88C	6776	87B	6822*	83A	6851*	85A		
6748	88C	6777	87B	6823*	84F	6852*	82B	**4900 'Hall' class 4-6-0**	
6749	87B	6778	88B	6824*	83G	6853*	84E	**5MT**	
6750	88C	6779	88B	6825*	83G	6854*	84B	6900	82A
6751	88B			6826*	83G	6855*	83D	6901*	84K
6752	88C	**6800 'Grange' class 4-6-0**		6827*	82B	6856*	84B	6902*	82F
6753	88C	**5MT**		6828*	84F	6857*	84F	6903*	87E
6754	88C	6800*	83G	6829*	83A	6858*	84G	6904*	84E
6755	86B	6801*	83G	6830*	82B	6859*	6C	6905*	87E
6756	86B	6802*	83D	6831*	6C	6860*	83G	6906*	84C
6757	86B	6803*	84F	6832*	82C	6861*	84B	6907*	83D
6758	88C	6804*	82B	6833*	82B	6862*	84B	6908*	82B
6759	86B	6805*	82C	6834*	81D	6863*	82B	6909*	87J
6760	86B	6806*	84K	6835*	82B	6864*	81D	6910*	81E
6761	87B	6807*	85A	6836*	83G	6865*	81D	6911*	83G
6762	87C	6808*	83G	6837*	83G	6866*	84E	6912*	83D
6763	87C	6809*	83G	6838*	83D	6867*	82B	6913*	83D
6764	86B	6810*	87F	6839*	84B	6868*	83B	6914*	82D
6765	88B	6811*	82B	6840*	86G	6869*	83D	6915*	82C
6766	87C	6812*	86A	6841*	6C	6870*	86A	6916*	85C
6767	88B	6813*	83A	6842*	82B	6871*	86G	6917*	85B
6768	87K	6814*	83A	6843*	84E	6872*	86G	6918*	87E
6769	88C	6815*	83B	6844*	87F	6873*	83D	6919*	82F
6770	88B	6816*	83D	6845*	82B	6874*	83B	6920*	81F
6771	88B	6817*	84K	6846*	82B	6875*	83B	6921*	85B
6772	86B	6818*	87F	6847*	86A	6876*	82B	6922*	81F
6773	88B	6819*	86G	6848*	83A	6877*	85A	6923*	81D

'5600' class 0-6-2T No 6678 moves slowly up to an adverse signal at the north end of Birmingham Snow Hill on Saturday 3 December 1955. Dating from February 1928, this was the second batch of these successful engines. This example was a familiar sight around the West Midlands, having a long association with Stourbridge shed in the 1950s and 1960s, remaining there until withdrawn in November 1964 and sold to Cashmore's at Great Bridge for scrap.

Michael Mensing

Above: The modified Halls, introduced in 1944, were a Hawksworth development of the earlier type with larger superheater, one-piece main frames and a plate framed bogie. No 6960 *Raveningham Hall* was the second to appear in February and was delivered to Old Oak Common. This view on Tuesday 3 May 1955 was recorded at West Bromwich when the engine was based at Reading after transfer from London in September 1953. There it remained until August 1963 when it was added to Oxford's allocation, and withdrawn in June 1964. It was rescued from Barry dump and can now be seen in the care of the Severn Valley Railway.

G. W. Sharpe

Below: A long way from home at Plymouth Laira is 'Grange' class 4-6-0 No 6816 *Frankton Grange* on Shrewsbury shed in 1955. This was a variation of the 'Hall', with smaller wheels but with a bigger tractive effort. No 6816 appeared in December 1936 and started life at Wolverhampton Oxley. From 1955 to 1964 the engine was based in the West Country including Bristol before a move to Worcester in July 1965, from where it was immediately withdrawn. *G. W. Sharpe*

No.	Shed		No.	Shed
6924*	84B		6986*	82B
6925*	82B		6987*	85A
6926*	84B		6988*	83A
6927*	81D		6989*	85C
6928*	86C		6990*	81A
6929*	84C		6991*	81C
6930*	85A		6992*	85C
6931*	83F		6993*	82F
6932*	86C		6994*	82D
6933*	83A		6995*	83B
6934*	83G		6996*	83B
6935*	82D		6997*	82A
6936*	82A		6998*	86C
6937*	81F		6999*	86C
6938*	83C			

4073 'Castle' class 4-6-0 7P

No.	Shed
6939*	86C
6940*	83D
6941*	84K
6942*	84B
6943*	86C
6944*	84G
6945*	82F
6946*	86C
6947*	85A
6948*	86C
6949*	84A
6950*	85A
6951*	86C
6952*	81E
6953*	81F
6954*	82A
6955*	82D
6956*	84A
6957*	82A
6958*	82A

7000*	83A
7001*	81A
7002*	87E
7003*	87E
7004*	81A
7005*	85A
7006*	85B
7007*	85A
7008*	81F
7009*	87E
7010*	81A
7011*	82A
7012*	87E
7013*	85A
7014*	82A
7015*	82C
7016*	86C
7017*	81A
7018*	87E
7019*	82A

6959 'Modified Hall' class 4-6-0 5MT

No.	Shed
6959*	81A
6960*	81D
6961*	81A
6962*	81A
6963*	84K
6964*	84A
6965*	83D
6966*	84C
6967*	82C
6968*	81D
6969*	86C
6970*	81F
6971*	84E
6972*	82A
6973*	81A
6974*	81A
6975*	84A
6976*	84C
6977*	82B
6978*	83D
6979*	84C
6980*	84G
6981*	82A
6982*	82B
6983*	81E
6984*	85C
6985*	85B

7020*	86C
7021*	87E
7022*	86C
7023*	86C
7024*	81A
7025*	81A
7026*	84A
7027*	81A
7028*	87E
7029*	83A
7030*	81A
7031*	83D
7032*	81A
7033*	81A
7034*	82A
7035*	85B
7036*	81A
7037*	82C

7200 class 2-8-2T 8F

No.	Shed
7200	87E
7201	82B
7202	88A
7203	86A
7204	85C
7205	88A
7206	86G
7207	87E
7208	86E
7209	87E
7210	86A
7211	87F
7212	81F
7213	86J
7214	86A
7215	87F
7216	86J
7217	87E
7218	86A
7219	86A
7220	86G
7221	86J
7222	85C
7223	86E
7224	87D
7225	87F
7226	87D
7227	86A
7228	87F
7229	86A
7230	86E
7231	86A
7232	86A
7233	86G
7234	86G
7235	86G
7236	87E
7237	86E
7238	81F
7239	81F
7240	87F
7241	82B
7242	86A
7243	87B
7244	87E
7245	86A
7246	81F
7247	86A
7248	87E
7249	88A
7250	82B
7251	86E
7252	88A
7253	86A

4300 class 2-6-0 4MT

No.	Shed
7300	82D
7301	85C
7302	82D
7303	82B
7304	83B
7305	84J
7306	87H
7307	85C
7308	85C
7309	84G
7310	84J
7311	83B
7312	85B
7313	84J
7314	85C
7315	84C
7316	83C
7317	84E
7318	87H
7319	86A
7320	87F
7321	82C

7400 class 0-6-0PT 2F

No.	Shed
7400	87G
7401	87G
7402	89C
7403	84J
7404	81F
7405	89A
7406	89C
7407	87G
7408	82F
7409	84J
7410	89A
7411	81F
7412	81F
7413	82C
7414	84J
7415	82C
7416	85C
7417	89C
7418	82C
7419	87G
7420	85C
7421	82C
7422	83F
7423	86J
7424	82C
7425	87G
7426	86G
7427	83A
7428	84F
7429	84F
7430	84F
7431	84J
7432	84F
7433	84J
7434	89A
7435	84F
7436	81F
7437	85C
7438	84E
7439	87K
7440	84J
7441	84F
7442	84J
7443	84J
7444	87G
7445	88A
7446	83E
7447	84J
7448	84F
7449	84F

5700 class 0-6-0PT 3F

No.	Shed		No.	Shed
7700	85D		7707	85C
7701	87A		7708	81D
7702	84D		7709	83E
7703	86H		7710	81E
7704	87D		7711	83E
7705	84F		7712	86B
7706	87B		7713	84E
			7714	6C
			7715	83E
			7716	83C
			7717	88D
			7718	87D
			7719	82B
			7720	86B
			7721	86B
			7722	88B
			7723	85B
			7724	86G
			7725	86F
			7726	88A
			7727	82D
			7728	82B
			7729	82B
			7730	81C
			7731	81C
			7732	81C
			7733	87B
			7734	81A
			7735	84E
			7736	86A
			7737	87A
			7738	88B
			7739	87A
			7740	86G
			7741	85B
			7742	87A
			7743	87A
			7744	87B
			7745	87F
			7746	86F
			7747	87J
			7748	82D
			7749	82B
			7750	85A
			7751	88B
			7752	86F
			7753	86F
			7754	84H
			7755	87G
			7756	87D
			7757	87A
			7758	84E
			7759	84B
			7760	81F
			7761	83C
			7762	83D
			7763	84C
			7764	86E
			7765	87F
			7766	88D
			7767	87A
			7768	86A
			7769	87A
			7770	86F
			7771	86A

The last few 'Castles' were built under BR control and this portrait of No 7029 *Clun Castle* on Shrewsbury shed in 1955 was an example. Entering traffic in May 1950, Newton Abbot was the first allocation. Subsequent moves were to Plymouth Laira in December 1956, back to Newton Abbot in March 1957, Old Oak Common in August 1962 and Gloucester in October 1964. Withdrawn in December 1965, it was secured for preservation and is at Tyseley Locomotive Works (Birmingham Railway Museum).

G. W. Sharpe

A view of Whitland East signalbox in May 1955 with '7200' class 2-8-2T No 7203 approaching on a lengthy freight. Another rebuild, this was formerly No 5278 and was converted in September 1934 then allocated to Newport Ebbw Junction. When this scene was recorded it had become Llanelly based, moving from Ebbw Junction the previous February. It was withdrawn in December from Severn Tunnel Junction and sold to King's at Norwich for scrap. *G. W. Sharpe*

Designed by Collett for freight work, this '7400' class 0-6-0PT No 7439, ex-works on Barry shed in July 1956, had been built after Nationalisation in October 1948 and first allocated to Llanelly. Moving to Swansea Victoria in June 1950, it stayed there until a move to Carmarthen in February 1955. There it stayed until 1964 when, after a short stay at Neath, history repeated itself and in July it returned to Llanelly, withdrawal coming seven months later. *G. W. Sharpe*

No.	Shed	No.	Shed
7772	88D	7786	87A
7773	86J	7787	87E
7774	86H	7788	81D
7775	86H	7789	86E
7776	87F	7790	82B
7777	81D	7791	81A
7778	86F	7792	82C
7779	88A	7793	82B
7780	82B	7794	82C
7781	86A	7795	82B
7782	82A	7796	86G
7783	82B	7797	84B
7784	82D	7798	86F
7785	87F	7799	87A

7800 'Manor' class 4-6-0 5MT

No.	Shed	No.	Shed
7800*	84K	7815*	83D
7801*	84K	7816*	83E
7802*	89C	7817*	84J
7803*	89C	7818*	84E
7804*	87G	7819*	89A
7805*	85C	7820*	83D
7806*	83A	7821*	84E
7807*	84K	7822*	84K
7808*	85B	7823*	84J
7809*	83D	7824*	83D
7810*	85B	7825*	87G
7811*	84G	7826*	87G
7812*	83A	7827*	84K
7813*	83A	7828*	84G
7814*	83D	7829*	87G

6959 'Modified Hall' class 4-6-0 5MT

No.	Shed
7900*	81F
7901*	82A
7902*	81A
7903*	81A
7904*	81A
7905*	83D
7906*	81D
7907*	82B
7908*	82B
7909*	83D
7910*	81C
7911*	81F
7912*	84E
7913*	84E
7914*	82C
7915*	84B
7916*	83A
7917*	82D
7918*	84E
7919*	81D
7920*	85A
7921*	84K
7922*	84K
7923*	82C
7924*	82D
7925*	83G
7926*	85B
7927*	81D
7928*	85A
7929*	84E

8100 class 2-6-2T 4MT

No.	Shed
8100	84D
8101	85D
8102	87H
8103	87G
8104	87A
8105	85A
8106	85A
8107	87H
8108	84E
8109	84D

9400 class 0-6-0PT 4F

No.	Shed	No.	Shed	No.	Shed
8400	84C	8434	81A	8467	87F
8401	86E	8435	81E	8468	84E
8402	86C	8436	86H	8469	88B
8403	83A	8437	84F	8470	88A
8404	83A	8438	84F	8471	88A
8405	84C	8439	86H	8472	82C
8406	86A	8440	86A	8473	83G
8407	84C	8441	88B	8474	87F
8408	87C	8442	87A	8475	87C
8409	83G	8443	87D	8476	87C
8410	87B	8444	86J	8477	87F
8411	84A	8445	86J	8478	88A
8412	83F	8446	86F	8479	82D
8413	82B	8447	86C	8480	85A
8414	88B	8448	86F	8481	88A
8415	84E	8449	84B	8482	88A
8416	88B	8450	86E	8483	87C
8417	84E	8451	83A	8484	88A
8418		8452	84C	8485	83F
8419	84F	8453	86A	8486	83F
8420	88F	8454	87B	8487	85B
8421	83F	8455	88C	8488	85B
8422	83D	8456	83C	8489	88A
8423	87B	8457	88B	8490	87B
8424	88B	8458	85A	8491	82B
8425	83D	8459	84C	8492	82B
8426	83D	8460	88F	8493	86H
8427	85A	8461	82C	8494	86H
8428	84B	8462	84A	8495	88A
8429	88B	8463	87E	8496	85A
8430	81D	8464	88B	8497	86F
8431	87D	8465	88B	8498	86F
8432	81A	8466	87B	8499	86A
8433	81A				

5700 class 0-6-0PT 3F

No.	Shed	No.	Shed	No.	Shed
8700	84E	8734	84A	8767	81A
8701	85C	8735	88C	8768	81A
8702	82B	8736	88D	8769	81A
8703	82B	8737	82B	8770	81A
8704	84F	8738	87H	8771	81A
8705	84A	8739	86D	8772	81A
8706	87K	8740	86F	8773	81A
8707	81A	8741	82B	8774	81C
8708	87F	8742	84F	8775	87A
8709	83D	8743	88B	8776	86C
8710	86A	8744	82D	8777	86G
8711	86A	8745	82E	8778	86A
8712	86F	8746	82B	8779	82C
8713	82B	8747	82B	8780	88A
8714	82B	8748	86F	8781	85B
8715	87A	8749	87F	8782	87A
8716	86G	8750	81C	8783	82C
8717	85B	8751	81A	8784	87A
8718	85D	8752	81C	8785	87F
8719	83D	8753	81C	8786	86H
8720	87C	8754	81A	8787	84C
8721	86F	8755	86G	8788	86G
8722	88B	8756	81A	8789	87E
8723	86C	8757	81A	8790	82B
8724	87C	8758	81C	8791	84F
8725	6C	8759	81A	8792	84F
8726	84A	8760	81A	8793	82C
8727	85D	8761	81A	8794	86A
8728	86C	8762	81A	8795	82B
8729	84K	8763	81A	8796	86B
8730	82B	8764	81A	8797	84F
8731	85D	8765	81A	8798	84A
8732	87F	8766	86A	8799	86E
8733	83E				

9000 'Dukedog' class 4-4-0 2P

No.	Shed
9000	89C
9003	89C
9004	89C
9005	89C
9008	89C
9009	89C
9010	89A
9011	82C
9012	89C
9013	89C
9014	89C
9015	81F

One of the batch of 10 'Manors' built after Nationalisation, No 7828 *Odney Manor* leaves Shrewsbury in 1955 on the 'Cambrian Coast Express'. Built in December 1950 and first allocated to Neath, it moved two years later to Shrewsbury where it stayed until May 1961, then moving to Wrexham Croes Newydd, then Machynlleth in March 1963, and back to Shrewsbury in January 1965. Withdrawal came in October the same year followed by storage at Barry Docks until 1981. Rescued for preservation, it currently enjoys life at the West Somerset Railway.

G. W. Sharpe

Another scene at Shrewsbury in 1955 with 'Modified Hall' No 7915 *Mere Hall* paired with a non-standard self-weighing tender. Entering traffic in March 1950 and going to Wolverhampton Stafford Road, then on to Oxley in April 1951, its only move then was to Birmingham Tyseley in October 1962, from where it was withdrawn in October 1965.

G. W. Sharpe

We move to Worcester shed in May 1956 to view '8100' class 2-6-2T No 8106 alongside another 85A resident, 'Castle' No 5086 *Viscount Horne*. No 8106 was a Collett rebuild in June 1939 from older Churchward 2-6-2T No 5126 and spent many years at Worcester. It was still there when withdrawn in December 1963.

G. W. Sharpe

An interesting comparison in pannier tank types at Exeter shed in April 1956. Both '9400' class No 8456 and '5700' class No 9765 belonged to 83C at the time. No 9765 had been built at Swindon in September 1935 and first allocated to St Blazey, while No 8456 had entered traffic in February 1950 at Taunton, as a delivery from Yorkshire Engine Co, moving on to Exeter two months later. No 9765 had joined the allocation in April 1953 from Plymouth Laira and remained until withdrawn in December 1961. No 8456 transferred to Southall in November 1958 and remained there until withdrawal in October 1963. *G. W. Sharpe*

Arriving from the Cambrian route into Shrewsbury in 1956 is 'Dukedog' 4-4-0 No 9018 and an unidentified '4300' 2-6-0. The 'Dukedogs' were 1930s rebuilds using 'Bulldog' class frames and this one appeared in April 1938. Withdrawal came in June 1960 from Oswestry. *G. W. Sharpe*

A look at the last batch of '4300' class 2-6-0s to be built sees No 9308 at Old Oak Common in March 1956. Built in 1932, it went new to 81A and was withdrawn in September 1962 from Shrewsbury as No 7330, the renumbering taking place in June 1957. *P. H. Groom*

Above: This portrait of '9400' class 0-6-0PT No 9430 was taken at its home shed Neath in 1955, where it had arrived new from R. Stephenson & Hawthorn in October 1950. In July 1961 it took up new duties as a Lickey banker at Bromsgrove, moving away in October 1964 to Bristol Barrow Road before its withdrawal in June 1965.
R. H. G. Simpson

Below: Another '5700' class 0-6-0PT with a difference, this time with condensing gear, No 9700 runs into Paddington with empty stock in 1954. Dating from February 1931, it spent its whole time allocated to Old Oak Common, finally going to Swindon Works in October 1963 for scrapping.
G. W. Sharpe

Number	Shed
9016	89C
9017	89C
9018	89C
9020	89C
9021	89C
9022	89C
9023	82C
9024	89C
9025	89C
9026	89A
9027	89A
9028	84J

4300 class 2-6-0 4MT

Number	Shed
9300	86C
9301	81C
9302	81F
9303	84E
9304	86C
9305	81C
9306	81D
9307	84B
9308	81D
9309	81C
9310	87G
9311	81F
9312	84A
9313	81C
9314	84B
9315	81C
9316	84B
9317	84B
9318	84F
9319	84E

9400 class 0-6-0PT 4F

Number	Shed
9400	82C
9401	81D
9402	81D
9403	81F
9404	81D
9405	81D
9406	81B
9407	81C
9408	84B
9409	81C
9410	81A
9411	81A
9412	81A
9413	81E
9414	81A
9415	81B
9416	81F
9417	81E
9418	81A
9419	81A
9420	81A
9421	81B
9422	81A
9423	81A
9424	81B
9425	84C
9426	84C
9427	86H
9428	84A
9429	85A
9430	87A
9431	87B
9432	84E
9433	83D
9434	83F
9435	84A
9436	87A
9437	87B
9438	85B
9439	83C
9440	83A
9441	
9442	87A
9443	87F
9444	87B
9445	85B
9446	87A
9447	87B
9448	87A
9449	84C
9450	86H
9451	87A
9452	87A
9453	82B
9454	87B
9455	87B
9456	87B
9457	87B
9458	86A
9459	86C
9460	86H
9461	86C
9462	83A
9463	83G
9464	85B
9465	87F
9466	85A
9467	83D
9468	87F
9469	87F
9470	88C
9471	85B
9472	87F
9473	87A
9474	87F
9475	85A
9476	82C
9477	84F
9478	87A
9479	87F
9480	85A
9481	82B
9482	86A
9483	87B
9484	87E
9485	87C
9486	87F
9487	87B
9488	82B
9489	87D
9490	86A
9491	87C
9492	87F
9493	86C
9494	88B
9495	82B
9496	84A
9497	83C

5700 class 0-6-0PT 3F

Number	Shed
9600	82C
9601	82E
9602	87J
9603	86C
9604	82A
9605	82B
9606	87C
9607	86J
9608	84E
9609	86J
9610	82A
9611	81F
9612	82D
9613	84F
9614	84E
9615	82D
9616	86A
9617	87B
9618	88D
9619	85C
9620	82F
9621	84A
9622	88D
9623	83A
9624	84H
9625	87D
9626	82B
9627	87A
9628	82D
9629	83C
9630	84H
9631	88C
9632	86A
9633	83A
9634	87B
9635	84E
9636	84F
9637	86A
9638	88D
9639	84H
9640	81F
9641	81C
9642	82F
9643	88D
9644	86A
9645	87D
9646	83B
9647	83B
9648	86C
9649	86F
9650	86G
9651	6C
9652	87H
9653	81F
9654	81F
9655	83E
9656	84G
9657	84G
9658	81A
9659	81A
9660	86F
9661	81A
9662	86A
9663	83B
9664	86A
9665	85C
9666	87G
9667	86A
9668	83A
9669	84J
9670	83B
9671	83D
9672	84G
9673	83E
9674	86A
9675	88D
9676	88C
9677	88B
9678	83A
9679	88B
9680	84E
9681	86F
9682	84E
9700	81A
9701	81A
9702	81A
9703	81A
9704	81A
9705	81A
9706	81A
9707	81A
9708	81A
9709	81A
9710	81A
9711	83D
9712	86J
9713	86C
9714	87H
9715	84B
9716	83D
9717	85C
9718	83B
9719	84F
9720	82C
9721	82C
9722	81B
9723	86C
9724	84E
9725	81A
9726	81C
9727	85B
9728	84K
9729	82B
9730	86G
9731	86J
9732	82E
9733	84E
9734	87A
9735	87B
9736	87B
9737	87B
9738	87E
9739	84B
9740	84G
9741	84H
9742	84H
9743	87F
9744	87D
9745	86E
9746	86A
9747	88D
9748	83G
9749	81D
9750	87A
9751	81A
9752	84B
9753	84E
9754	81A
9755	83E
9756	87A
9757	83B
9758	81A
9759	86C
9760	87J
9761	87E
9762	82D
9763	81D
9764	82E
9765	83C
9766	87B
9767	84F
9768	84B
9769	88B
9770	83D
9771	82B
9772	82C
9773	82C
9774	84H
9775	87E
9776	88B
9777	87E
9778	86C
9779	87A
9780	86D
9781	81B
9782	84F
9783	87A
9784	81A
9785	87B
9786	87A
9787	87F
9788	87F
9789	81B
9790	82C
9791	81D
9792	87A
9793	84J
9794	84K
9795	82C
9796	86G
9797	86G
9798	84E
9799	87B

M7 class 0-4-4T 2P

Number	Shed
30021	72A
30022	70C
30023	72A
30024	72A

No.	Shed
30025	72A
30026	70C
30027	70C
30028	70C
30029	71A
30030	71A
30031	71A
30032	71A
30033	71A
30034	72D
30035	72D
30036	72D
30037	72D
30038	70B
30039	72D
30040	72D
30041	70B
30042	70B
30043	70B
30044	72A
30045	72A
30046	72A
30047	75D
30048	75D
30049	75D
30050	75D
30051	75D
30052	75A
30053	75A
30054	70F
30055	70F
30056	71B
30057	71B
30058	71B
30059	71B
30060	71B

USA class 0-6-0T 3F

No.	Shed
30061	71I
30062	71I
30063	71I
30064	71I
30065	71I
30066	71I
30067	71I
30068	71I
30069	71I
30070	71I
30071	71I
30072	71I
30073	71I
30074	71I

B4 class 0-4-0T 1F

No.	Shed
30082	71A
30083	71A
30084	74C
30086	74C
30087	71B
30088	72D
30089	72D
30093	71B
30094	72D
30096	71A
30102	72D

M7 class 0-4-4T 2P

No.	Shed
30104	71B
30105	71B
30106	71B
30107	71B
30108	75D
30109	70C
30110	70C
30111	71B
30112	71B

T9 class 4-4-0 3P

No.	Shed
30117	71A
30120	71A

M7 class 0-4-4T 2P

No.	Shed
30123	70A
30124	70A
30125	71A
30127	71A
30128	71B
30129	75A
30130	71A
30131	72C
30132	70A
30133	70A

G6 class 0-6-0T 2F

No.	Shed
30160	70E
30162	71B

02 class 0-4-4T 0P

No.	Shed
30177	71A
30179	71A
30182	72C
30183	72D
30192	72D
30193	72A
30199	72A
30200	72F
30203	72F
30207	70F
30212	71B
30216	72D
30223	71B
30224	70A
30225	72D
30229	71A
30230	70B
30232	72A
30233	71A
30236	72D

G6 class 0-6-0T 2F

No.	Shed
30238	70C

M7 class 0-4-4T 2P

No.	Shed
30241	70A
30242	70A
30243	70A
30244	70A
30245	70A
30246	70C
30247	72E
30248	70A
30249	70A
30250	72E
30251	72E
30252	72E
30253	72E
30254	72E
30255	72E
30256	72E

G6 class 0-6-0T 2F

No.	Shed
30258	70D
30260	71B
30266	72B
30270	72B
30274	71H
30277	70C

T9 class 4-4-0 3P

No.	Shed
30283	71A
30284	71A
30285	71A
30287	71A
30288	71A
30289	71A
30300	71A
30301	72B
30304	72B

700 class 0-6-0 3F

No.	Shed
30306	71A
30308	70C
30309	72B

T9 class 4-4-0 3P

No.	Shed
30310	71A
30313	72B

700 class 0-6-0 3F

No.	Shed
30315	72A
30316	71A
30317	72B

M7 class 0-4-4T 2P

No.	Shed
30318	71B
30319	70A
30320	70A
30321	70A
30322	70A
30323	72A
30324	70C

700 class 0-6-0 3F

No.	Shed
30325	70C
30326	70C
30327	72B

M7 class 0-4-4T 2P

No.	Shed
30328	70C

H15 class 4-6-0 4P5F

No.	Shed
30330	72B
30331	72B
30332	72B
30333	72B
30334	72B
30335	72B

T9 class 4-4-0 3P

No.	Shed
30337	70C
30338	70A

700 class 0-6-0 3F

No.	Shed
30339	70B
30346	70B

G6 class 0-6-0T 2F

No.	Shed
30349	70C

700 class 0-6-0 3F

No.	Shed
30350	70C
30352	70B
30355	70B

M7 class 0-4-4T 2P

No.	Shed
30356	70F
30357	70F

700 class 0-6-0 3F

No.	Shed
30368	70D

M7 class 0-4-4T 2P

No.	Shed
30374	72A
30375	71A
30376	71A
30377	71A
30378	71A
30379	71A

L12 class 4-4-0 2P

No.	Shed
30434	70C

N15 'King Arthur' class 4-6-0 5P

No.	Shed
30448*	72B
30449*	72B
30450*	72B
30451*	72B
30452*	72B
30453*	72B
30454*	72B
30455*	70A
30456*	70A
30457*	70A

D15 class 4-4-0 3P

No.	Shed
30465	70A
30467	70A

H15 class 4-6-0 4P5F

No.	Shed
30473	71A
30474	71A
30475	71A
30476	71A
30477	71A
30478	71A

M7 class 0-4-4T 2P

No.	Shed
30479	71A
30480	71A
30481	71A

H15 class 4-6-0 4P5F

No.	Shed
30482	70A
30483	70A
30484	70A
30485	70A
30486	70A
30487	70A
30488	70A
30489	70A
30490	70A
30491	70A

G16 class 4-8-0T 8F

No.	Shed
30492	70B
30493	70B
30494	70B
30495	70B

S15 class 4-6-0 6F

No.	Shed
30496	70B
30497	70B
30498	70B
30499	70B
30500	70B
30501	70B
30502	70B
30503	70B
30504	70B
30505	70B
30506	70B
30507	70B
30508	70B
30509	70B
30510	70B
30511	70B
30512	70B
30513	70B
30514	70B
30515	70B

H16 class 4-6-2T 6F

No.	Shed
30516	70B
30517	70B
30518	70B
30519	70B
30520	70B

H15 class 4-6-0 4P5F

No.	Shed
30521	70A
30522	70A
30523	70A
30524	70A

Q class 0-6-0 4F

No.	Shed
30530	71A
30531	71A
30532	71A
30533	75C
30534	75C
30535	71A
30536	71A
30537	75C

Above: Eastleigh shed is host to Exmouth Junction-based 'M7' class 0-4-4T No 30025 in 1954. Dating back to February 1899, this Drummond LSWR engine survived until 10 May 1964, its last allocation being Salisbury, and was one of the last in service. *G. W. Sharpe*

Below: The USA 0-6-0Ts were acquired from the War Department in December 1946 and had been built by the Porter and Vulcan firms of America in 1942 and 1943. They were used as dock shunters at Southampton, where this scene was recorded in July 1957 with No 30073. Displaced by diesel shunters, six of the class became departmental engines. No 30073 was not so lucky and was withdrawn on 8 January 1967. *G. W. Sharpe*

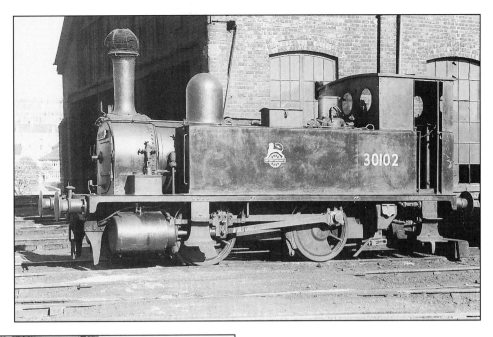

A second 'B4' preserved is No 30102 at Bressingham Steam Museum. This 1955 view is at Plymouth Friary shed where this little engine spent many years before going to Eastleigh in November 1958 when dock shunting duties were turned over to diesels. Note the spark arrestor on the chimney, essential when working in the timber yards at Oreston. Later in 1958 transfer took place to Bournemouth, but a return was made to Eastleigh in October 1961 before withdrawal on 15 September 1963. *G. W. Sharpe*

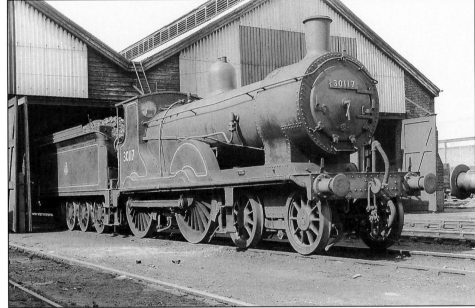

The graceful lines of 'T9' class 4-4-0 No 30117 are shown in this view at Eastleigh shed in May 1955. Built at the Nine Elms Works of the LSWR in July 1899, this member of the class received a superheater in November 1927 and was withdrawn from Eastleigh on 22 July 1961. *G. W. Sharpe*

'G6' class 0-6-0T No 30160 on Reading South shed on Sunday 7 August 1955. Designed by Adams with later modifications by Drummond, this one dated from March 1900. It had been transferred to Reading in May 1952 from Nine Elms, moving on to Basingstoke in December 1956 from where withdrawal was actioned on 25 April 1959. *G. W. Sharpe*

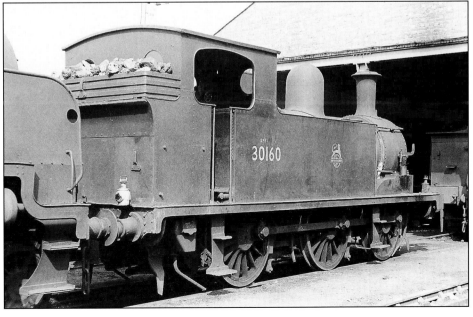

'O2' class 0-4-4T No 30212, built in May 1892, is alongside Bournemouth shed on carriage shunting duties in May 1955. Eastleigh claimed the engine in September 1956, where it remained until withdrawn on 5 December 1959 and cut up in the works the next month. *G. W. Sharpe*

Ex-works on Eastleigh shed on Thursday 23 August 1956 awaiting return to its home shed at Salisbury is '700' class 0-6-0 No 30317. It was built in May 1897 for the LSWR to a Drummond design; the class became extinct in December 1962. No 30317 went to Exmouth Junction in April 1958 and was withdrawn on 22 July 1961, coming back to Eastleigh Works for scrapping. *G. W. Sharpe*

The robust lines of Drummond's 'H15' class 4-6-0 No 30335 are caught in this view on Eastleigh shed in June 1955. This locomotive had been completely rebuilt in November 1914 with two cylinders from an 'E14' class four-cylinder 4-6-0. Allocated to Salisbury at Nationalisation, it spent January to June 1950 at Feltham, then went on to Nine Elms before returning to Salisbury in October the same year for the rest of its days until it was withdrawn on 6 June 1959. *G. W. Sharpe*

Not long out of works, Urie-designed 'N15' 'King Arthur' class 4-6-0 No 30456 *Sir Galahad* looks superb at home at Nine Elms shed in 1954. Built in 1925, this was then the front-line passenger engine of the day. No 30456 was withdrawn on 14 May 1960 when allocated to Basingstoke, the last class member bowing out in 1962.

G. W. Sharpe

Boscombe on the Bournemouth to Eastleigh line is the location for this view of 'H15' class 4-6-0 No 30485 on Monday 30 August 1954 with a semifast. This was a 1955 withdrawal, going from Nine Elms on 9 April.

G. W. Sharpe

Eastleigh shed in 1953 with ex-works 'G16' class 4-8-0T No 30494 awaiting return to its hump shunting duties at Feltham. Built in August 1921 to a Urie design for the then newly constructed marshalling yard at Feltham, it spent its whole career along with three companions at 70B, not being withdrawn until well after diesel shunters had appeared, on 8 December 1962.

R. H. G. Simpson

Another long-serving member of the Feltham fleet was No 30497, an 'S15' class 4-6-0, seen at Eastleigh shed on Thursday 23 August 1956. March 1920 was the production date for this Urie express freight engine. Withdrawal came on 7 July 1963, still based at Feltham, then storage, until March 1964 when it was towed to Cohens at Kettering for scrap. *G. W. Sharpe*

Another type associated with Feltham was the five-member 'H16' class of 4-6-2T. This example, No 30517, was built in November 1921 and photographed at Nine Elms shed in July 1957. Withdrawn on 29 December 1962, this was the last active member of the class. Stored at Feltham shed until May 1963, it was then cut up at Eastleigh Works. *G. W. Sharpe*

Nine Elms shed in 1955 is seen with its own 'H15' class 4-6-0 No 30522 awaiting work. This was one of the batch built in 1924 and entered traffic in July. Leaving Nine Elms in May 1959 to pastures new at Salisbury, it was withdrawn on 23 September 1961 and cut up at Eastleigh Works. *R. H. G. Simpson*

30538	75C
30539	75C
30540	75C
30541	71B
30542	71A
30543	71A
30544	75D
30545	75D
30546	75D
30547	75C
30548	71B
30549	71B

0395 class 0-6-0 2F

30564	72A
30566	71A
30567	70B
30568	70B
30569	70B
30570	70B
30572	70B
30573	70B
30574	70C
30575	70C
30577	70C
30578	70C
30579	70C
30580	70C

0415 class 4-4-2T 1P

30582	72A
30583	72A
30584	72A

0298 class 2-4-0T 0P

30585	72F
30586	72F
30587	72F

C14 class 0-4-0T 0P

30588	71A
30589	71A

M7 class 0-4-4T 2P

30667	72A
30668	72A
30669	72A
30670	72A
30671	72A
30673	72B
30674	72B
30675	70C
30676	72A

700 class 0-6-0 3F

30687	70B
30688	70B
30689	70B
30690	71B
30691	72A
30692	70A
30693	70C
30694	70A
30695	71B
30696	70B
30697	70A
30698	70A
30699	70A
30700	70A
30701	70A

T9 class 4-4-0 3P

30702	72B
30705	70D
30706	71B
30707	72C
30708	72A
30709	72A
30710	72A
30711	72A
30712	72A
30715	72A
30717	72A
30718	70A
30719	70A
30721	72B
30724	70D
30726	70F
30727	72A
30728	71B
30729	70F
30730	70F
30732	70F

N15 'King Arthur' class 4-6-0 5P

30736*	71B
30737*	71B
30738*	71B
30739*	71B
30740*	71B
30741*	71B
30742*	71B
30743*	71B
30744*	70A
30745*	70D
30746*	71A
30747*	71A
30748*	71A
30749*	70D
30750*	70A
30751*	70A
30752*	70A
30753*	70D
30755*	70A

757 class 0-6-2T 1P2F

30757*	72D
30758*	72D

N15 'King Arthur' class 4-6-0 5P

30763*	73A
30764*	73A
30765*	73A
30766*	73A
30767*	73A
30768*	73A
30769*	73A
30770*	73A
30771*	73A
30772*	73C
30773*	73A
30774*	73A
30775*	74C
30776*	74C
30777*	74C
30778*	70A
30779*	70A
30780*	70A
30781*	70A
30782*	71B
30783*	71B
30784*	71A
30785*	71A
30786*	71A
30787*	71A
30788*	71A
30789*	71A
30790*	71A
30791*	73A
30792*	73A
30793*	73A
30794*	73A
30795*	73A
30796*	74C
30797*	74C
30798*	74C
30799*	73B
30800*	73B
30801*	73B
30802*	74A
30803*	74A
30804*	74A
30805*	74A
30806*	73C

S15 class 4-6-0 6F

30823	72B
30824	72B
30825	72B
30826	72B
30827	72B
30828	72B
30829	72B
30830	72B
30831	72B
30832	72B
30833	70B
30834	70B
30835	75B
30836	75B
30837	75B
30838	70B
30839	70B
30840	70B
30841	72A
30842	72A
30843	72A
30844	72A
30845	72A
30846	72A
30847	72B

LN 'Lord Nelson' class 4-6-0 7P

30850*	71A
30851*	71A
30852*	71A
30853*	71A
30854*	71A
30855*	71A
30856*	71A
30857*	71A
30858*	70A
30859*	70A
30860*	70A
30861*	71B
30862*	71B
30863*	71B
30864*	71B
30865*	71B

V 'Schools' class 4-4-0 5P

30900*	74E
30901*	74E
30902*	74E
30903*	74E
30904*	74E
30905*	74E
30906*	74E
30907*	74E
30908*	74E
30909*	74E
30910*	74E
30911*	74B
30912*	74B
30913*	74B
30914*	74B
30915*	73A
30916*	74B
30917*	74B
30918*	74B
30919*	74C
30920*	74C
30921*	74C
30922*	74B
30923*	74C
30924*	73B
30925*	73B
30926*	73B
30927*	73B
30928*	73B
30929*	73B
30930*	73B
30931*	73B
30932*	73B
30933*	73B
30934*	73B
30935*	73B
30936*	73B
30937*	73B
30938*	73B
30939*	73B

Z class 0-8-0T 6F

30950	74D
30951	75E
30952	74A
30953	71H
30954	72A
30955	74A
30956	75A
30957	72B

C class 0-6-0 2F

31004	74B

H class 0-4-4T 1P

31005	73A

R1 class 0-6-0T 2F

31010	74A

C class 0-6-0 2F

31018	73C

E1 class 4-4-0 3P

31019	73A

P class 0-6-0T 0F

31027	74C

C class 0-6-0 2F

31033	73C
31037	74A

R1 class 0-6-0T 2F

31047	74C

01 class 0-6-0 2F

31048	74A

C class 0-6-0 2F

31054	73C
31059	73C
31061	73C
31063	73C

01 class 0-6-0 2F

31064	74A
31065	74C

E1 class 4-4-0 3P

31067	73A

C class 0-6-0 2F

31068	73B

R1 class 0-6-0T 2F

31069	74C

C class 0-6-0 2F

31071	73B

D class 4-4-0 2P

31075	75B

C class 0-6-0 2F

31086	73B
31102	73B

R1 class 0-6-0T 2F

31107	74C

Above: 'Q' class No 30543 seen on Eastleigh shed in May 1955. An Eastleigh engine for many years, in November 1962 it was moved to Horsham, then on to Three Bridges, then Brighton, and finally in May 1964 to Redhill where it was withdrawn on 20 December 1964. Along with No 30542, this was the last of the class. Stored at Eastleigh and Nine Elms, it was cut up at Ward's yard at Grays, Essex, in May 1965. *G. W. Sharpe*

Below: An elderly engine, but still useful, at Eastleigh shed in May 1955, '0395' class 0-6-0 No 30566 is seen. Dating back to October 1885, it was an Adams design for the LSWR. This was an Eastleigh inhabitant for its entire British Railways existence and was the last but one to be withdrawn on 7 February 1959. *G. W. Sharpe*

Adams 4-4-2T No 30583 dating from March 1885 is shown at Axminster on a Lyme Regis train on Monday 27 August 1956. Originally a class of 71 engines, three survived into the 1960s, all going in 1961. No 30583 lives on at the Bluebell Railway after withdrawal on 22 July 1961. *G. W. Sharpe*

Wadebridge in July 1957 sees Beattie Well Tank No 30587 outside the goods shed. A remarkable survivor from May 1874, it had been considerably rebuilt and renewed including receiving a Drummond boiler. All the other members of the class had been scrapped as long ago as 1898, but three remained for Wenford Bridge mineral line duties. All three were withdrawn in December 1962, and two remain in preservation, including this one which is at the South Devon Railway 'Primrose Line'. *G. W. Sharpe*

Another 'three member' class, the 'C14' 0-4-0Ts had two based at Eastleigh and one in service stock. No 30589 is taking a rest inside Eastleigh shed on Thursday 26 July 1951. Dating from January 1907, this engine was originally built as a 2-2-0T for railmotor work and later rebuilt for shunting duties at Southampton Docks. *G. W. Sharpe*

'T9' class 4-4-0 No 30709 at Exmouth Junction shed in July 1956. One of the batch built in 1899 by Dübs & Co, this was a West Country engine for many years, based at 72A and withdrawn in July 1961.
G. W. Sharpe

'King Arthur' class 4-6-0 No 30750 *Morgan Le Fay* is seen down from London and gracing the shed yard at Salisbury in 1956. Built in October 1922, this was included in the withdrawal list for 1957 and succumbed on 6 July after transfer from Nine Elms to Basingstoke only six weeks before. The name was transferred to Standard 4-6-0 No 73112 in April 1960.
R. H. G. Simpson

'S15' class 4-6-0 No 30839, allocated to Feltham, is seen at Eastleigh shed on Saturday 28 August 1954. Put to traffic in May 1936 and first allocated to Hither Green, this engine was withdrawn from Feltham on 19 September 1965 and reduced to scrap metal at Bird's yard at Risca, South Wales.
G. W. Sharpe

'Lord Nelson' class 4-6-0 No 30853 *Sir Richard Grenville* seen at home at Eastleigh shed in May 1955 after a visit to the works earlier in the year. Built in September 1928, and based at Eastleigh from December 1948 through to withdrawal on 3 March 1962, it returned to its birthplace, Eastleigh Works, for cutting up. *G. W. Sharpe*

'Schools' class 4-4-0 No 30937 *Epsom* at Folkestone Warren on Monday 1 August 1955. This member of the class dated from July 1935 and had gone new to Bricklayers Arms shed, where it served for many years. Seen here fitted with multiple-jet blastpipe and large-diameter chimney, this was the most powerful 4-4-0 to run in Britain. Modernisation caught up with No 30937 in 1962 when allocated to Nine Elms, withdrawal being sanctioned on 8 December. *L. Hanson*

The 'Z' class 0-8-0Ts were introduced in 1929 and equipped with three cylinders for heavy yard shunting. They were also used in their last years as banking engines for the stiff climb from Exeter St Davids to the Central station. This scene, recorded in March 1956 at Ashford shed, shows No 30951 awaiting its next assignment. It joined the rest of its classmates at Exmouth Junction in 1959 from where it was withdrawn on 24 November 1962. *P. H. Groom*

C class 0-6-0 2F

| 31112 | 73D |
| 31113 | 74C |

R1 class 0-6-0T 2F

| 31128 | 74C |

D1 class 4-4-0 3P

| 31145 | 74C |

R1 class 0-6-0T 2F

| 31147 | 74A |

C class 0-6-0 2F

| 31150 | 74C |

R1 class 0-6-0T 2F

| 31154 | 74C |

H class 0-4-4T 1P

31158	73D
31161	73D
31162	74E
31164	74D

E1 class 4-4-0 3P

| 31165 | 73B |

E class 4-4-0 1P

| 31166 | 74D |

R1 class 0-6-0T 2F

| 31174 | 74E |

H class 0-4-4T 1P

| 31177 | 74D |

P class 0-6-0T 0F

| 31178 | 74C |

H class 0-4-4T 1P

| 31184 | 74D |

C class 0-6-0 2F

| 31191 | 74C |

H class 0-4-4T 1P

| 31193 | 74D |

C class 0-6-0 2F

31218	74A
31219	74A
31221	74A
31223	74A
31225	73B
31227	73D
31229	73D

H class 0-4-4T 1P

| 31239 | 74D |

C class 0-6-0 2F

31242	73D
31243	74C
31244	74D

| 31245 | 74B |

D1 class 4-4-0 3P

| 31246 | 74C |
| 31247 | 74C |

C class 0-6-0 2F

31252	74B
31253	70C
31255	73E
31256	73E

01 class 0-6-0 2F

| 31258 | 74C |

H class 0-4-4T 1P

31259	74D
31261	73A
31263	73A
31265	73A
31266	73A

C class 0-6-0 2F

| 31267 | 73B |
| 31268 | 73E |

H class 0-4-4T 1P

| 31269 | 74E |

C class 0-6-0 2F

31270	74D
31271	74B
31272	74D

H class 0-4-4T 1P

| 31274 | 74E |
| 31276 | 74A |

C class 0-6-0 2F

| 31277 | 74D |

H class 0-4-4T 1P

| 31278 | 74C |
| 31279 | 74E |

C class 0-6-0 2F

31280	73B
31287	73B
31293	73B
31294	73B

H class 0-4-4T 1P

| 31295 | 74E |

C class 0-6-0 2F

| 31297 | 73B |
| 31298 | 74B |

H class 0-4-4T 1P

31305	73E
31306	73B
31307	73D
31308	73D
31309	75B
31310	75A

C class 0-6-0 2F

| 31317 | 74C |

H class 0-4-4T 1P

31319	75A
31320	75A
31321	73A
31322	75F

P class 0-6-0T 0F

| 31323 | 74C |

H class 0-4-4T 1P

| 31324 | 74B |

P class 0-6-0T OF

| 31325 | 75A |

H class 0-4-4T 1P

31326	74B
31327	74A
31328	74C
31329	74C

R1 class 0-6-0T 2F

31335	74E
31337	74C
31339	74A
31340	74C

01 class 0-6-0 2F

| 31370 | 74A |

N class 2-6-0 4P5F

31400	74A
31401	74A
31402	74A
31403	74A
31404	74A
31405	74A
31406	74A
31407	74A
31408	73B
31409	73A
31410	73A
31411	73A
31412	73A
31413	73A
31414	73A

01 class 0-6-0 2F

31425	74C
31430	74C
31434	74C

C class 0-6-0 2F

| 31461 | 73A |

D1 class 4-4-0 3P

| 31470 | 73E |

C class 0-6-0 2F

| 31480 | 73C |
| 31481 | 73E |

D1 class 4-4-0 3P

| 31487 | 73E |

D class 4-4-0 2P

| 31488 | 70E |

D1 class 4-4-0 3P

31489	73E
31492	73E
31494	73E

C class 0-6-0 2F

| 31495 | 73D |

D class 4-4-0 2P

| 31496 | 70C |

E1 class 4-4-0 3P

| 31497 | 73B |

C class 0-6-0 2F

| 31498 | 73C |

H class 0-4-4T 1P

| 31500 | 74A |
| 31503 | 73E |

E1 class 4-4-0 3P

| 31504 | 73A |

D1 class 4-4-0 3P

| 31505 | 73D |

E1 class 4-4-0 3P

| 31506 | 73A |
| 31507 | 73B |

C class 0-6-0 2F

| 31508 | 73D |

D1 class 4-4-0 3P

| 31509 | 73D |

C class 0-6-0 2F

| 31510 | 73D |

H class 0-4-4T 1P

| 31512 | 74A |

C class 0-6-0 2F

| 31513 | 74A |

H class 0-4-4T 1P

31517	75F
31518	73D
31519	74E
31520	75F
31521	74A
31522	74A
31523	74D
31530	74D
31531	74C
31533	73B
31540	73B
31542	73B

| 31543 | 74D |
| 31544 | 74D |

D1 class 4-4-0 3P

| 31545 | 73D |

H class 0-4-4T 1P

| 31548 | 74D |

D class 4-4-0 2P

| 31549 | 74A |

H class 0-4-4T 1P

31550	73A
31551	73A
31552	73A
31553	73B
31554	74D

P class 0-6-0T 0F

31555	73A
31556	75A
31557	73A
31558	75A

C class 0-6-0 2F

| 31573 | 73A |

D class 4-4-0 2P

| 31574 | 74A |

C class 0-6-0 2F

| 31575 | 73A |
| 31576 | 73A |

D class 4-4-0 2P

| 31577 | 74A |

C class 0-6-0 2F

31578	73A
31579	73A
31581	73A
31582	73A
31583	73A
31584	73A
31585	74D

D class 4-4-0 2P

| 31586 | 70C |

C class 0-6-0 2F

31588	74D
31589	74A
31590	74D

D class 4-4-0 2P

| 31591 | 75B |

C class 0-6-0 2F

| 31592 | 74B |
| 31593 | 70C |

U class 2-6-0 4P3F

| 31610 | 72C |
| 31611 | 75B |

Above: A visitor to Brighton shed from Faversham is 'D1' class 4-4-0 No 31487 in 1955. This was a rebuild from the Wainwright 'D' class with the addition of superheaters, piston valves and other modifications. This one had been built in July 1902 and rebuilt in June 1921. Allocations in BR days included Faversham, Stewarts Lane, Tonbridge, and finally Bricklayers Arms from where it was withdrawn on 25 February 1961.
G. W. Sharpe

Below: As a comparison, this is an original 'D' class 4-4-0 which escaped rebuilding: No 31586 seen at Reading Southern shed in February 1955. This was one of four withdrawn during 1955, on 3 September, allocated to Guildford. One remains in preservation, No 31737, withdrawn on 3 November 1956 from Guildford, which is now at the National Railway Museum.
P. H. Groom

31612	75B	31722	73B	**U class 2-6-0 4P3F**	
31613	71A	31723	73B	31790	72C
31614	75B	31724	75E	31791	72C
31615	75B	31725	75D	31792	72C
31616	70C			31793	72C
31617	70A	**D1 class 4-4-0 3P**		31794	72C
31618	71A	31727	74D	31795	72C
31619	71A			31796	72C
31620	71A	**D class 4-4-0 2P**		31797	70C
31621	71A	31734	74D	31798	70C
31622	70C			31799	70C
31623	72C	**D1 class 4-4-0 3P**		31800	70C
31624	70C	31735	73B	31801	71A
31625	70C			31802	73E
31626	71A	**D class 4-4-0 2P**		31803	73E
31627	70C	31737	74D	31804	73E
31628	70C			31805	70F
31629	70A	**D1 class 4-4-0 3P**		31806	70A
31630	70C	31739	73B	31807	70F
31631	70C	31741	73B	31808	70F
31632	71C	31743	73A	31809	70F
31633	70D	31749	73A		
31634	70OD			**N class 2-6-0 4P5F**	
31635	72B	**L1 class 4-4-0 3P**		31810	73A
31636	72B	31753	74C	31811	73A
31637	70F	31754	74C	31812	73A
31638	70F	31755	74C	31813	72B
31639	72B	31756	74A	31814	72B
		31757	74A	31815	73D
R class 0-4-4T 1P		31758	74A	31816	73D
31661	74C	31759	74A	31817	74C
31666	74D			31818	74C
		L class 4-4-0 3P		31819	74C
C class 0-6-0 2F		31760	74D	31820	74C
31681	73D	31761	74D	31821	74C
31682	73D	31762	74D		
31683	73D	31763	74D	**N1 class 2-6-0 4P5F**	
31684	73D	31764	74E	31822	73C
31686	73C	31765	74D		
31687	73C	31766	74D	**N class 2-6-0 4P5F**	
31688	73C	31767	74E	31823	73B
31689	73C	31768	74E	31824	73B
31690	73C	31769	74E	31825	73B
31691	73C	31770	74D	31826	73B
31692	73C	31771	74D	31827	73B
31693	73C	31772	74A	31828	73B
31694	73C	31773	74D	31829	73B
31695	73C	31774	74A	31830	72A
		31775	74A	31831	72A
R1 class 0-4-4T 1P		31776	74A	31832	72A
31698	74D	31777	74A	31833	72A
31704	74D	31778	74A	31834	72A
		31779	74B	31835	72A
C class 0-6-0 2F		31780	74B	31836	72A
31711	73D	31781	74B	31837	72A
31712	73D			31838	72A
31713	73D	**L1 class 4-4-0 3P**		31839	72A
31714	73E	31782	74A	31840	72A
31715	73E	31783	73B	31841	72A
31716	74D	31784	73B	31842	72E
31717	74D	31785	73B	31843	72E
31718	73A	31786	73B	31844	72A
31719	73A	31787	73B	31845	72A
31720	73E	31788	73B	31846	72A
31721	74E	31789	73B	31847	72A

31848	72A	31916	73C
31849	72A	31917	75C
31850	73E	31918	75C
31851	72A	31919	75C
31852	73E	31920	75C
31853	73B	31921	73A
31854	73C	31922	73C
31855	73C	31923	73C
31856	73C	31924	73C
31857	73C	31925	73C
31858	73C		
31859	73C	**E1R class 0-6-2T 1P2F**	
31860	73C	32094	72D
31861	73C	32095	72D
31862	75B	32096	72E
31863	75B		
31864	75B	**E2 class 0-6-0T 3F**	
31865	75B	32100	73A
31866	75B	32101	73A
31867	75B	32102	73A
31868	75B	32103	73A
31869	75B	32104	73A
31870	73B	32105	73A
31871	73B	32106	73A
31872	73B	32107	73A
31873	73B	32108	74C
31874	73B	32109	74C
31875	73B		
		E1 class 0-6-0T 1P2F	
N1 class 2-6-0 4P5F		32113	71A
31876	73C		
31877	73C	**E1R class 0-6-2T 1P 2F**	
31878	73C	32124	72A
31879	73C	32135	72A
31880	73C		
		E1 class 0-6-0T 1P2F	
U1 class 2-6-0 4P3F		32138	70F
31890	73B	32139	70F
31891	73B	32151	71A
31892	73C		
31893	73C	**E3 class 0-6-2T 2F**	
31894	75B	32165	75A
31895	75B	32166	75A
31896	75B	32167	75A
31897	75B	32168	70E
31898	75B	32169	75A
31899	75B	32170	75A
31900	75A		
31901	75A	**N15X 'Remembrance'**	
31902	75A	**class 4-6-0 4P**	
31903	75A	32327*	70D
31904	73A	32328*	70D
31905	73A	32329*	70D
31906	73A	32330*	70D
31907	73A	32331*	70D
31908	74D	32332*	70D
31909	74D	32333*	70D
31910	74D		
		K class 2-6-0 4P5F	
W class 2-6-4T 6F		32337	70F
31911	73C	32338	75A
31912	73C	32339	75A
31913	73C	32340	75A
31914	73A	32341	75A
31915	73A	32342	75A

Maunsell 'U' class 2-6-0 No 31624 seen at Nine Elms shed in August 1956. Built at Ashford in February 1929, this was the two-cylinder type based on earlier rebuilds from the 'K' class 2-6-4Ts. Under BR ownership it operated from Bournemouth, Dorchester in 1950, Guildford from November 1950, Eastleigh from August 1953 to October 1953, then back to Guildford, and finally Nine Elms in July 1956, remaining there until withdrawn on 14 June 1964. *R. H. G. Simpson*

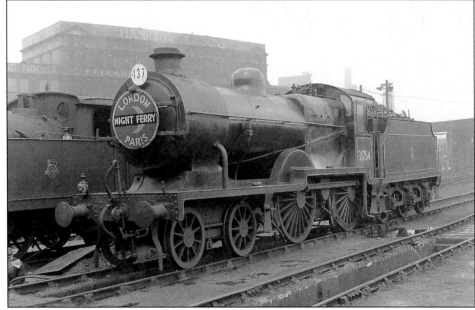

'L1' class 4-4-0 No 31754 at Stewarts Lane in May 1955 after duty on the Dover to London 'Night Ferry' service as a pilot engine for this arduous turn diagrammed for a Pacific. These were a Maunsell design and built by the North British Loco Co. No 31754 entered traffic in March 1926 and was based at Dover from 1948 until June 1959 when Nine Elms took charge. Withdrawal came on 18 November 1961. *G. W. Sharpe*

The older 'L' class 4-4-0 from the drawing board of Wainwright for the SE&CR, No 31781 is seen at Dover on Thursday 4 August 1955. This was one of 10 built by Borsig in Berlin in July 1914 as Ashford was too busy with other work. The German-built engines were the only examples to be fitted with Schmidt-type superheaters, and the only standard gauge steam locomotives to be built in Germany for an English railway company. They were delivered within days of the outbreak of World War 1. No 31781 remained on Ramsgate's allocation from 1948 until June 1959 when it was transferred to Nine Elms, promptly being withdrawn on receipt on the 6th and sent to Ashford for scrapping. *L. Hanson*

'U' class 2-6-0 No 31790 at Exmouth Junction shed in 1953 was a rebuild from the ill-fated Maunsell 'K' class 2-6-4Ts, the conversion work being carried out at Eastleigh in June 1928. The original engine was No A790 *River Avon* dating from June 1917. The rebuilding was a result of a derailment at speed outside Sevenoaks on 21 August 1927 of No A800 *River Cray*, in which 13 were killed and 43 injured. The accident was due to the instability of the class at speed creating dangerous oscillations on poor track. No 31790 was withdrawn on 9 May 1965 after six years' allocation at Guildford.

G. W. Sharpe

'N' class 2-6-0 No 31859 at its home base Hither Green in 1955. Dating from April 1925, this was one of the 50 built at Woolwich Arsenal and completed at Ashford. No 31859 moved on in later years to Norwood Junction, Stewarts Lane and Guildford before settling at Exmouth Junction in August 1963 from where it was withdrawn in September 1964.

R. H. G. Simpson

Another Hither Green view in 1955, this time with 'N1' 2-6-0 No 31879 on show alongside 'W' class 2-6-4T No 31913. This was the three-cylinder version of the 'N' class and only six were built: the first, No 31822 in March 1923, and the remainder in 1930. All were withdrawn towards the end of 1962 after the complete batch had been transferred in June 1962 to Stewarts Lane from Tonbridge. No 31879 was withdrawn on 17 November.

R. H. G. Simpson

Redhill shed on Sunday 17 April 1955 sees 'U1' class 2-6-0 No 31906 being topped up with water ready for its run back to London where it was based at Stewarts Lane. The three-cylinder version of the 'U' class, 21 were built, the first being a rebuild of 'K1' class 2-6-4T No A890. The rest were constructed at Eastleigh Works in 1931, this one being completed in September. Withdrawal came on 22 December 1962 when based at Norwood Junction. For the record, other engines at Redhill shed on this date were Nos 30540, 30835, 30837, 31259, 31309, 31630, 31814, 31862, 31863, 31866, 31867, 31895, 31899, 32448, 32449, 32450, 32451, 32507, 32512, 32552, 32560, 32561, 33024 and 80011.   *K. C. H. Fairey*

The 'W' class was a three-cylinder 2-6-4T design by Maunsell for shunting and freight work. The first five were built at Eastleigh in 1932 and the remaining 10 at Ashford in 1935 and 1936. This is No 31924, which was built in February 1936, seen at Hither Green shed in July 1957. It lasted in service until 26 July 1964, by then based at Feltham.

G. W. Sharpe

At Eastleigh shed in 1957 is 'E2' class 0-6-0T No 32105 awaiting return to Stewarts Lane. This was a class of only 10 engines introduced by Billington between 1913 and 1915 for the LB&SCR at Brighton Works. No 32105 was put to traffic in June 1915 and spent many years at its London base. In September 1959 it moved across the capital to Norwood Junction and in December 1961 to Southampton for dock shunting, withdrawal coming on 15 September 1962.

R. H. G. Simpson

Number	Shed
32343	75A
32344	75E
32345	75E
32346	75E
32347	75E
32348	75E
32349	70F
32350	75E
32351	75E
32352	75E
32353	75E

D3 class 0-4-4T 1P

Number	Shed
32390	75A

E6X class 0-6-2T 3F

Number	Shed
32407	75C

E6 class 0-6-2T 3F

Number	Shed
32408	73B
32409	73B
32410	73B

E6X class 0-6-2T 3F

Number	Shed
32411	75C

E6 class 0-6-2T 3F

Number	Shed
32412	73B
32413	75C
32414	75C
32415	73B
32416	75C
32417	75C
32418	75C

H2 class 4-4-2 4P

Number	Shed
32421*	75A
32422*	75A
32424*	75A
32425*	75A
32426*	75A

C2X class 0-6-0 2F

Number	Shed
32434	75A
32437	75A
32438	75A
32440	75A
32441	75A
32442	75A
32443	75C
32444	75C
32445	75C
32446	75C
32447	75C
32448	75B
32449	75B
32450	75B
32451	75B

E3 class 0-6-2T 2F

Number	Shed
32453	73B
32454	74D
32455	73A
32456	74D
32458	73B
32459	73B
32460	73B
32461	73B
32462	73B

E4 class 0-6-2T 2MT

Number	Shed
32463	75D
32464	75D
32465	75D

E4X class 0-6-2T 2MT

Number	Shed
32466	75C

E4 class 0-6-2T 2MT

Number	Shed
32467	75D
32468	75D
32469	75D
32470	75D
32471	73B
32472	73B
32473	73B
32474	73B
32475	75A
32476	70A

E4X class 0-6-2T 2MT

Number	Shed
32477	75C
32478	75C

E4 class 0-6-2T 2MT

Number	Shed
32479	70F
32480	75E
32481	75E
32482	75A
32484	75C
32485	75A
32486	72B
32487	70C
32488	74D

E4X class 0-6-2T 2MT

Number	Shed
32489	75C

E4 class 0-6-2T 2MT

Number	Shed
32490	70C
32491	71A
32492	71A
32493	70A
32494	75A
32495	70F
32496	75A
32497	70A
32498	70A
32499	70A
32500	70A
32501	70E
32502	70E
32503	74D
32504	75A
32505	70F
32506	72B
32507	75B
32508	75A
32509	70F
32510	71A
32511	75A
32512	75B
32513	75A
32514	75A
32515	75A
32516	75E
32517	75F
32518	75A
32519	75E
32520	75E

C2X class 0-6-0 2F

Number	Shed
32521	75D
32522	75D
32523	75D
32524	73B
32525	73B
32526	73B
32527	73B
32528	75E
32529	75E
32532	75E
32534	75E
32535	75E
32536	75E
32537	75E
32538	75E
32539	75A
32540	75A
32541	75D
32543	75C
32544	75C
32545	75C
32546	75C
32547	75C
32548	70F
32549	70F
32550	70F
32551	73B
32552	73B
32553	73B
32554	73B

E4 class 0-6-2T 2MT

Number	Shed
32556	71A
32557	71A
32558	71A
32559	71A
32560	75B
32561	75B
32562	71A
32563	71A
32564	73B
32565	73B
32566	75A

E5 class 0-6-2T 2MT

Number	Shed
32568	70D

E5X class 0-6-2T 2MT

Number	Shed
32570	75D

E5 class 0-6-2T 2MT

Number	Shed
32571	75C

E5X class 0-6-2T 2MT

Number	Shed
32576	75D

E4 class 0-6-2T 2MT

Number	Shed
32577	75A
32578	74E
32579	71A
32580	74D
32581	75F
32582	75F

E5 class 0-6-2T 2MT

Number	Shed
32583	70D

E5X class 0-6-2T 2MT

Number	Shed
32586	75A

E5 class 0-6-2T 2MT

Number	Shed
32593	74C

E1 class 0-6-0T 1P2F

Number	Shed
32606	71I

E1R class 0-6-2T 1P2F

Number	Shed
32608	72E
32610	72E

A1X 'Terrier' class 0-6-0T 0P

Number	Shed
32636	75A
32640	70F
32646	75A
32650	70F
32655	74E
32661	70F
32662	75A
32670	74E
32677	70F
32678	74E

E1 class 0-6-0T 1P2F

Number	Shed
32689	71I
32694	70F

E1R class 0-6-2T 1P2F

Number	Shed
32695	72A
32696	72E
32697	72A

Q1 class 0-6-0 5F

Number	Shed
33001	70C
33002	70C
33003	70C
33004	70C
33005	70C
33006	70B
33007	70B
33008	70B
33009	70B
33010	70B
33011	70B
33012	70B
33013	70B
33014	73C
33015	73A
33016	70B
33017	73A
33018	70B
33019	70C
33020	71A
33021	71A
33022	70C
33023	71A
33024	74D
33025	70C
33026	70B
33027	70B
33028	74D
33029	74D
33030	74D
33031	74D
33032	74D
33033	74D
33034	74D
33035	74D
33036	74D
33037	73C
33038	73A
33039	74E
33040	74E

'West Country' class 4-6-2 7P6F

Number	Shed
34001*	72A
34002*	72A
34003*	72A
34004*	72A
34005*	70A
34006*	70A
34007*	70A
34008*	70A
34009*	70A
34010*	70A
34011*	70A
34012*	70A
34013*	72A
34014*	72A
34015*	72A
34016*	72A
34017*	73A
34018*	70A
34019*	70A
34020*	70A
34021*	72A
34022*	72A
34023*	72A
34024*	72A
34025*	72A
34026*	72A
34027*	72A
34028*	72A
34029*	72A
34030*	72A
34031*	72A
34032*	72A
34033*	72A
34034*	72A
34035*	72D
34036*	72D
34037*	72D

An unrebuilt 'E4', No 32560, is shown on Redhill shed on Sunday 17 April 1955. Originally named *Pembury* and built in November 1901, withdrawal came on 13 August 1958 at Nine Elms after transfer from Redhill in August 1957.

K. C. H. Fairey

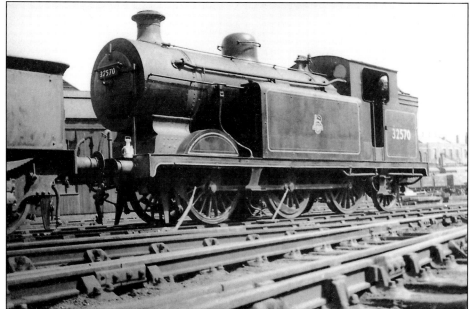

Another Billington tank engine, this time 'E5X' class 0-6-2T No 32570 at Brighton shed on Sunday 17 April 1955. Again, only four had been rebuilt from 'E5s', this one in March 1911, the original engine being built in December 1902 and named *Armington*. Brighton was the last allocation when withdrawn on 14 January 1956. Other engines sharing the hospitality of Brighton shed on the date of this photograph were Nos 30129, 30542, 30840, 31310, 31325, 31556, 31724, 31725, 31890, 31900, 31901, 31903, 32103, 32167, 32169, 32338, 32339, 32341, 32342, 32343, 32347, 32390, 32424, 32425, 32426, 32434, 32437, 32438, 32440, 32441, 32468, 32482, 32485, 32511, 32513, 32515, 32516, 32566, 32574, 32577, 34045, 34046, 34047, 34065, 42091, 80016, 80019 and diesel shunters 13092, 13093, 13094 and 13100. *K. C. H. Fairey*

Fratton shed in May 1955 is the setting for 'A1X' 'Terrier' class 0-6-0T No 32661. If long life is a sign of a successful engine, then these little Stroudley engines must qualify. This example first took to the rails in October 1875 and was rebuilt in January 1912 with a new boiler, the removal of wing plates and splasher sandboxes, and new sandboxes being fitted beneath the running plate. No 32661 lasted until 28 April 1963, by then allocated to Eastleigh, and was broken up in August 1963 over at the Works. No fewer than eight remain in preservation.

G. W. Sharpe

Above: Ugly but powerful, the Bulleid 'Q1s' certainly were noticeable. This is No 33007 at Feltham shed in 1956 with sister engine No 33026 alongside. Built during World War 2 to help a chronic shortage of powerful freight locomotives, they were without any unnecessary fittings such as footplating and handholds to save on materials and weight. Even the boiler lagging was as light as possible, with the weight of the cladding being transferred to the frames. All this resulted in a locomotive 14 tons lighter than a conventional engine of similar size. No 33007 entered traffic in July 1942 and was first allocated to Guildford. For its British Railways career it operated from Feltham, other than a short stay at Hither Green in 1953. Withdrawn on 26 January 1964, it was cut up at Cashmore's at Newport 11 months later. *Ken Hunt*

Below: 'West Country' 4-6-2 No 34005 *Barnstaple* at Nine Elms shed in March 1956 with the unique longer-than-normal smoke deflectors. Built in July 1945, it was first allocated to Exmouth Junction and was the first to be rebuilt in June 1957. Withdrawal took place on 2 October 1966 at Bournemouth shed. *P. H. Groom*

'Battle of Britain' 4-6-2 No 34079 *141 Squadron* enters Dover Marine on an express from London on Thursday 4 August 1955. Built in 1948 and first allocated to Ramsgate, it remained in this unrebuilt form until withdrawn on 27 February 1966 from Eastleigh shed. *L. Hanson*

Entering Bournemouth on the 'Bournemouth Belle' is Nine Elms-based 'Merchant Navy' 4-6-2 No 35015 *Rotterdam Lloyd* in May 1955. Built in March 1945, it was allocated new to Nine Elms where it remained on allocation until May 1956 when Stewarts Lane took over its maintenance. Moving back to Nine Elms in June 1959 after being rebuilt one year earlier, it remained at 70A until withdrawn on 23 February 1964. *G. W. Sharpe*

Ryde shed on the Isle of Wight in May 1958 sees Stroudley 'E1' class 0-6-0T No 4 *Wroxall* on shed. Dating from November 1878, it had gone to the island in June 1933 and was renumbered from No 131 and renamed from *Gournay*. Withdrawal came on 22 October 1960 and it was the last active member of the class of four on the island, leaving only one other, No 32694, on the mainland. *P. H. Groom*

34038*	72D	34097*	74B	W17*	70H	40043	1C
34039*	75A	34098*	74B	W18*	70H	40044	1A
34040*	71A	34099*	74B	W19*	70H	40045	53B
34041*	71A	34100*	74B	W20*	70H	40046	1A
34042*	71A	34101*	73A	W21*	70H	40047	1A
34043*	71B	34102*	73A	W22*	70H	40048	84G
34044*	71B	34103*	73A	W23*	70H	40049	1A
34045*	75A	34104*	73A	W24*	70H	40050	1A
34046*	75A	34105*	71B	W25*	70G	40051	1A
34047*	75A	34106*	71B	W26*	70G	40052	9E
34048*	75A	34107*	71B	W27*	70G	40053	9E
		34108*	71B	W28*	70G	40054	1A

'Battle of Britain' class 4-6-2 7P6F

34049*	72B			W29*	70G	40055	9E
34050*	72B			W30*	70G	40056	53B

'Battle of Britain' class 4-6-2 7P6F

34051*	72B	34109*	71B	W31*	70G	40057	53B
34052*	72B	34110*	71B	W32*	70G	40058	84G

'Merchant Navy' class 4-6-2 8P

34053*	72B			W33*	70G	40059	53B
34054*	72B	35001*	72A	W34*	70G	40060	53B
34055*	72B	35002*	72A	W35*	70G	40061	53B
34056*	72A	35003*	72A	W36*	70G	40062	26F
34057*	72A	35004*	72A			40063	26A
34058*	72A	35005*	70A			40064	1A
34059*	72A	35006*	72B			40065	26A
34060*	72A	35007*	72B	**Fowler 2-6-2T 3MT**		40066	1A
34061*	72A	35008*	72A	40001	1A	40067	9F
34062*	72A	35009*	72B	40002	1A	40068	1A
34063*	70A	35010*	70A	40003	2C	40069	1A
34064*	70A	35011*	70A	40004	1A	40070	11A
34065*	73A	35012*	70A	40005	84G		
34066*	73A	35013*	72A	40006	1A	**Stanier 2-6-2T 3MT**	
34067*	73A	35014*	71B	40007	1A	40071	9B
34068*	73A	35015*	70A	40008	84G	40072	24E
34069*	72A	35016*	70A	40009	9E	40073	3C
34070*	73A	35017*	70A	40010	1C	40074	20E
34071*	73A	35018*	70A	40011	11A	40075	20D
34072*	74C	35019*	70A	40012	53B	40076	2C
34073*	74C	35020*	70A	40013	26A	40077	9A
34074*	74C	35021*	70A	40014	26F	40078	2C
34075*	74B	35022*	71B	40015	26A	40079	16D
34076*	74B	35023*	72A	40016	1A	40080	3C
34077*	74B	35024*	72A	40017	9E	40081	9B
34078*	74B	35025*	70A	40018	1A	40082	20C
34079*	74B	35026*	73A	40019	1A	40083	6G
34080*	74B	35027*	73A	40020	1C	40084	3B
34081*	74B	35028*	73A	40021	14B	40085	3C
34082*	74B	35029*	74C	40022	14C	40086	6G
34083*	74B	35030*	74C	40023	14A	40087	2B
34084*	74B			40024	14C	40088	6C
34085*	74B	**LOCOMOTIVES**		40025	14A	40089	9F
34086*	74B	**ALLOCATED TO**		40026	14C	40090	20E
34087*	73A	**THE ISLE OF WIGHT**		40027	14B	40091	86G
34088*	73A			40028	14B	40092	14B
34089*	73A	**E1 class 0-6-0T 1P2F**		40029	14B	40093	9A
34090*	73A	W1*	70G	40030	14A	40094	9F
		W2*	70G	40031	14B	40095	6G
'West Country' class 4-6-2 7P6F		W3*	70G	40032	14B	40096	14B
		W4*	70G	40033	14B	40097	86K
34091*	73A			40034	14B	40098	86G
34092*	73A	**O2 class 0-4-4T OP**		40035	14B	40099	24E
34093*	71B	W14*	70H	40036	14B	40100	14B
34094*	71B	W15*	70H	40037	14B	40101	6C
34095*	71B	W16*	70H	40038	14B	40102	6C
34096*	74B			40039	14C	40103	24E
				40040	14B	40104	2B
				40041	11A	40105	87K
				40042	1A		

40106	9B
40107	9A
40108	3E
40109	24E
40110	6C
40111	14B
40112	20E
40113	9F
40114	20E
40115	21A
40116	22A
40117	20E
40118	3E
40119	14B
40120	20G
40121	6C
40122	3B
40123	6G
40124	9F
40125	3B
40126	2C
40127	8E
40128	6C
40129	3B
40130	6G
40131	6C
40132	6C
40133	6G
40134	8D
40135	6C
40136	9A
40137	8D
40138	9B
40139	20C
40140	20C
40141	87K
40142	14B
40143	8B
40144	6C
40145	86G
40146	15C
40147	20E
40148	20A
40149	21A
40150	60B
40151	60B
40152	65D
40153	65D
40154	65D
40155	20E
40156	2C
40157	2C
40158	65P
40159	66C
40160	14B
40161	86K
40162	20G
40163	20G
40164	24E
40165	15D
40166	14B
40167	14B
40168	16D
40169	20A
40170	68B

76

Ryde shed in 1954 sees Adams 'O2' No 23 *Totland* on shed. This had been No 188 on the mainland and built in October 1890, going to the island in April 1925. This was one of the first to be withdrawn on the island on 13 August 1955.

G. W. Sharpe

Ex-works fully lined out and repainted at Derby shed in April 1956 is Fowler 2-6-2T No 40030, fitted with condensing gear and awaiting return to Cricklewood. Along with No 40021, this engine had had an interesting transfer in August 1953 to Beattock for banking duties and remained there until transfer back to London in June 1954. Built in March 1931, and originally numbered 15529, it was withdrawn during the week ended 29 August 1959 from Kentish Town.

G. W. Sharpe

A non-condensing example of Fowler's 2-6-2Ts is No 40042 at Willesden shed in 1956. Built in June 1931, it was withdrawn during the week ended 22 July 1961 from Willesden and broken up at Crewe Works.

R. H. G. Simpson

Above: Bristol-based Stanier 2-6-2T No 40116 moves out of Bristol Temple Meads on a Bath to Portishead local on Saturday 9 July 1955. Built at Derby in August 1935, it was first allocated to Birmingham Bournville. After its time at Bristol, it moved north to Wrexham Rhosddu in August 1958, a year later to Birkenhead, then on to Bangor in July 1961, where it was withdrawn during the week ended 24 November 1962.   *G. W. Sharpe*

Below: By 1955 four of the Stanier 2-6-2Ts had been fitted with larger type 6B boilers, with another two being equipped in 1956. No 40148, seen here at Pontefract in 1955, had its new boiler fitted in November 1942. This was an attempt to improve the steaming abilities of these engines, but no real advantage was recorded. No 40148 had first been allocated to Huddersfield in September 1937, and by 1948 was spending its time on commuter trains out of St Pancras allocated to Kentish Town. In December 1951 it returned to Yorkshire to Leeds Holbeck and remained a northern engine, going to Royston in June 1959 from where it was withdrawn on 23 August 1962.   *G. W. Sharpe*

40171	86K	40421	2E	40569	71G	40635	10C	**LMS Compound 4-4-0 4P**
40172	14B	40426	22A	40570	67B	40636	67A	40900	16A
40173	3C	40433	9F	40571	67B	40637	67A	40902	68B
40174	24E	40434	10C	40572	67B	40638	67D	40903	64D
40175	16D	40439	21B	40573	67B	40640	67C	40904	64D
40176	65D	40443	5C	40574	67C	40641	67A	40906	67A
40177	65D	40447	5A	40575	67C	40642	67A	40907	19B
40178	20E	40448	12A	40576	68B	40643	67B	40908	67A
40179	20D	40450	10C	40577	68B	40644	67B	40909	67A
40180	3D	40452	15C	40578	67D	40645	67B	40910	9E
40181	20C	40453	17B	40579	67D	40646	5C	40912	68B
40182	15C	40454	16A	40580	6K	40647	67C	40913	67A
40183	20G	40458	16A	40581	25G	40648	61A	40915	67B
40184	20G	40461	5C	40582	12A	40649	67A	40916	66A
40185	68B	40463	21B	40583	5A	40650	61A	40917	21B
40186	65D	40464	2E	40584	25G	40651	68A	40920	67C
40187	65D	40472	20F	40585	26C	40652	12A	40921	63A
40188	65D	40482	9A	40586	26C	40653	2E	40924	63A
40189	65D	40485	15C	40587	27D	40654	11B	40925	6G
40190	27C	40486	22A	40588	27A	40655	12A	40926	5A
40191	27C	40487	16A	40589	6K	40656	12D	40927	17A
40192	27C	40489	22B	40590	67C	40657	2E	40928	21B
40193	20A	40491	18C	40592	67B	40658	6A	40929	17D
40194	27C	40493	16A	40593	67B	40659	5A	40930	22B
40195	27C	40495	6K	40594	67A	40660	5A	40931	17D
40196	27C	40501	3C	40595	67A	40661	67B	40932	22B
40197	27C	40502	18C	40596	67A	40663	61A	40933	3E
40198	27C	40504	16A	40597	67B	40664	67C	40934	22B
40199	27C	40509	71H	40598	67A	40665	67B	40935	16A
40200	65D	40511	21A	40599	67A	40666	67D	40936	3E
40201	8D	40513	17A	40600	61A	40667	67D	40937	24A
40202	8B	40518	20A	40601	71G	40668	67D	40938	63B
40203	8E	40519	17B	40602	68A	40669	67D	40939	63C
40204	2B	40520	17D	40603	61A	40670	67C	41045	11E
40205	2C	40521	20C	40604	67A	40671	6K	41048	15D
40206	3D	40522	5A	40605	67B	40672	1C	41049	15D
40207	3B	40525	17B	40606	67D	40673	10B	41050	17A
40208	6G	40526	17B	40607	67D	40674	9A	41053	15C
40209	6C	40527	71H	40608	67D	40675	6K	41059	15D
		40531	3C	40609	67D	40676	10C	41060	5A
		40534	2E	40610	67C	40677	2E	41061	20E
Fowler 4-4-0 2P		40535	16A	40611	68C	40678	5C	41062	19B
40323	20A	40536	12A	40612	67B	40679	6K	41063	19B
40326	17A	40537	18C	40613	68A	40680	27D	41064	21B
		40538	19B	40614	68B	40681	24D	41065	11E
Johnson/Fowler 4-4-0 2P		40540	22B	40615	68A	40682	26C	41066	9E
40332	5A	40541	22B	40616	68C	40683	2E	41067	20E
40337	18C	40542	15C	40617	67B	40684	27A	41068	20A
40356	12A	40543	15C	40618	67B	40685	26C	41069	22B
40362	11E	40548	6G	40619	67B	40686	67B	41070	19B
40364	17B	40550	18C	40620	67A	40687	67B	41071	19B
40377	6G	40552	20D	40621	67A	40688	67B	41072	19B
40396	12A	40553	16A	40622	61A	40689	67B	41073	21B
40402	5A	40556	18C	40623	68C	40690	25G	41075	15C
40404	17A	40557	18C	40624	67D	40691	27A	41076	2A
40405	9A	40559	6G	40625	67D	40692	12A	41077	17A
40407	17A	40562	20E	40626	67D	40693	9A	41078	22B
40409	15C			40627	67A	40694	12D	41079	15D
40411	16A	**LMS 4-4-0 2P**		40628	6K	40695	12D	41081	11E
40412	12A	40563	71H	40629	6A	40696	71G	41083	17A
40413	5A	40564	71H	40630	20D	40697	71G	41085	24A
40414	20F	40565	10B	40631	10B	40698	71G	41086	6G
40416	17A	40566	67B	40632	20G	40699	12A	41088	17A
40418	17A	40567	5A	40633	17B	40700	71G	41089	15C
40419	5A	40568	71G	40634	71H			41090	3E
40420	10B								

Above: Built under Fowler in April 1921 for the SD&JR as No 69, 2P 4-4-0 No 40326 is at home on Derby shed in December 1955. This was to the same design as the rebuilt Midland 4-4-0s, but with detail differences. It was withdrawn during the week ended 12 May 1956, still on Derby's allocation. *G. W. Sharpe*

Below: Johnson/Fowler 4-4-0, No 40550 is out in the cold at Chinley on the 10.50am Manchester Central to Sheffield Midland on Friday 14 January 1955. Rebuilt in January 1915, it lasted until the week ended 13 June 1959 based at Nottingham and was cut up at Derby Works. *Initial Photographics/R. J. Buckley*

Built by the LMS in October 1928, 2P 4-4-0 No 40598 is captured on film at the now long-closed Glasgow St Enoch station in April 1954. Many of the class gave good service in the southwest of Scotland, including this one, which operated from Glasgow Corkerhill shed until withdrawn on 12 November 1959. *G. W. Sharpe*

Fully lined out and repainted at Derby shed on Monday 2 May 1955 after a visit to the Works is LMS Compound 4-4-0 No 40925. Built in May 1927, this was the later version based on the Midland's Deeley design. No 40925 was based at Llandudno Junction for many years until moving on to Manchester Longsight for a short stay in June 1957, and to Birmingham Bournville the following December. The final move to Derby came in January 1959 from where it was withdrawn later the same year during the week ended 14 November.

Initial Photographics/R. J. Buckley

Compound No 40933 at its home shed Birmingham Monument Lane on Sunday 22 July 1956 paired with a high-sided tender. Only one of these tenders was fitted to any of these engines, and No 40933 had received it from No 40936 two years earlier. Dating from June 1927, No 40933 was withdrawn during April 1958 after transfer in December 1957 to Gloucester Barnwood.

G. W. Sharpe

No.	Code	No.	Code	No.	Code	No.	Code	No.	Code
41091	15D	41172	2A	41239	6H	41304	71A	41752	18D
41093	6G	41173	9E	41240	22A	41305	71A	41753	6C
41094	17A	41175	68B	41241	71G	41306	75E	41754	17A
41095	15C	41176	67A	41242	71G	41307	75E	41763	18D
41097	15C	41177	64C	41243	71G	41308	73E	41769	87K
41098	9E	41179	68B	41244	6K	41309	73E	41773	17A
41100	20A	41180	21A	41245	19B	41310	73E	41777	18D
41101	25G	41181	16A	41246	19B	41311	73E	41779	16A
41102	24E	41183	67C	41247	20E	41312	73E	41795	17A
41103	15D	41185	16A	41248	71H	41313	72A	41797	20B
41104	20A	41186	27C	41249	71H	41314	72A	41803	18D
41105	2A	41187	27C	41250	25F	41315	72D	41804	18D
41106	6A	41188	25G	41251	25A	41316	75F	41805	19C
41107	11E	41189	27A	41252	25A	41317	75F	41814	26G
41108	11E	41190	19B	41253	25A	41318	75F	41826	14A
41111	6G	41191	19B	41254	25G	41319	75F	41835	19C
41112	9E	41192	17A	41255	25G	41320	5A	41838	20B
41113	2A	41193	24E	41256	25G	41321	8B	41839	17B
41114	9E	41194	21B	41257	25G	41322	8B	41844	20D
41116	8A	41195	22B	41258	25G	41323	8B	41847	17A
41117	22B	41196	11E	41259	25G	41324	6H	41855	20F
41118	9E	41197	11E	41260	24F	41325	20F	41857	19A
41119	6G	41198	15C	41261	24F	41326	20F	41859	20B
41120	6A	41199	15D	41262	25F	41327	20F	41860	87K
41121	8A			41263	25F	41328	15A	41865	17B
41122	2A	**Ivatt 2-6-2T 2MT**		41264	25F	41329	15D	41875	19C
41123	9E	41200	6H	41265	20E			41878	17B
41124	6J	41201	86K	41266	20E	**Johnson 0-4-0ST 0F**		41879	21A
41126	65B	41202	86K	41267	20A	41516	17B	41885	16D
41127	68C	41203	86K	41268	15C	41518	18C	41889	17A
41128	65B	41204	86K	41269	15D	41523	17B		
41129	68C	41205	20G	41270	15D			**Stanier 0-4-4T 2P**	
41130	64D	41206	20G	41271	15D	**Deeley 0-4-0T 0F**		41900	11E
41131	66A	41207	14A	41272	15D	41528	18D	41901	5A
41132	67C	41208	14A	41273	15D	41529	18D	41902	3C
41135	68C	41209	19B	41274	20F	41530	22B	41903	11E
41136	11E	41210	8B	41275	20C	41531	18C	41904	11E
41137	20E	41211	2B	41276	1E	41532	18C	41905	9D
41140	21A	41212	6H	41277	6K	41533	18D	41906	9A
41142	67A	41213	2B	41278	15A	41534	18D	41907	9A
41143	16A	41214	2A	41279	2A	41535	17A	41908	1C
41144	16A	41215	6D	41280	3C	41536	17B	41909	1C
41147	64C	41216	6D	41281	26F	41537	22B		
41149	66D	41217	11B	41282	26F			**LT&S 4-4-2T 3P**	
41150	9E	41218	2E	41283	26F	**Johnson 0-6-0T 1F**		41928	33A
41151	9E	41219	2E	41284	27B	41661	20D	41936	30A
41152	11E	41220	1C	41285	27B	41671	14B	41938	15C
41153	6A	41221	11B	41286	2C	41672	14C	41939	33A
41154	9E	41222	1E	41287	10E	41682	16A	41940	16D
41155	67C	41223	6H	41288	10C	41686	40A	41941	33A
41156	21B	41224	6K	41289	10E	41699	87K	41942	33A
41157	6A	41225	3B	41290	10E	41702	26G	41943	16D
41158	6A	41226	3C	41291	73A	41706	22A	41944	30A
41159	9A	41227	2C	41292	73A	41708	18D	41945	33B
41160	5A	41228	2C	41293	73A	41710	17A	41946	33B
41161	9E	41229	5A	41294	71A	41712	14A	41947	16D
41162	2A	41230	6H	41295	73A	41713	14B	41948	33A
41163	9E	41231	6K	41296	72E	41720	22B	41949	30A
41164	6A	41232	6K	41297	72A	41724	14B	41950	33A
41165	2A	41233	6H	41298	72E	41725	84G	41951	30A
41166	8A	41234	6D	41299	73B	41726	17A	41952	30A
41167	5A	41235	6D	41300	73B	41734	6C	41966	18A
41168	9A	41236	6G	41301	73B	41739	18D	41969	33A
41169	9E	41237	6G	41302	73B	41748	22B	41970	30A
41170	9E	41238	6G	41303	75E	41749	18D	41971	20F

Number	Code
42348	5D
42349	8E
42350	9A
42351	9A
42352	8E
42353	9B
42354	9B
42355	9C
42356	9C
42357	9C
42358	5D
42359	11B
42360	5D
42361	16A
42362	9C
42363	9C
42364	11B
42365	9D
42366	9D
42367	9D
42368	9D
42369	9C
42370	9D
42371	9D
42372	11B
42373	16A
42374	34E
42375	5F
42376	11B
42377	20E
42378	5D
42379	9B
42380	20E
42381	9C
42382	9C
42383	21A
42384	25B
42385	87K
42386	9C
42387	87K
42388	87K
42389	1C
42390	87K
42391	9A
42392	11B
42393	11D
42394	87K
42395	11B
42396	11D
42397	9A
42398	9A
42399	9A
42400	5D
42401	11B
42402	11B
42403	11D
42404	11D
42405	25D
42406	25D
42407	25D
42408	25B
42409	25B
42410	25B
42411	25D
42412	25B
42413	25B
42414	25B
42415	6H
42416	6H
42417	6H
42418	6H
42419	3E
42420	3E
42421	3E
42422	3E
42423	10A
42424	11D

Stanier 2-6-4T 4MT

Number	Code
42425	6A
42426	8A
42427	11B
42428	11A
42429	11A
42430	9A
42431	5D
42432	11A
42433	24A
42434	24C
42435	24C
42436	24C
42437	24A
42438	24B
42439	24B
42440	5D
42441	3D
42442	10C
42443	5D
42444	6H
42445	8E
42446	2A
42447	5E
42448	8E
42449	5D
42450	6A
42451	6A
42452	9E
42453	10C
42454	10A
42455	6H
42456	10A
42457	11C
42458	5D
42459	8A
42460	6H
42461	6A
42462	10A
42463	9B
42464	11C
42465	10A
42466	8E
42467	9A
42468	5D
42469	9E
42470	3D
42471	5E
42472	26C
42473	27D
42474	24B
42475	24B
42476	24C
42477	25C
42478	9A
42479	8E
42480	24C
42481	24C
42482	3C
42483	24D
42484	24D
42485	24D
42486	26A
42487	2A
42488	3C
42489	3D
42490	24D
42491	24C
42492	24C
42493	11B
42494	5D

Stanier Three-cylinder 2-6-4T 4MT

Number	Code
42500	33C
42501	33C
42502	33C
42503	33C
42504	33C
42505	33C
42506	33C
42507	33C
42508	33C
42509	33C
42510	33C
42511	33C
42512	33C
42513	33C
42514	33C
42515	33C
42516	33C
42517	33C
42518	33C
42519	33C
42520	33C
42521	33C
42522	33C
42523	33C
42524	33C
42525	33C
42526	33C
42527	33C
42528	33C
42529	33C
42530	33C
42531	33C
42532	33A
42533	33A
42534	33A
42535	33A
42536	33A

Stanier 2-6-4T 4MT

Number	Code
42537	27D
42538	5C
42539	10A
42540	6A
42541	2A
42542	9A
42543	5D
42544	11A
42545	26C
42546	24B
42547	24B
42548	24A
42549	24A
42550	26A
42551	26F
42552	3D
42553	25C
42554	27D
42555	24B
42556	24C
42557	27D
42558	24D
42559	24D
42560	10C
42561	10C
42562	5C
42563	10C
42564	8A
42565	26C
42566	5A
42567	5D
42568	6A
42569	27D
42570	8A
42571	11B
42572	10A
42573	11A
42574	10C
42575	9A
42576	2A
42577	2A
42578	5C
42579	3E
42580	8E
42581	11B
42582	5D
42583	8A
42584	8E
42585	2A
42586	3C
42587	6A
42588	6H
42589	11E
42590	5D
42591	11A
42592	27D
42593	5D
42594	9A
42595	6A
42596	8E
42597	8E
42598	8E
42599	9A
42600	5D
42601	11A
42602	8A
42603	5D
42604	3C
42605	5F
42606	8B
42607	8B
42608	9A
42609	5D
42610	10A
42611	5E
42612	8E
42613	11C
42614	27D
42615	2A
42616	3D
42617	6H
42618	26A
42619	26D
42620	26D
42621	26A
42622	26A
42623	26A
42624	26A
42625	24E
42626	26C
42627	3C
42628	8E
42629	26C
42630	26C
42631	27D
42632	27D
42633	26C
42634	24A
42635	26C
42636	24E
42637	24E
42638	24E
42639	25E
42640	27D
42641	27D
42642	27D
42643	24A
42644	27D
42645	26B
42646	26B
42647	26B
42648	26B
42649	26D
42650	26D
42651	26A
42652	26C
42653	26C
42654	26C
42655	26C
42656	26C
42657	26C
42658	3D
42659	1E
42660	6A
42661	24A
42662	10C
42663	10A
42664	8A
42665	5F
42666	10A
42667	5D
42668	5D
42669	2A
42670	5D

Above: Corwen station on Sunday 2 October 1955 sees Stanier 2-6-4T No 42461. Built in September 1936 at Derby and first allocated to Macclesfield, by 1948 it was allocated to Manchester Longsight. In July 1953 it moved to Chester LMS shed and in September 1956 back to Manchester at Newton Heath. A brief stay at Lancaster from July to September 1958 was followed by six weeks at Manchester Agecroft before moving to Blackpool from where withdrawal came during the week ended 28 March 1964. The train seen here was the RCTS North Wales Rail Tour which started at Chester General at 10.50am and was formed of saloon stock with roof-boards. Included in the tour was the Dyserth Branch (which had lost its passenger service on 22 September 1930), Denbigh, Ruthin, the Brymbo Branch, Wrexham, Shotton, before returning to Chester, this time into Northgate station, arriving at 5.19pm after a run of 140 miles. *G. W. Sharpe*

Below: Superbly turned out at Derby shed, repainted and fully lined out on Friday 30 September 1955, is Stanier's three-cylinder 2-6-4T No 42513 awaiting return to Shoeburyness. Built for the LT&SR line in July 1934, it was first allocated to Leicester Midland before going to its intended route. It was withdrawn from Shoeburyness on 18 June 1962 along with the 28 remaining members of the class due to the electrification of the line. All were cut up at Doncaster Works. *Initial Photographics/R. J. Buckley*

42671 5D
42672 5F

Fairburn 2-6-4T 4MT

42673 2A
42674 3E
42675 5F
42676 9E
42677 5A
42678 33A
42679 33A
42680 14C
42681 33A
42682 14B
42683 9E
42684 33A
42685 14B
42686 14C
42687 33A
42688 66D
42689 66B
42690 66D
42691 66D
42692 66A
42693 62B
42694 66A
42695 66A
42696 66B
42697 66D
42698 66D
42699 66B

Hughes/Fowler 2-6-0 5MT

42700 25G
42701 26A
42702 26A
42703 26A
42704 26A
42705 26A
42706 24B
42707 26A
42708 26A
42709 26A
42710 26A
42711 26A
42712 25G
42713 26A
42714 26A
42715 26A
42716 24B
42717 24B
42718 24D
42719 26D
42720 68A
42721 26B
42722 26B
42723 26B
42724 26B
42725 26B
42726 26A
42727 26A
42728 26A
42729 24D
42730 26B
42731 26D

42732 26A
42733 26A
42734 26B
42735 66C
42736 65F
42737 65F
42738 63C
42739 67C
42740 66C
42741 66C
42742 67D
42743 67B
42744 67B
42745 67C
42746 65B
42747 1A
42748 68A
42749 68C
42750 26A
42751 68A
42752 68A
42753 26B
42754 21A
42755 26B
42756 17B
42757 68A
42758 21A
42759 14A
42760 17D
42761 21A
42762 20E
42763 17B
42764 21A
42765 24F
42766 26A
42767 17B
42768 17D
42769 16A
42770 20G
42771 20A
42772 9A
42773 9B
42774 20A
42775 9F
42776 5B
42777 5B
42778 9A
42779 3A
42780 65F
42781 2B
42782 3D
42783 2B
42784 20G
42785 5B
42786 8C
42787 1A
42788 9F
42789 26A
42790 21A
42791 21A
42792 17D
42793 68A
42794 19A
42795 20A
42796 24D

42797 19A
42798 20A
42799 17B
42800 63C
42801 63C
42802 65F
42803 65F
42804 64C
42805 67C
42806 67A
42807 64C
42808 67C
42809 67C
42810 11E
42811 5B
42812 1A
42813 5B
42814 9A
42815 5B
42816 21A
42817 2B
42818 17B
42819 26B
42820 26D
42821 24D
42822 17B
42823 16A
42824 21A
42825 17B
42826 17B
42827 21A
42828 24B
42829 17B
42830 64C
42831 68A
42832 68A
42833 68A
42834 68A
42835 68A
42836 68A
42837 68A
42838 26B
42839 14A
42840 24F
42841 24F
42842 24F
42843 24F
42844 24F
42845 25B
42846 21A
42847 17A
42848 9A
42849 8C
42850 66C
42851 5B
42852 2B
42853 3A
42854 2B
42855 14A
42856 5B
42857 21A
42858 9A
42859 9B
42860 26B
42861 25B

42862 25B
42863 25B
42864 26B
42865 26D
42866 25B
42867 24F
42868 26B
42869 24B
42870 1A
42871 26A
42872 17A
42873 17D
42874 17D
42875 68A
42876 68A
42877 68A
42878 26A
42879 67C
42880 66C
42881 68A
42882 68A
42883 68A
42884 68A
42885 68A
42886 68A
42887 68A
42888 68A
42889 26A
42890 67C
42891 66C
42892 68A
42893 68A
42894 68A
42895 68A
42896 68A
42897 68A
42898 68A
42899 68A
42900 68A
42901 68A
42902 68B
42903 68B
42904 67C
42905 67D
42906 67D
42907 68B
42908 67A
42909 68B
42910 67A
42911 67A
42912 68B
42913 68B
42914 5B
42915 3D
42916 17B
42917 9A
42918 9A
42919 5B
42920 14A
42921 5B
42922 21A
42923 9A
42924 9B
42925 26B
42926 25B

42927 67C
42928 11E
42929 3A
42930 9A
42931 1A
42932 5B
42933 5B
42934 9B
42935 9A
42936 9A
42937 1A
42938 9A
42939 5B
42940 5B
42941 6B
42942 9D
42943 9D
42944 2B

Stanier 2-6-0 5MT

42945 6B
42946 3D
42947 3D
42948 1A
42949 8E
42950 5B
42951 3D
42952 5B
42953 5A
42954 3D
42955 5B
42956 5B
42957 3D
42958 3D
42959 6B
42960 9A
42961 5A
42962 5B
42963 5A
42964 2B
42965 6B
42966 1A
42967 6C
42968 5B
42969 6C
42970 6C
42971 6B
42972 5B
42973 6B
42974 3D
42975 6B
42976 6B
42977 6C
42978 6C
42979 3D
42980 5B
42981 6C
42982 6B
42983 5B
42984 5B

Ivatt 2-6-0 4MT

43000 1D
43001 1D
43002 2B

The highly successful joint design of Hughes and Fowler, the 'Crab' 2-6-0s survived well into the 1960s, the last being withdrawn in January 1967. This is Leeds City station on Saturday 23 July 1955 and 'Crab' No 42721 is partnered with a 'Jubilee' on the 4.2pm Hull to Liverpool. Alongside is D49/2 'Hunt' class 4-4-0 No 62759 *The Craven*. No 42721 served from Manchester Agecroft shed for many years until Aintree received it in March 1957. It then had short stays from March 1962 at Wigan L&Y, Bolton, Lancaster, and finally in October 1963 returned to Agecroft where it was withdrawn on the 12th of the month and cut up at Horwich Works. *Initial Photographics/B. K. B. Green*

One of five 'Crabs' fitted with Reidinger rotary poppet valve gear in 1953, No 42825 is seen at Derby shed on Saturday 29 May 1954. Fitted as an experiment to improve performance, there was no marked change to the rest of the class fitted with standard Walschaerts valve gear. Previously the five engines had Lentz gear, but again there had been no improvement. All five were kept together and at Nationalisation were at Saltley, although Nos 42824 and 42825 strayed away to Bournville in February 1953, both returning to Saltley two months later. All five transferred to Burton in August 1954 and remained there until withdrawal, No 42825 going during the week ended 30 June 1962, the other four being withdrawn around the same time. *Initial Photographics/R. J. Buckley*

Stanier's 2-6-0 design first appeared in 1933 with No 42945 (numbered at first 13245), the first three going to Perth. This is No 42972, a January 1934 production first allocated to Willesden. When this photograph was taken in June 1955 at Shrewsbury shed it was a Crewe South engine. Reallocations included Stoke in November 1962, Bescot in March 1963 and Gorton at the beginning of January 1965 from where it was withdrawn three months later during the week ended 17 April.

G. W. Sharpe

43003	2B	43068	31D	43133	65A	43232	15C	43327	17B
43004	12D	43069	53A	43134	65A	43233	20C	43329	8B
43005	2B	43070	52B	43135	65A	43234	18D	43330	5B
43006	12D	43071	51A	43136	65A	43235	18B	43331	18B
43007	12D	43072	51D	43137	65A	43237	8B	43332	19A
43008	12D	43073	51D	43138	64F	43239	16D	43333	15C
43009	12D	43074	51D	43139	68E	43240	16A	43334	19A
43010	17A	43075	51A	43140	64E	43241	68A	43335	19A
43011	2B	43076	53A	43141	64E	43242	16C	43337	22B
43012	19A	43077	53A	43142	31D	43243	19C	43339	21A
43013	21A	43078	53A	43143	31D	43244	15B	43340	17B
43014	20B	43079	53A	43144	31D	43245	14C	43341	19A
43015	53A	43080	35A	43145	32G	43246	21A	43342	17D
43016	52B	43081	35A	43146	32G	43247	17B	43344	22A
43017	21A	43082	35A	43147	32G	43248	71H	43351	68A
43018	15C	43083	35A	43148	32G	43249	16A	43355	21B
43019	14A	43084	35A	43149	32G	43250	20C	43356	71H
43020	1D	43085	35A	43150	32G	43251	18A	43357	9B
43021	1D	43086	35A	43151	32G	43252	19A	43359	21B
43022	1D	43087	35A	43152	32G	43253	18B	43361	17A
43023	2B	43088	35A	43153	32G	43254	19A	43367	15A
43024	1D	43089	31A	43154	32G	43256	17B	43368	17A
43025	10E	43090	31D	43155	32G	43257	20F	43369	16A
43026	10E	43091	31D	43156	32G	43258	22B	43370	17D
43027	17A	43092	31D	43157	32F	43259	17A	43371	16A
43028	10E	43093	31D	43158	32F	43261	14A	43373	22B
43029	10E	43094	50C	43159	32F	43263	21B	43374	21A
43030	52B	43095	50C	43160	32F	43266	18B	43378	16A
43031	14A	43096	50C	43161	32F	43267	20C	43379	16C
43032	19B	43097	50C			43268	9D	43381	21A
43033	16A	43098	50C			43271	11E	43386	18D
43034	2B	43099	53A	**Johnson 0-6-0 3F**		43273	17D	43387	9D
43035	2B	43100	53A	43174	15D	43274	9D	43388	19A
43036	21A	43101	51D	43178	20F	43275	9A	43389	3D
43037	19C	43102	51D	43180	19C	43277	84G	43392	20B
43038	53A	43103	53A	43181	19C	43278	9D	43394	84G
43039	20A	43104	31D	43183	20D	43281	9B	43395	17B
43040	16A	43105	31D	43185	17A	43282	8B	43396	6K
43041	17A	43106	31D	43186	21C	43284	21A	43398	8B
43042	19A	43107	31D	43187	9B	43286	17B	43399	2E
43043	52B	43108	31D	43188	17B	43287	16C	43400	17D
43044	20B	43109	31D	43189	5B	43290	17D	43401	16A
43045	15C	43110	31D	43192	16A	43292	18A	43402	17A
43046	21A	43111	31D	43193	17B	43294	17A	43405	18A
43047	21A	43112	20F	43194	71H	43295	20F	43406	17B
43048	17A	43113	20F	43200	17A	43298	18D	43410	3C
43049	17A	43114	19A	43201	71J	43300	9D	43411	15C
43050	51D	43115	19A	43203	21B	43301	68A	43419	71J
43051	51D	43116	20A	43204	71J	43305	16C	43427	22A
43052	50C	43117	20A	43205	15C	43306	17B	43428	15D
43053	53A	43118	14A	43207	5B	43307	14A	43429	17A
43054	51K	43119	16A	43208	19C	43308	3D	43431	16D
43055	51C	43120	14A	43210	21A	43309	18A	43433	21A
43056	51A	43121	14A	43211	18C	43310	18D	43435	21A
43057	51A	43122	53A	43212	18C	43312	17B	43436	71H
43058	35A	43123	50C	43213	22B	43313	15D	43440	14A
43059	35A	43124	53A	43214	21A	43314	8B	43441	21A
43060	35A	43125	50C	43216	71H	43315	17A	43443	21A
43061	35A	43126	52C	43218	71H	43317	18B	43444	22A
43062	35A	43127	35C	43219	21A	43318	17A	43446	20C
43063	35A	43128	52C	43222	15D	43321	20C	43449	20D
43064	35A	43129	52B	43223	21A	43323	17A	43453	18A
43065	35A	43130	53A	43224	18D	43324	17A	43454	15D
43066	35A	43131	53A	43225	19C	43325	19C	43456	20B
43067	35A	43132	65A	43226	17A	43326	15C	43457	9A

Ivatt-designed 2-6-0 No 43001 is seen at Willesden shed in March 1956 as originally built in December 1947 with a double-chimney. This was replaced by a single-chimney later in 1956. First allocated to Crewe South, it moved to Bletchley during the week ended 6 March 1948 then to Devons Road at the end of December 1950, remaining at Bow until October 1957 when it moved to Nuneaton. In October 1962 Bescot became its home, and the wheel turned full circle when it returned to Crewe South in June 1963. Here it remained, apart from a brief stay at Stoke in 1966, until withdrawal during the week ended 16 September 1967. *P. H. Groom*

Melton Constable station on Saturday 6 August 1955 sees Ivatt 2-6-0 No 43150 on the 10.35am Peterborough to Yarmouth. A large number of the type went new to East Anglia and ex-M&GN sheds, including No 43150 which was sent to Melton Constable shed when released from Doncaster Works to traffic on 7 November 1951. Its first transfer was to Stratford in February 1959 and then out to Peterborough New England in February 1960 where it remained until withdrawn on 3 January 1965. King's yard at Norwich conducted the last rites two months later.
Initial Photographics/B. K. B. Green

Johnson 3F 0-6-0 No 43268 at Friden is seen on an Ian Allan special for Buxton on Sunday 25 September 1955. The 11-coach special had started at St Pancras at 9.30am with over 350 enthusiasts on board hauled to Derby by 'Royal Scot' 4-6-0 No 46100 *Royal Scot*. At Derby Compounds Nos 40917 and 41077 took over for the remainder of the journey to Buxton. At Whatstandwell a stop was made so that those wanting a run over the Cromford and High Peak line could leave the train and board buses to Cromford Wharf. The excursionists then had to ascend on foot Sheep Pasture incline to Middleton Top to join a train of open wagons for the journey over Hopton incline to Friden, hauled by North London Railway 0-6-0Ts Nos 58850 and 58860. This was where No 43268 was waiting with a train of corridor stock for the run to Buxton. Here the Compounds returned the trippers to Derby, and No 46100 to London to arrive at 9.15pm. Luckily it was a sunny day, and the cost for the whole trip was 30s (£1.50) adult fare and 17s 6d (87p) for an accompanied juvenile. Light lunch and full dinner could be taken for 12s 6d (62p). *Initial Photographics/R. J. Buckley*

No.	Shed	No.	Shed	No.	Shed	No.	Shed	No.	Shed
43459	17A	43618	8B	43749	19A	43848	65B	43914	20C
43462	21C	43619	17B	43750	17D	43849	65B	43915	5D
43463	19C	43620	21A	43753	18A	43850	18B	43916	20F
43464	22A	43621	84G	43754	15C	43851	20B	43917	16A
43468	16C	43622	68A	43755	22B	43852	20D	43918	17D
43469	17B	43623	17B	43756	19A	43853	22B	43919	14B
43474	15D	43624	21A	43757	26G	43854	9F	43920	18D
43476	20C	43627	21A	43759	84G	43855	21A	43921	17C
43482	21A	43629	15C	43760	17D	43856	18B	43922	68A
43484	21A	43630	26G	43762	84G	43857	18D	43923	18A
43490	21A	43631	18A	43763	21A	43858	17B	43924	22B
43491	84G	43633	8B	43766	17A	43859	17A	43925	17A
43494	17B	43634	16D	43770	15D	43860	18B	43926	22A
43496	17D	43636	68A	43771	20E	43861	15A	43927	26G
43497	20D	43637	16A	43773	16C	43863	18D	43928	16A
43499	18A	43638	26G			43864	5D	43929	17D
43502	3C	43639	20D	**Deeley 0-6-0 3F**		43865		43930	15A
43506	22B	43644	21A	43775	19A	43866	18B	43931	20B
43507	21A	43645	22B	43776	17D	43867	18B	43932	21B
43509	20D	43650	18A	43778	17B	43868	68A	43933	18A
43510	17A	43651	9G	43781	19A	43869	17C	43934	14A
43514	68A	43652	17B	43784	20E	43870	15C	43935	14A
43515	18D	43656	20D	43785	15D	43871	20B	43936	16A
43520	21A	43657	8B	43786	2B	43872	19C	43937	15C
43521	21B	43658	17C	43787	8B	43873	15D	43938	21A
43522	16D	43660	19C	43789	20C	43874	16D	43939	21A
43523	21A	43664	19C	43790	15C	43875	21A	43940	21A
43524	18D	43665	15D	43791	21A	43876	15D	43941	21A
43529	15D	43668	21B	43793	18A	43877	6E	43942	20C
43531	15A	43669	19C	43795	18A	43878	21A	43943	18A
43538	9G	43673	21A	43798	21A	43879	17A	43944	20F
43544	21A	43674	21A	43799	15C	43880	18B	43945	9F
43546	18D	43675	21B	43800	19A	43881	17D	43946	21A
43548	17A	43676	15C	43803	21A	43882	19A	43947	14A
43550	17A	43678	68A	43806	15C	43883	66B	43948	17B
43553	20C	43679	84G	43808	15A	43884	63B	43949	21A
43558	16A	43680	21A	43809	17B	43885	18B	43950	19C
43562	5B	43681	20B	43810	18A	43886	18D	43951	21A
43565	14C	43682	17C	43812	21A	43887	22B	43952	27D
43568	21A	43684	21A	43814	19C	43888	14C	43953	17B
43570	84G	43686	20E	43815	17B	43889	15B	43954	16A
43572	17A	43687	21B	43817	21A	43890	11E	43955	17A
43574	17B	43690	21A	43822	84G	43891	18C	43956	16A
43575	18D	43693	21A	43823	18A	43892	17B	43957	35C
43578	17A	43698	21A	43825	18A	43893	20F	43958	16A
43579	20B	43705	20C	43826	18A	43894	17C	43959	18C
43580	18B	43709	17B	43828	18A	43895	16C	43960	20F
43581	84G	43710	15C	43829	15D	43896	12A	43961	18A
43583	21B	43711	16D	43832	18A	43897	24D	43962	16A
43584	17A	43712	22A			43898	15B	43963	21A
43585	20G	43714	20D	**Fowler 0-6-0 4F**		43899		43964	14B
43586	20B	43715	19A	43835	17C	43900	18D	43965	17B
43587	17B	43717	9A	43836	6B	43901	14A	43966	18B
43593	22A	43721	15D	43837	21B	43902	68A	43967	15D
43594	21A	43723	18C	43838	17A	43903	16C	43968	20A
43595	19A	43727	16D	43839	17A	43904	6B	43969	18A
43596	16C	43728	15C	43840	17A	43905	14A	43970	16C
43598	17A	43729	16A	43841	1E	43906	20C	43971	15D
43599	21A	43731	19A	43842	9D	43907	16C	43972	16A
43600	84G	43734	22A	43843	15C	43908	6B	43973	68A
43605	18D	43735	17A	43844	19A	43909	21A	43974	18A
43607	19A	43737	20B	43845	21A	43910	16A	43975	14B
43608	17B	43742	20E	43846	22B	43911	21A	43976	17B
43612	26G	43745	17A	43847	17A	43912	21A	43977	15A
43615	8B	43748	15C			43913	20F	43978	19C

Above: The Deeley version of the 3F 0-6-0 is shown here in the shape of No 43784 at Shipley in May 1955 after transfer to Bradford Manningham shed from Skipton in March 1954. Built at Derby in 1903, No 43784 remained at Bradford until declared redundant on 12 September 1960 and was stored until August 1961 when it was sold to Cashmore's at Great Bridge for scrap.   *G. W. Sharpe*

Below: When Fowler took over from Deeley at Derby he continued the Midland tradition of 0-6-0s by building his own version rated at 4F. This was in reality a variation on the previous designs, but with superheated boilers. The first two appeared in 1911 and were thoroughly tested until mass production started in 1917 and continued until 1922, 192 engines being built. This is No 43854 at Derby shed on Friday 16 September 1955 after a works visit, and was one of a batch built in 1918. In 1948 it was based at Peterborough Spital Bridge, moving on to Heaton Mersey in October 1952. December 1958 was the month of transfer to Coalville, where it remained until withdrawn during the week ended 6 June 1964. Cashmore's at Great Bridge carried out the cutting up.   *G. W. Sharpe*

No.	Shed	No.	Shed	No.	Shed	No.	Shed	No.	Shed
43979	15A	44042	26G	44107	20C	44172	17D	44237	8B
43980	11D	44043	15D	44108	21A	44173	18B	44238	20B
43981	6G	44044	20A	44109	17C	44174	19A	44239	35C
43982	16A	44045	22B	44110	35C	44175	22B	44240	27D
43983	16A	44046	17D	44111	19C	44176	21A	44241	17D
43984	11E	44047	18A	44112	17A	44177	17A	44242	2E
43985	21A	44048	17B	44113	17C	44178	9F	44243	14B
43986	21A	44049	17A	44114	26G	44179	21A	44244	18C
43987	20B	44050	17D	44115	3C	44180	17C	44245	19C
43988	18A	44051	14A	44116	1A	44181	68A	44246	5D
43989	21B	44052	14B	44117	6B	44182	15C	44247	35C
43990	18A	44053	18C	44118	18B	44183	68A	44248	21A
43991	17A	44054	18C	44119	26G	44184	15C	44249	18D
43992	17B	44055	17B	44120	3D	44185	21A	44250	18A
43993	18D	44056	25D	44121	12A	44186	2E	44251	63A
43994	18A	44057	3E	44122	18D	44187	21A	44252	17C
43995	18A	44058	6E	44123	22B	44188	18B	44253	63A
43996	67A	44059	11B	44124	17B	44189	68A	44254	63A
43997	16C	44060	12A	44125	5E	44190	18A	44255	65B
43998	18B	44061	2E	44126	5E	44191	18B	44256	65B
43999	20F	44062	25D	44127	19C	44192	11A	44257	63A
44000	20F	44063	5E	44128	19C	44193	63A	44258	63A
44001	67A	44064	2A	44129	18D	44194	65B	44259	14A
44002	19C	44065	6B	44130	18B	44195	16A	44260	17C
44003	20C	44066	18D	44131	16A	44196	66A	44261	8B
44004	21A	44067	1C	44132	16A	44197	20F	44262	17D
44005	16C	44068	5D	44133	18A	44198	67A	44263	21A
44006	18B	44069	9A	44134	17D	44199	68B	44264	22B
44007	20F	44070	18D	44135	22A	44200	18A	44265	17B
44008	68A	44071	19C	44136	18A	44201	21A	44266	22A
44009	68A	44072	1E	44137	21A	44202	16C	44267	18D
44010	18D	44073	6B	44138	21A	44203	21A	44268	16C
44011	63B	44074	5D	44139	16A	44204	21A	44269	22A
44012	18A	44075	9B	44140	16C	44205	16C	44270	14B
44013	19C	44076	2E	44141	20C	44206	16C	44271	9B
44014	18B	44077	5D	44142	17A	44207	20A	44272	22B
44015	22A	44078	3C	44143	17B	44208	1A	44273	35C
44016	68A	44079	5E	44144	9F	44209	22B	44274	20C
44017	17D	44080	9F	44145	18A	44210	14B	44275	9E
44018	17D	44081	12A	44146	71H	44211	21A	44276	20G
44019	25A	44082	16C	44147	18D	44212	19A	44277	20F
44020	17A	44083	11D	44148	17C	44213	21A	44278	15B
44021	16A	44084	21A	44149	20G	44214	17A	44279	17C
44022	26G	44085	17C	44150	21A	44215	16A	44280	10E
44023	17A	44086	11B	44151	16A	44216	20E	44281	67B
44024	5F	44087	22B	44152	35C	44217	18A	44282	20G
44025	26G	44088	18A	44153	20B	44218	27E	44283	66A
44026	21A	44089	19C	44154	18A	44219	2E	44284	18B
		44090	9F	44155	9G	44220	27D	44285	18B
LMS 0-6-0 4F		44091	18A	44156	17C	44221	27D	44286	9F
44027	3B	44092	21A	44157	18A	44222	20F	44287	19A
44028	17D	44093	5D	44158	16A	44223	16A	44288	18C
44029	14A	44094	20B	44159	67B	44224	17A	44289	18A
44030	16A	44095	16A	44160	21A	44225	27D	44290	20C
44031	17A	44096	71G	44161	18A	44226	21A	44291	26G
44032	6B	44097	35C	44162	18C	44227	21A	44292	11D
44033	16A	44098	20D	44163	17D	44228	14A	44293	22B
44034	15C	44099	20D	44164	17A	44229	18B	44294	18C
44035	22B	44100	17B	44165	21A	44230	21A	44295	17A
44036	19C	44101	17D	44166	17C	44231	15C	44296	22A
44037	19C	44102	71H	44167	22B	44232	19C	44297	14A
44038	27E	44103	17C	44168	17D	44233	18A	44298	14B
44039	16A	44104	18D	44169	17A	44234	65B	44299	18D
44040	26G	44105	27D	44170	20D	44235	21A	44300	5E
44041	20F	44106	18A	44171	21A	44236	9E	44301	5B

The LMS standard goods 4F 0-6-0, based on the Fowler version, was introduced in 1924, the last not appearing until 1941 after a gap of nine years between 1928 and 1937. Derby shed on Tuesday 1 June 1954 has No 44142 on shed in ex-works condition paired with a self-weighing tender. This was one of the 1925 batch built at Crewe Works and spent its entire post-Nationalisation days based at Derby. It was withdrawn during the week ended 12 December 1959 and stored alongside Derby station until May 1960 when, unusually, it went to Doncaster Works for scrapping.

Initial Photographics/R. J. Buckley

LMS 4F 0-6-0 No 44383 is seen at Stoke-on-Trent on Saturday 23 April 1955. This was an example built by the North British Locomotive Company in 1926 and also remained at one allocation from 1948, in this instance Stoke. It was withdrawn during the week ended 28 November 1959 and scrapped at Crewe Works.

Initial Photographics/ R. J. Buckley

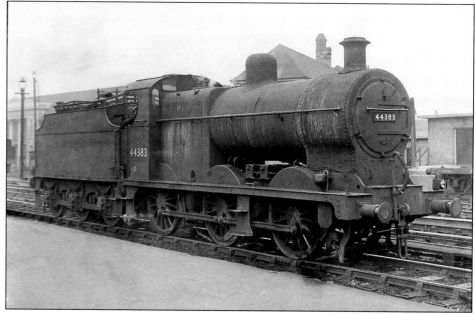

The 4Fs were often used on passenger turns and this view at Spondon on Saturday 19 June 1954 shows No 44602, paired with a high-sided tender, on the 12.12pm Derby to Nottingham. Built at Derby in August 1940 and first allocated to Cricklewood, by 1948 it was a Derby engine, moving to Rowsley in March 1955 and Gorton in May 1962, from where withdrawal took place during the week ended 29 August 1964. This was another purchase by Cashmore's at Great Bridge for scrap. *Initial Photographics/R. J. Buckley*

44302	3D	44367	6K	44432	5D	44497	1A	44562	20B
44303	10E	44368	11B	44433	17B	44498	5D	44563	14B
44304	17A	44369	17A	44434	17B	44499	5D	44564	17D
44305	6H	44370	1A	44435	17B	44500	5D	44565	17D
44306	11A	44371	18D	44436	17B	44501	20A	44566	17D
44307	6B	44372	1A	44437	19A	44502	5D	44567	22B
44308	5D	44373	5D	44438	10E	44503	5E	44568	19A
44309	5D	44374	5D	44439	3B	44504	5D	44569	22A
44310	5D	44375	5D	44440	1A	44505	12D	44570	20B
44311	26A	44376	18A	44441	1D	44506	3E	44571	21A
44312	67B	44377	5D	44442	1A	44507	5D	44572	17C
44313	16A	44378	17A	44443	1C	44508	5D	44573	19A
44314	63A	44379	9F	44444	3C	44509	35C	44574	15A
44315	68A	44380	17A	44445	6H	44510	11A	44575	15A
44316	17B	44381	1A	44446	20C	44511	11B	44576	19C
44317	15D	44382	9B	44447	1E	44512	3E	44577	16A
44318	63B	44383	5D	44448	3C	44513	5D	44578	16A
44319	67B	44384	9F	44449	12D	44514	3E	44579	20G
44320	65F	44385	5D	44450	5E	44515	21A	44580	21A
44321	18B	44386	5E	44451	1A	44516	21A	44581	14A
44322	63B	44387	11B	44452	5E	44517	3D	44582	20A
44323	67B	44388	2A	44453	5E	44518	35C	44583	21A
44324	68A	44389	6G	44454	11A	44519	35C	44584	20B
44325	67B	44390	12D	44455	5D	44520	21A	44585	16A
44326	68A	44391	2E	44456	9G	44521	35C	44586	20B
44327	17D	44392	9E	44457	19A	44522	35C	44587	22B
44328	63A	44393	5D	44458	20D	44523	71G	44588	17D
44329	67A	44394	16D	44459	11D	44524	2E	44589	16C
44330	67B	44395	2A	44460	24D	44525	6G	44590	18D
44331	67B	44396	8E	44461	12D	44526	17B	44591	17B
44332	17B	44397	1A	44462	25D	44527	17B	44592	3E
44333	21A	44398	24D	44463	21A	44528	17B	44593	1E
44334	17A	44399	11A	44464	27D	44529	14A	44594	11B
44335	20B	44400	20E	44465	15B	44530	14A	44595	5B
44336	20D	44401	16A	44466	22A	44531	14B	44596	5D
44337	20D	44402	17A	44467	20B	44532	14B	44597	17B
44338	20D	44403	15C	44468	20F	44533	16A	44598	18B
44339	9D	44404	18D	44469	11D	44534	22A	44599	17B
44340	9B	44405	5D	44470	16C	44535	15B	44600	17B
44341	9G	44406	21A	44471	25D	44536	22A	44601	22B
44342	5E	44407	9F	44472	16A	44537	22A	44602	17A
44343	1C	44408	16A	44473	1A	44538	17B	44603	18C
44344	5B	44409	17A	44474	25D	44539	17C	44604	20D
44345	3C	44410	18C	44475	18D	44540	17A	44605	18B
44346	12A	44411	22A	44476	35C	44541	27E	44606	18D
44347	11B	44412	16A	44477	19A	44542	17A		
44348	1D	44413	21A	44478	5D	44543	26A	**Stanier 4-6-0 5MT**	
44349	9A	44414	16A	44479	24D	44544	27D	44658	14B
44350	9E	44415	16D	44480	16A	44545	17A	44659	21A
44351	11B	44416	16D	44481	27E	44546	16A	44660	21A
44352	1E	44417	71H	44482	18B	44547	20F	44661	17A
44353	5D	44418	21A	44483	24D	44548	5D	44662	20A
44354	1A	44419	17A	44484	5D	44549	12D	44663	15C
44355	22A	44420	17A	44485	25D	44550	20C	44664	21A
44356	8B	44421	9F	44486	26G	44551	17B	44665	19B
44357	9A	44422	71G	44487	11B	44552	17B	44666	21A
44358	5D	44423	15C	44488	3C	44553	22A	44667	17A
44359	5B	44424	22A	44489	8E	44554	17C	44668	68A
44360	3D	44425	16C	44490	3E	44555	16A	44669	68A
44361	3E	44426	19A	44491	2E	44556	17D	44670	68A
44362	18A	44427	21A	44492	3B	44557	71G	44671	68A
44363	1C	44428	17A	44493	6B	44558	71G	44672	68A
44364	1E	44429	17D	44494	8E	44559	71G	44673	68A
44365	12D	44430	18B	44495	12D	44560	71G	44674	68A
44366	6B	44431	20F	44496	5D	44561	71G	44675	68A

44676	68A	44741	9A	44806	15C	44871	5D	44936	12A
44677	65B	44742	9A	44807	5A	44872	3D	44937	9A
44678	6J	44743	22A	44808	10C	44873	3C	44938	9E
44679	5A	44744	20A	44809	17A	44874	11A	44939	12A
44680	5A	44745	22A	44810	21A	44875	1A	44940	24A
44681	6J	44746	20A	44811	21B	44876	3D	44941	9A
44682	5A	44747	22A	44812	15C	44877	68A	44942	3E
44683	5A	44748	9A	44813	21A	44878	68A	44943	20A
44684	5A	44749	9A	44814	21A	44879	63A	44944	19A
44685	5A	44750	9A	44815	17A	44880	65B	44945	21A
44686	9A	44751	9A	44816	14B	44881	65B	44946	25F
44687	9A	44752	9A	44817	14B	44882	68A	44947	24E
44688	27A	44753	20A	44818	17A	44883	68A	44948	25B
44689	27A	44754	20A	44819	17A	44884	68A	44949	25B
44690	27A	44755	20A	44820	63A	44885	63A	44950	24E
44691	27A	44756	20A	44821	21A	44886	68A	44951	25F
44692	27A	44757	20A	44822	14B	44887	27C	44952	64D
44693	25F	44758	5A	44823	26B	44888	21A	44953	64D
44694	25F	44759	5A	44824	25A	44889	24E	44954	62B
44695	25F	44760	9A	44825	14B	44890	26A	44955	64D
44696	26A	44761	5A	44826	20A	44891	26A	44956	65A
44697	26A	44762	5A	44827	5A	44892	11A	44957	65A
44698	63A	44763	5A	44828	20A	44893	26A	44958	68A
44699	63A	44764	5A	44829	3B	44894	26A	44959	63A
44700	64D	44765	5A	44830	19B	44895	25G	44960	63A
44701	64D	44766	5A	44831	2A	44896	3D	44961	63A
44702	65B	44767	27A	44832	5B	44897	68A	44962	21A
44703	68A	44768	8A	44833	2A	44898	68A	44963	21A
44704	63A	44769	8A	44834	5B	44899	68A	44964	21A
44705	63A	44770	5A	44835	84G	44900	68A	44965	21A
44706	67A	44771	1A	44836	2A	44901	68A	44966	21A
44707	66A	44772	8A	44837	2A	44902	68A	44967	65B
44708	10C	44773	8A	44838	1A	44903	68A	44968	65A
44709	11A	44774	14A	44839	17A	44904	11A	44969	66B
44710	6A	44775	21A	44840	5A	44905	11A	44970	65B
44711	2A	44776	21A	44841	21A	44906	8A	44971	12A
44712	2A	44777	14A	44842	21A	44907	8A	44972	63D
44713	2A	44778	24E	44843	20A	44908	65A	44973	63D
44714	2A	44779	24E	44844	3D	44909	2A	44974	63D
44715	2A	44780	25B	44845	26G	44910	6A	44975	63D
44716	2A	44781	26B	44846	14B	44911	5A	44976	63D
44717	9E	44782	26B	44847	17A	44912	25F	44977	63D
44718	60A	44783	60A	44848	19B	44913	6H	44978	63A
44719	60A	44784	60A	44849	20A	44914	3A	44979	63A
44720	63A	44785	65B	44850	66B	44915	2A	44980	63A
44721	63A	44786	66A	44851	19B	44916	1A	44981	14B
44722	60A	44787	60A	44852	20A	44917	71G	44982	24E
44723	60A	44788	60A	44853	20A	44918	16A	44983	20A
44724	60A	44789	60A	44854	20A	44919	21A	44984	14B
44725	68A	44790	68A	44855	19A	44920	21A	44985	14B
44726	68A	44791	67A	44856	17A	44921	63A	44986	19B
44727	68A	44792	68A	44857	20A	44922	65B	44987	26B
44728	27C	44793	64D	44858	19A	44923	65B	44988	24E
44729	27C	44794	61B	44859	21A	44924	63A	44989	27C
44730	24E	44795	68A	44860	2A	44925	63A	44990	25F
44731	24E	44796	63A	44861	16A	44926	24E	44991	60A
44732	24E	44797	63A	44862	2A	44927	24E	44992	60A
44733	24E	44798	60A	44863	2A	44928	25A	44993	68A
44734	26A	44799	60A	44864	6J	44929	24E	44994	64C
44735	26A	44800	8B	44865	6J	44930	24E	44995	65A
44736	26A	44801	63A	44866	2A	44931	63A	44996	65A
44737	24E	44802	19A	44867	2A	44932	24A	44997	63A
44738	6G	44803	26G	44868	6J	44933	26A	44998	63A
44739	6G	44804	21A	44869	1A	44934	26A	44999	63A
44740	6G	44805	21A	44870	2A	44935	9A	45000	2A

Above: No 44740 was a 'Black Five' variant seen here at Colwyn Bay on a Llandudno-bound train in June 1955. Entering traffic at Crewe North from Crewe Works during the week ended 29 May 1948, it was equipped with Caprotti valve gear. Moving on to Llandudno Junction after running in at 5A during the week ended 26 June 1948, it stayed here working the Manchester expresses until withdrawn during the week ended 13 April 1963 and returned to Crewe for scrapping.
G. W. Sharpe

Below: Similar to No 44740 with Caprotti valve gear, No 44755 also had a double-chimney and Timken roller bearings as seen here in 1957 in the goods yard at Shrewsbury. Built at Crewe and entering traffic during the week ended 1 May 1948, it went new to Derby shed. This would not be for long as, during the week ended 12 June 1948, it was sent to Leeds Holbeck where it settled for a long stay until September 1961 when Stockport Edgeley acquired it. Two months later it went to Liverpool Speke Junction and withdrawal came during the week ended 16 November 1963.
G. W. Sharpe

Above: Camden shed in May 1955 sees double-chimney and Timken roller bearing-fitted 'Black Five' No 44766. This was the last Stanier 4-6-0 to enter traffic under the LMS, going into stock at Crewe North during the week ended 27 December 1947 from Crewe Works. Resident at Crewe until July 1959, when Birmingham Monument Lane added it to its roster, it moved to Bescot later in 1959 and to Stourbridge in March 1966, Llandudno Junction three months later, then Chester LMS shed in October, and back to Crewe at South shed in May 1967. It was withdrawn during the week ended 19 August 1967. *P. H. Groom*

Below: In July 1955 'Standard Black Five' No 44841 starts the climb from Bromsgrove on to the Lickey Incline with a freight. Built in October 1944 at Crewe Works, it started its career at Saltley and, apart from spending October 1958 at Leicester Central shed, remained on allocation until April 1965 when Wolverhampton Oxley added it to its engines. Withdrawn during the week ended 22 October 1966, it remained stored at Oxley until January 1967 when it made the short journey to Cashmore's at Great Bridge for scrap. *G. W. Sharpe*

A number of Class 5s were fitted with boilers that had the dome and top feed combined as shown here on No 45017 in ex-works condition in June 1955 at Shrewsbury when allocated to Carnforth, where it had been transferred from Liverpool Edge Hill during the week ended 11 August 1951. May 1959 saw a move to Wigan Springs Branch, and July 1963 to Southport. The next year, in June, Manchester Newton Heath acquired the engine, and the following November it moved to Trafford Park. August 1965 saw it back at Carnforth where it survived until the very end of steam, being withdrawn during the week ended 10 August 1968. As it was built in May 1935, and first allocated to Inverness, it was amongst the oldest to remain active right to the end.   *G. W. Sharpe*

Glasgow St Rollox shed in 1955 sees named 'Black Five' No 45156 *Ayrshire Yeomanry*. Built by Armstrong Whitworth in July 1935, it was first allocated to Crewe North and went on to Scotland in 1936 when it received its name. Transferred south to Manchester Newton Heath in April 1957, it then served from Bolton in December 1962, Warrington in May 1963, Liverpool Edge Hill from July 1963 to May 1968, then to Manchester Patricroft for two months, and finally Rose Grove in July for the final weeks until the end of steam, being withdrawn during the week ended 10 August 1968.

G. W. Sharpe

A final look at a 'Black Five' with a difference, this time No 45298 with a self-weighing tender at Shrewsbury shed in April 1955. Built in December 1936 by Armstrong Whitworth and first allocated to Liverpool Edge Hill, during the week ended 28 February 1948 it moved to Shrewsbury from Crewe North where it settled until June 1964 when it moved to Bangor. After time at other North Wales sheds, it went to Crewe South in June 1967 from where withdrawal took place later in the year during the week ended 16 September.

G. W. Sharpe

45001	6B	45066	60A	45131	5B	45196	8B	45261	25B
45002	2A	45067	5B	45132	3D	45197	12A	45262	19A
45003	1A	45068	27A	45133	11A	45198	5B	45263	15C
45004	10A	45069	8A	45134	5B	45199	10C	45264	17A
45005	8A	45070	12A	45135	10A	45200	24E	45265	21A
45006	9E	45071	5A	45136	60B	45201	25A	45266	67B
45007	68A	45072	11A	45137	10C	45202	26A	45267	14B
45008	66B	45073	5B	45138	68A	45203	26A	45268	21A
45009	66B	45074	5B	45139	12A	45204	25A	45269	21A
45010	67B	45075	25G	45140	12A	45205	24B	45270	5B
45011	65A	45076	25G	45141	11B	45206	24F	45271	8B
45012	68A	45077	27C	45142	10C	45207	25F	45272	21A
45013	68A	45078	24A	45143	84G	45208	25F	45273	22A
45014	2E	45079	25G	45144	6H	45209	24B	45274	22A
45015	3B	45080	25G	45145	84G	45210	25F	45275	6B
45016	63B	45081	68A	45146	9A	45211	25G	45276	8A
45017	11A	45082	68A	45147	1A	45212	24F	45277	14B
45018	68A	45083	68A	45148	5A	45213	63A	45278	1A
45019	11A	45084	63B	45149	5D	45214	65B	45279	14B
45020	8A	45085	66B	45150	2A	45215	25B	45280	21A
45021	2E	45086	64C	45151	66B	45216	27A	45281	68A
45022	64C	45087	64D	45152	66B	45217	8E	45282	2A
45023	64C	45088	16A	45153	65B	45218	25B	45283	84G
45024	1A	45089	1A	45154*	65B	45219	25F	45284	26A
45025	1A	45090	60A	45155	65B	45220	26A	45285	14B
45026	10A	45091	2E	45156*	65B	45221	15C	45286	12A
45027	1A	45092	11A	45157*	65B	45222	25B	45287	3B
45028	5B	45093	5B	45158*	65B	45223	26A	45288	12A
45029	66B	45094	3D	45159	65B	45224	26A	45289	10A
45030	67A	45095	10C	45160	67A	45225	26A	45290	10C
45031	26G	45096	10B	45161	64C	45226	24A	45291	11B
45032	8B	45097	1A	45162	61B	45227	27A	45292	2E
45033	5A	45098	60A	45163	68A	45228	27A	45293	12A
45034	5B	45099	66B	45164	63A	45229	27A	45294	10C
45035	8B	45100	68A	45165	63A	45230	12A	45295	12A
45036	67A	45101	25A	45166	67A	45231	3D	45296	12A
45037	12A	45102	26A	45167	63A	45232	26A	45297	19B
45038	5B	45103	26A	45168	63A	45233	26A	45298	84G
45039	8A	45104	26A	45169	68B	45234	26A	45299	12A
45040	21A	45105	26A	45170	63A	45235	5A	45300	5A
45041	5B	45106	12A	45171	63A	45236	11B	45301	5A
45042	10C	45107	24F	45172	63A	45237	25B	45302	5B
45043	6A	45108	5B	45173	67A	45238	19A	45303	8A
45044	5B	45109	9A	45174	67A	45239	9E	45304	10C
45045	6J	45110	6J	45175	67A	45240	5A	45305	8A
45046	11B	45111	5B	45176	66B	45241	11A	45306	11A
45047	63A	45112	68A	45177	65B	45242	8A	45307	5A
45048	5B	45113	8A	45178	65B	45243	8A	45308	3C
45049	63A	45114	3D	45179	60A	45244	12A	45309	66B
45050	2A	45115	65B	45180	6J	45245	63A	45310	3B
45051	3E	45116	65B	45181	8A	45246	12A	45311	6J
45052	3D	45117	63A	45182	10C	45247	6B	45312	10C
45053	63A	45118	68A	45183	64C	45248	12A	45313	10A
45054	11A	45119	65B	45184	12A	45249	8A	45314	10A
45055	10A	45120	68A	45185	5B	45250	8A	45315	12A
45056	19B	45121	66B	45186	21A	45251	67A	45316	10C
45057	10C	45122	68A	45187	2A	45252	8B	45317	11B
45058	3D	45123	68A	45188	10C	45253	14B	45318	24E
45059	14A	45124	60A	45189	5B	45254	5A	45319	60A
45060	5B	45125	63A	45190	84G	45255	8B	45320	60A
45061	27C	45126	68A	45191	2E	45256	8A	45321	8B
45062	19A	45127	64C	45192	60A	45257	5D	45322	3D
45063	25G	45128	5B	45193	11A	45258	12A	45323	12A
45064	1A	45129	10C	45194	67A	45259	10C	45324	1A
45065	3D	45130	6B	45195	3C	45260	16A	45325	6B

45326	11A
45327	11A
45328	8B
45329	12A
45330	68A
45331	6G
45332	10B
45333	8E
45334	68A
45335	14A
45336	26A
45337	26B
45338	26B
45339	25A
45340	25B
45341	25G
45342	21A
45343	8A
45344	3C
45345	12A
45346	8E
45347	9E
45348	12A
45349	3D
45350	1A
45351	12A
45352	10C
45353	5B
45354	8B
45355	65B
45356	65B
45357	63A
45358	63B
45359	63B
45360	60A
45361	60A
45362	67A
45363	68A
45364	68A
45365	63A
45366	63A
45367	63A
45368	12A
45369	5B
45370	3D
45371	12A
45372	2A
45373	5A
45374	1A
45375	2A
45376	8A
45377	10C
45378	10C
45379	2A
45380	8A
45381	1A
45382	6J
45383	11B
45384	62B
45385	6J
45386	11B
45387	1A
45388	8A
45389	63A
45390	3E
45391	5B
45392	2E
45393	8A
45394	2A
45395	3C
45396	65B
45397	3D
45398	8A
45399	8A
45400	65B
45401	10C
45402	5A
45403	2A
45404	1A
45405	3B
45406	84G
45407	21A
45408	10A
45409	12A
45410	8A
45411	10C
45412	12A
45413	8A
45414	12A
45415	27A
45416	3A
45417	6H
45418	3D
45419	2A
45420	10C
45421	8A
45422	84G
45423	65B
45424	10C
45425	10A
45426	10C
45427	11A
45428	10C
45429	2A
45430	2A
45431	2A
45432	68B
45433	66B
45434	5A
45435	25A
45436	24E
45437	2A
45438	12A
45439	3B
45440	71G
45441	2A
45442	10C
45443	65B
45444	10C
45445	12A
45446	5A
45447	19A
45448	3D
45449	10A
45450	26G
45451	12A
45452	63A
45453	60A
45454	10A
45455	68A
45456	63A
45457	63A
45458	63A
45459	63A
45460	63A
45461	60A
45462	66B
45463	63A
45464	63A
45465	63A
45466	68A
45467	63A
45468	65B
45469	63A
45470	63A
45471	65B
45472	63A
45473	63A
45474	63A
45475	63A
45476	60A
45477	60A
45478	60A
45479	60A
45480	68B
45481	68A
45482	65B
45483	63A
45484	66B
45485	66B
45486	62B
45487	63A
45488	63A
45489	67A
45490	67A
45491	68A
45492	63A
45493	2A
45494	12A
45495	8B
45496	63A
45497	63A
45498	66B
45499	65B

'Patriot' class 4-6-0 6P

45500*	12A
45501*	9A
45502*	12A
45503*	5A
45504*	5A
45505*	9A
45506*	5A
45507*	5A
45508	10B
45509*	17A
45510	5A
45511*	1A

'Rebuilt Patriot' class 4-6-0 7P

45512*	12A

'Patriot' class 4-6-0 6P

45513	5A

'Rebuilt Patriot' class 4-6-0 7P

45514*	1B

'Patriot' class 4-6-0 6P

45515*	8A
45516*	5A
45517	1A
45518*	8A
45519*	9A
45520*	9A

Rebuilt 'Patriot' class 4-6-0 7P

45521*	8A
45522*	1B
45523*	1B

'Patriot' class 4-6-0 6P

45524*	5A

'Rebuilt Patriot' class 4-6-0 7P

45525*	8A
45526*	12A
45527*	8A
45528	5A
45529*	5A
45530*	9A
45531*	8A
45532*	1B

'Patriot' class 4-6-0 6P

45533*	8A

Rebuilt 'Patriot' class 4-6-0 7P

45534*	8A
45535*	8A
45536*	9A

'Patriot' class 4-6-0 6P

45537*	12A
45538*	8A
45539*	9A

Rebuilt 'Patriot' class 4-6-0 7P

45540*	9A

'Patriot' class 4-6-0 6P

45541*	12A
45542	12A
45543*	12A
45544	5A

Rebuilt 'Patriot' class 4-6-0 7P

45545*	1B

'Patriot' class 4-6-0 6P

45546*	1A
45547	5A
45548*	5A
45549	12A
45550	8A
45551	12A

'Jubilee' class 4-6-0 6P

45552*	12A
45553*	9A
45554*	16A
45555*	3B
45556*	5A
45557*	14B
45558*	10C
45559*	10C
45560*	16A
45561*	22A
45562*	20A
45563*	10C
45564*	20A
45565*	20A
45566*	20A
45567*	8A
45568*	20A
45569*	20A
45570*	17A
45571*	24E
45572*	22A
45573*	20A
45574*	24E
45575*	14B
45576*	19B
45577*	22A
45578*	9A
45579*	14B
45580*	24E
45581*	25G
45582*	10B
45583*	12A
45584*	24E
45585*	17A
45586*	5A
45587*	9A
45588*	24E
45589*	20A
45590*	19B
45591*	5A
45592*	1B
45593*	12A
45594*	19B
45595*	9A
45596*	8A
45597*	20A
45598*	14B
45599*	12A
45600*	10C
45601*	1B
45602*	22A
45603*	8A
45604*	5A
45605*	20A
45606*	1B
45607*	19B
45608*	20A
45609*	19B
45610*	17A
45611*	16A
45612*	14B

Shrewsbury shed is seen again in 1955 and on the turntable is 'Patriot' 4-6-0 No 45501 *St Dunstans*. This and No 45500 had parts included from former withdrawn 'Claughton' class engines and were distinguishable from other class members by having larger centred driving wheels and fluted side rods. No 45501 was built in November 1930 and based at Manchester Longsight from the week ended 5 June 1948 after transfer from Liverpool Edge Hill, remaining at 9A until June 1958 when sent to Crewe North. From here during its last years of service it went to Carnforth, Mold Junction, Warrington, and finally Carlisle Upperby in September 1960 from where it was withdrawn during the week ended 26 August 1961.

G. W. Sharpe

One of the unnamed 'Patriots', No 45544 runs into Shrewsbury past Coton Hill sidings on a local in May 1955. It had been transferred to Liverpool Edge Hill from Crewe North the previous January and stayed at 8A until July 1959 when it transferred to Carlisle Upperby. Returning south to Warrington in September 1960, it was withdrawn during the week ended 9 December 1961.

G. W. Sharpe

In 1946 a start was made on rebuilding the 'Patriots' with Stanier Type 2A tapered boilers, new smokeboxes, double-chimneys, new cabs and Stanier tenders. No 45531 *Sir Frederick Harrison* was dealt with in December 1947 and is seen here at Manchester Exchange on the 9.10am from Liverpool Lime Street on Saturday 30 April 1955. At the time of the rebuild it was a Wolverhampton Bushbury engine, and moved on to Camden during the week ended 28 May 1949, replaced at Bushbury by a 'Jubilee'. Camden returned it to Bushbury during the week ended 1 October 1949 and at the beginning of June 1950 Bushbury lost it again, to Liverpool Edge Hill, where it stayed until April 1962. Reallocations then were frequent to Derby, Wigan Springs Branch, Carlisle Upperby, and Carlisle Kingmoor in September 1964. Withdrawal was authorised during the week ended 30 October 1965.

Initial Photographics/R. J. Buckley

45613*	8A	45647*	3B	45680*	9A	45713*	68A	45741*	3B
45614*	14B	45648*	14B	45681*	8A	45714*	68A	45742*	3B
45615*	14B	45649*	14B	45682*	22A	45715*	68A		
45616*	14B	45650*	14B	45683*	19B	45716*	68A	**'Royal Scot' class 4-6-0 7P**	
45617*	5A	45651*	22A	45684*	5A	45717*	27A	46100*	1B
45618*	9E	45652*	9E	45685*	22A	45718*	68A	46101*	5A
45619*	20A	45653*	24E	45686*	1B	45719*	24E	46102*	66A
45620*	16A	45654*	19B	45687*	67A	45720*	67A	46103*	20A
45621*	67A	45655*	9E	45688*	3B	45721*	8A	46104*	66A
45622*	9E	45656*	19B	45689*	9A	45722*	12A	46105*	66A
45623*	8A	45657*	68A	45690*	22A	45723*	9A	46106*	5A
45624*	9A	45658*	20A	45691*	68A	45724*	68A	46107*	66A
45625*	1A	45659*	20A	45692*	63A	45725*	19B	46108*	20A
45626*	17A	45660*	22A	45693*	67A	45726*	5A	46109*	20A
45627*	14B	45661*	26A	45694*	20A	45727*	63A	46110*	8A
45628*	9E	45662*	22A	45695*	25G	45728*	68A	46111*	9A
45629*	9E	45663*	22A	45696*	68A	45729*	68A	46112*	20A
45630*	12A	45664*	19B	45697*	68A	45730*	68A	46113*	20A
45631*	9A	45665*	67A	45698*	27A	45731*	68A	46114*	9A
45632*	9A	45666*	12A	45699*	22A	45732*	68A	46115*	9A
45633*	10B	45667*	16A	45700*	26A	45733*	3B	46116*	12A
45634*	1A	45668*	10C	45701*	26A	45734*	3B	46117*	20A
45635*	26A	45669*	1B	45702*	26A			46118*	5A
45636*	16A	45670*	8A	45703*	5A	**'Rebuilt Jubilee' class 4-6-0 7P**		46119*	5A
45638*	9A	45671*	26A	45704*	68A			46120*	5A
45639*	20A	45672*	1B	45705*	25G	45735*	1B	46121*	66A
45640*	68A	45673*	63A	45706*	26A	45736*	5A	46122*	9A
45641*	14B	45674*	5A	45707*	67A			46123*	8A
45642*	26A	45675*	20A	45708*	25G	**'Jubilee' class 4-6-0 6P**		46124*	8A
45643*	12A	45676*	1B	45709*	9A	45737*	3B	46125*	5A
45644*	9A	45677*	67A	45710*	26A	45738*	3B	46126*	12A
45645*	10C	45678*	5A	45711*	67A	45739*	20A	46127*	5A
45646*	25G	45679*	68A	45712*	26A	45740*	3B	46128*	9A

'Jubilee' class 4-6-0 No 45610 *Gold Coast* leaves Derby on the 12.40pm Newcastle to Bristol on Monday 26 April 1954. Built to a Stanier design in July 1934 at Crewe, it was first allocated to Camden. A Derby-allocated engine for most of its BR days, it was renamed *Ghana* in December 1958. After spending a year on Burton on Trent's books in 1962, it was back at Derby when withdrawn during the week ended 11 January 1964.

Initial Photographics/R. J. Buckley

No.	Shed
46129*	5A
46130*	9A
46131*	9A
46132*	9A
46133*	20A
46134*	6J
46135*	12A
46136*	12A
46137*	5A
46138*	5A
46139*	1B
46140*	9A
46141*	12A
46142*	1B
46143*	9A
46144*	1B
46145*	20A
46146*	1B
46147*	1B
46148*	5A
46149*	8A
46150*	12A
46151*	5A
46152*	8A
46153*	8A
46154*	1B
46155*	5A
46156*	5A
46157*	8A
46158*	8A
46159*	5A
46160*	9A
46161*	9A
46162*	1B
46163*	5A
46164*	8A
46165*	12A
46166*	5A
46167*	5A
46168*	1B
46169*	9A
46170*	1B

'Princess Royal' class 4-6-2 8P

No.	Shed
46200*	8A
46201*	5A
46203*	5A
46204*	8A
46205*	8A
46206*	5A
46207*	8A
46208*	8A
46209*	5A
46210*	5A
46211*	5A
46212*	5A

'Princess Coronation' class 4-6-2 8P

No.	Shed
46220*	66A
46221*	66A
46222*	66A
46223*	66A
46224*	66A
46225*	5A
46226*	12A
46227*	66A
46228*	12A
46229*	1B
46230*	66A
46231*	66A
46232*	66A
46233*	5A
46234*	5A
46235*	5A
46236*	1B
46237*	1B
46238*	12A
46239*	1B
46240*	1B
46241*	1B
46242*	1B
46243*	5A
46244*	1B
46245*	1B
46246*	5A
46247*	1B
46248*	5A
46249*	5A
46250*	1B
46251*	8A
46252*	5A
46253*	1B
46254*	1B
46255*	12A
46256*	1B
46257*	1B

Ivatt 2-6-0 2MT

No.	Shed
46400	22A
46401	15B
46402	15B
46403	15B
46404	15B
46405	25C
46406	27A
46407	25C
46408	25C
46409	25C
46410	26A
46411	26A
46412	27B
46413	27A
46414	27A
46415	25A
46416	27A
46417	27A
46418	26A
46419	26A
46420	8D
46421	8D
46422	8D
46423	8D
46424	8D
46425	3A
46426	3A
46427	3D
46428	10A
46429	5D
46430	5D
46431	1A
46432	10A
46433	1A
46434	10A
46435	27A
46436	25C
46437	25C
46438	25A
46439	27B
46440	17A
46441	11E
46442	20F
46443	17A
46444	15B
46445	2D
46446	2D
46447	12D
46448	10A
46449	12C
46450	19A
46451	19A
46452	20F
46453	20A
46454	17A
46455	12C
46456	12D
46457	12D
46458	12D
46459	12D
46460	61A
46461	61A
46462	64A
46463	62B
46464	62B
46465	31A
46466	31A
46467	31A
46468	30E
46469	30E
46470	51F
46471	51H
46472	51F
46473	51F
46474	51H
46475	51A
46476	51H
46477	51H
46478	51H
46479	51A
46480	51H
46481	51H
46482	51F
46483	27A
46484	26A
46485	26B
46486	26B
46487	26A
46488	12D
46489	12D
46490	3A
46491	12C
46492	3D
46493	10A
46494	5D
46495	15B
46496	15B
46497	20A
46498	20A
46499	18C
46500	18C
46501	16D
46502	16A
46503	89A
46504	89A
46505	89A
46506	89A
46507	82A
46508	89B
46509	89A
46510	89A
46511	89A
46512	89A
46513	89A
46514	89A
46515	89A
46516	89B
46517	89B
46518	89B
46519	89B
46520	89B
46521	89B
46522	89B
46523	89A
46524	89B
46525	82B
46526	82B
46527	82B

Webb 2-4-2T 1P

No.	Shed
46604	2C
46616	87K

LMS/BR 0-4-0ST 0F

No.	Shed
47000	17D
47001	27A
47002	27A
47003	18C
47004	18C
47005	6C
47006	6C
47007	6C
47008	10B
47009	6C

Fowler 0-6-0T 2F

No.	Shed
47160	6F
47161	24F
47162	64A
47163	64C
47164	6F
47165	24F
47166	6F
47167	66D
47168	66D
47169	66D

Sentinel 0-4-0T

No.	Shed
47181	10E
47182	67C
47183	84G
47184	5B
47190	71G
47191	71G

Johnson 0-6-0T 3F

No.	Shed
47200	14B
47201	11E
47202	14B
47203	14A
47204	14B
47205	14B
47206	14A
47207	14A
47208	14A
47209	14A
47210	14A
47211	14A
47212	14B
47213	14A
47214	14A
47215	14A
47216	14A
47217	14A
47218	14A
47219	14A
47220	14A
47221	14A
47222	20E
47223	15D
47224	14A
47225	21A
47226	14A
47227	15C
47228	19A
47229	14B
47230	87K
47231	17B
47232	87K
47233	17B
47234	18A
47235	19A
47236	19A
47237	22B
47238	19C
47239	20D
47240	14A
47241	14B
47242	14B
47243	14B
47246	14B
47247	18A
47248	14A
47249	20B
47250	17A
47251	14A
47252	15D
47253	17B
47254	20A
47255	20E
47256	87K
47257	17B
47258	87K
47259	87K

One of the two rebuilt 'Jubilee' class, No 45736 *Phoenix*, passes Gayton loops in Northamptonshire on a northbound express on Saturday 9 July 1955. Built in 1936, it was rebuilt with a '2A' boiler and double-chimney in 1942. Serving from several West Coast sheds, the last allocation was Carlisle Kingmoor and it was withdrawn during the week ended 26 September 1964, to be scrapped at Hughes Bolckows yard at North Blyth.   *L. Hanson*

A rare visitor to Shrewsbury shed in April 1954 is 'Royal Scot' 4-6-0 No 46102 *Black Watch* as a result of a visit to Crewe Works for a light intermediate repair. Built by the North British Loco Co in September 1927 it was rebuilt with a 2A tapered boiler and double-chimney in October 1949. Reallocated to Glasgow Polmadie from Carlisle Kingmoor in April 1942, it remained at 66A until October 1962 when it was sent to Glasgow Corkerhill along with No 46104, another long-time resident of Polmadie. Whether they carried out any duties is not recorded but they were both withdrawn during the week ended 29 December the same year.   *G. W. Sharpe*

The 'odd one out' in the 'Royal Scot' class was No 46106 *Gordon Highlander* with BR straight-sided smoke deflectors, fitted in 1954. The engine is seen at Lichfield Trent Valley on a southbound express working in April 1955, with LMS 2P 4-4-0 No 40633 on the high-level line with a Burton train. Built in 1927, and rebuilt in September 1949, the engine was allocated to 15 different depots during its operating days, including a short stay at Leicester Central in 1962 from 12 May to 30 June. It was withdrawn during the week ended 8 December 1962 from Carlisle Upperby.

G. W. Sharpe

Above: Awaiting return to service in April 1954 at Crewe after a light casual repair at the works is 'Royal Scot' No 46137 *The Prince of Wales's Volunteers South Lancashire*. This was the last to be rebuilt and was called back to Crewe Works in January 1955 for a heavy general repair and rebuild. Withdrawal came during the week ended 3 November 1962 from Carlisle Upperby and it was scrapped at Crewe Works the following May after storage at Carlisle. *G. W. Sharpe*

Below: 'Princess Royal' class 4-6-2 No 46201 *Princess Elizabeth* powers an express on the Crewe to Shrewsbury line in February 1955. Built in November 1933 and first allocated to Camden, later allocations included Crewe North, Liverpool Edge Hill, Glasgow Polmadie, Carlisle Kingmoor and Carlisle Upperby from where withdrawal took place during the week ended 20 October 1962. Placed in store at Upperby and Kingmoor for a further year, this superb engine was saved for us to still enjoy at the Midland Railway Centre. *G. W. Sharpe*

'Princess Royal' 4-6-2 No 46205 *Princess Victoria* is seen near Shrewsbury shed in June 1957. Built in August 1935, this was the only engine in the class with a modified motion bracket. It was withdrawn during the week ended 25 November 1961 from Willesden after a period in store.

G. W. Sharpe

'Princess Coronation' class 4-6-2 No 46226 *Duchess of Norfolk* is seen at Shrewsbury station on a running-in turn after a heavy general repair at Crewe Works in May 1954. Built in May 1938 as a streamlined engine, the casing was removed on 27 November 1948. During its BR years the allocations were between Camden, Crewe North, Liverpool Edge Hill and Carlisle Upperby where the engine was allocated from 20 October 1956 to withdrawal during the week ended 12 September 1964.

G. W. Sharpe

'Princess Coronation' 4-6-2 No 46229 *Duchess of Hamilton* is seen on Crewe North shed with the 'Mid-Day Scot' headboard giving a clue to her duties. Built in September 1938 in streamlined form, the casing was removed on 10 January 1948. As a reminder the engine retained its sloping smokebox front until 1957 when a conventional one was fitted. At Nationalisation the engine was Crewe North-based, moving to Camden in April 1948, and back to Crewe in September 1949. It went back to Camden in July 1952, moving again to Crewe in October 1960 and finally to Liverpool Edge Hill in March 1961, from where withdrawal took place during the week ended 15 February 1964. It is still part of our heritage through preservation and has been seen in main line action in recent years.

G. W. Sharpe

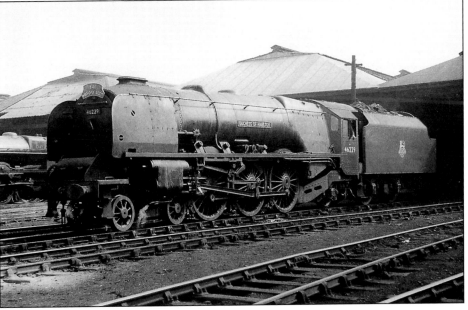

The Ivatt 2MT 2-6-0 first appeared in December 1946 and continued to be built until April 1953. This is No 46454 seen hard at work in Ashwood Dale nearing its Buxton destination on a train from Derby on Tuesday 6 September 1955. Built at Crewe, it entered traffic during the week ended 29 April 1950 allocated to Derby, where it remained until transfer to Burton in June 1957. Leicester Midland then became its home in July 1958, and it went back to Derby in November 1960. The final move was to Birmingham Saltley in January 1961 from where it was withdrawn during the week ended 8 October 1966. *E. R. Morten*

Derby shed is the setting for this view of Ivatt 2-6-0 No 46484 on Tuesday 22 June 1954 fitted with a narrow chimney, a characteristic trademark of Darlington Works construction. Released to traffic during the week ended 27 October 1951 to Manchester Newton Heath shed, it remained there until June 1962, when it transferred to Lees shed at Oldham. April 1964 saw the engine based at Wigan Springs Branch and then moving on to Liverpool Bank Hall in June 1965, finally settling at Buxton in November of the same year. Withdrawal came during the week ended 1 July 1967 and following storage at Buxton until November it was sent to Buttigiegs at Newport for scrap.

Initial Photographics/R. J. Buckley

Introduced in 1932 and built by Kitsons to a specification by Stanier, this 0-4-0ST No 47000 was first allocated to Gloucester Barnwood for dock shunting. At first numbered 1540, it was renumbered 7000 in 1934. A proposal to renumber to 250 in 1945 was dropped. In 1948 it was based at Burton and in April 1952 was moved to Rowsley to take up work on the Cromford & High Peak line, and is here seen at Middleton Top in June 1955. It moved to Derby in January 1959 and remained there, except for a brief loan to Westhouses in May 1960, until withdrawn during the week ended 8 October 1966. *G. W. Sharpe*

Greenock Ladyburn shed in June 1954 with the Fowler-designed short-wheelbase 0-6-0T for dock shunting, No 47167. Built in 1929, this was a Greenock engine at Nationalisation until withdrawn on 7 July 1960, apart from a three-month stay at Birkenhead from 3 July to 18 September 1948.

G. W. Sharpe

Although outside the limit for photographs taken around 1955, as this is such a rare shot, it had to be included. Photographed at Sutton Oak shed in July 1951 is unique Sentinel single-speed locomotive No 47184. Built in 1931 for industrial use, it was taken into LMS stock in 1932. At Nationalisation it was at Sutton Oak and moved to Preston during the week ended 26 March 1949, to return to Sutton Oak one week later. During the week ended 2 September 1950 it went to Wrexham Rhosddu, to return during the week ended 24 February 1951. It said its last goodbye to the Sutton Oak St Helens shed during the week ended 8 December 1951 to join the allocation at Crewe South, remaining there until withdrawal during the week ended 10 December 1955.

G. W. Sharpe

Another Sentinel type, with a chain drive, No 47182 is seen at Ayr shed in 1955. Built in 1930, it was based at Ayr for many years through to withdrawal on 10 February 1956. It was one of two based in Scotland, the other being No 68138 at Kelso, which later joined No 47182 at Ayr (see photo later in this book).

R. H. G. Simpson

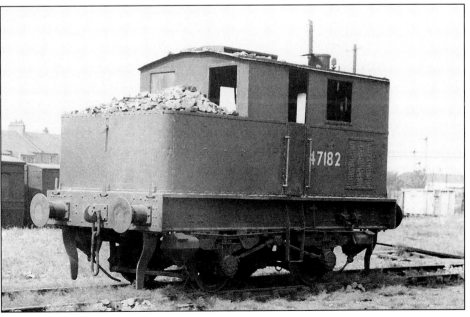

A third type of Sentinel locomotive, No 47191, is seen at Derby shed on Sunday 8 June 1952 after a visit to the works and awaiting return to Radstock. Built in May 1929 for the Somerset & Dorset Railway, and acquired by the LMS in 1930, No 47191 was withdrawn on 20 August 1959 and cut up at Crewe Works after being sent there from Radstock ostensibly for repairs. *Author's collection*

Johnson 0-6-0T No 47239 is seen at Derby shed on Friday 4 June 1954 after a works visit for light repair. Built in May 1902, its original Midland number was 2760, then it was renumbered 1939 in 1907 and 7239 under the LMS. Allocated to Normanton from the week ended 28 August 1948 after transfer from Leeds Stourton, it moved on to York in April 1958 and was withdrawn on 26 September 1961.

Initial Photographics/R. J. Buckley

A number of Johnson 3F 0-6-0Ts were fitted with condensing apparatus for working through the London tunnels. This example, No 47247, is at Derby shed on Monday 14 June 1954 awaiting entry to the works still with LMS on the tank side. Built in June 1902 as Midland No 2768, it was renumbered 1947 in 1907 and 7247 in March 1935. At Nationalisation it was a Toton engine, moving to Staveley Barrow Hill during the week ended 17 March 1951 then back to Toton during the week ended 31 December 1954. Here it stayed until withdrawn during the week ended 29 August 1959 and it was then placed in store at Badnalls Wharf, Norton Bridge, until August 1960 when it was sold to Cashmore's at Great Bridge for scrap.

Initial Photographics/R. J. Buckley

LMS 0-6-0T 3F

47260	14B	47291	10B	47323	11B	47355	1C	47387	8B
47261	14C	47292	12D	47324	6C	47356	1B	47388	8C
47262	33A	47293	10B	47325	8A	47357	8A	47389	6A
47263	18D	47294	3A	47326	12A	47358	1B	47390	12D
47264	15A	47295	12A	47327	8E	47359	1B	47391	12A
47265	15A	47296	3C	47328	33A	47360	10B	47392	8A
47266	5B	47297	6A	47329	67A	47361	1A	47393	10E
47267	9A	47298	10E	47330	5B	47362	8B	47394	6G
47268	8B	47299	2E	47331	66A	47363	3B	47395	9A
47269	2A	47300	33A	47332	66A	47364	10C	47396	3A
47270	5D	47301	21C	47333	22A	47365	10C	47397	3B
47271	20B	47302	1D	47334	20D	47366	10E	47398	3B
47272	18C	47303	21C	47335	20D	47367	2B	47399	10C
47273	15A	47304	1D	47336	26G	47368	6J	47400	9A
47274	15C	47305	21C	47337	12D	47369	9A	47401	10C
47275	71G	47306	33A	47338	5B	47370	5D	47402	8A
47276	21C	47307	1D	47339	11A	47371	6B	47403	12A
47277	16A	47308	21C	47340	12A	47372	6B	47404	8A
47278	18C	47309	8E	47341	9A	47373	8C	47405	20D
47279	15A	47310	1D	47342	1A	47374	6A	47406	11A
47280	5B	47311	33A	47343	9A	47375	6A	47407	8A
47281	5D	47312	33A	47344	5D	47376	8B	47408	12A
47282	33A	47313	21A	47345	9A	47377	12A	47409	11A
47283	14B	47314	1D	47346	9B	47378	1A	47410	11A
47284	8C	47315	1D	47347	9A	47379	2A	47411	8A
47285	2B	47316	71G	47348	1D	47380	5D	47412	1A
47286	2B	47317	11A	47349	1D	47381	11E	47413	10B
47287	11B	47318	2E	47350	6K	47382	3A	47414	5B
47288	10E	47319	10B	47351	33A	47383	6A	47415	12A
47289	9B	47320	8E	47352	8B	47384	5B	47416	8A
47290	12D	47321	6J	47353	8A	47385	8A	47417	17A
		47322	11B	47354	1B	47386	24B	47418	20A

Another engine on Derby shed on 14 June 1954 awaiting works attention was LMS 'Jinty' 0-6-0T No 47352, with the 1948 British Railways lettering on the tank side. Built in 1926 by the North British Engine Co, it was originally numbered 16435. This was a Warrington Dallam engine from January 1948 to withdrawal during the week ended 12 March 1960. It was stored on Warrington shed until September 1961 and then sent to the Central Wagon Co at Wigan for scrapping.

Initial Photographics/R. J. Buckley

No.	Shed	No.	Shed	No.	Shed	No.	Shed
47419	20E	47485	17B	47549	15D	47616	5B
47420	20A	47486	1D	47550	22A	47618	12A
47421	20C	47487	8A	47551	18A	47619	18D
47422	16A	47488	1D	47552	22A	47620	18D
47423	18C	47489	8A	47554	14C	47621	10C
47424	18D	47490	8C	47555	33A	47622	6C
47425	21C	47491	1A	47556	12A	47623	20B
47426	18D	47492	1A	47557	71G	47624	19A
47427	20F	47493	8C	47558	1D	47625	18D
47428	20F	47494	1D	47559	1D	47626	18D
47429	33A	47495	1D	47560	1D	47627	6C
47430	10C	47496	71G	47561	1D	47628	6F
47431	5B	47497	1D	47562	20F	47629	17A
47432	19A	47498	8A	47563	19A	47630	18D
47433	14A	47499	1D	47564	1D	47631	16A
47434	14A	47500	1E	47565	21C	47632	20B
47435	14A	47501	1D	47566	8E	47633	5E
47436	20A	47502	21C	47567	25G	47634	20C
47437	14B	47503	11C	47568	25G	47635	22B
47438	20C	47504	6A	47569	25G	47636	19A
47439	8C	47505	1A	47570	25G	47637	18D
47440	26G	47506	22B	47571	25G	47638	21A
47441	15C	47507	6C	47572	25A	47639	11E
47442	15C	47508	25E	47573	25A	47640	20B
47443	20B	47509	25E	47574	26B	47641	17B
47444	10E	47510	25A	47575	24B	47642	15A
47445	5E	47511	1D	47576	24B	47643	17B
47446	20D	47512	33A	47577	24B	47644	14B
47447	17D	47513	19A	47578	26B	47645	14B
47448	20C	47514	1D	47579	26B	47646	6B
47449	17C	47515	1D	47580	25A	47647	5D
47450	5B	47516	5B	47581	20C	47648	5D
47451	5D	47517	1D	47582	25A	47649	5C
47452	10E	47518	1D	47583	26B	47650	6B
47453	10E	47519	8A	47584	26B	47651	8C
47454	20F	47520	1A	47585	26B	47652	8B
47455	18D	47521	1E	47586	24B	47653	5C
47457	17D	47522	1B	47587	5D	47654	8B
47458	33A	47523	5B	47588	5C	47655	87K
47459	17D	47524	5B	47589	20B	47656	6B
47460	17D	47525	12D	47590	5C	47657	8B
47461	17D	47526	5B	47591	8B	47658	5D
47462	20C	47527	1B	47592	CW	47659	10B
47463	20B	47528	9A	47593	12D	47660	17A
47464	17B	47529	1B	47594	2B	47661	5B
47465	71G	47530	6C	47595	5E	47662	5B
47466	18B	47531	1A	47596	5D	47664	12A
47467	1B	47532	11E	47597	8A	47665	5C
47468	11E	47533	15C	47598	5E	47666	12A
47469	11E	47534	15C	47599	5D	47667	1B
47470	11E	47535	18C	47600	6A	47668	1B
47471	11E	47536	66A	47601	9B	47669	1B
47472	10B	47537	66A	47602	5B	47670	5B
47473	3B	47538	20B	47603	8B	47671	1B
47474	1A	47539	22B	47604	12D	47672	6F
47475	1A	47540	66A	47605	11B	47673	9A
47476	6J	47541	60A	47606	5C	47674	6F
47477	87K	47542	71G	47607	22B	47675	1A
47478	87K	47543	15A	47608	5B	47676	1A
47479	87K	47544	22A	47609	5D	47677	2A
47480	87K	47545	18D	47610	5D	47678	22A
47481	87K	47546	19C	47611	19A	47679	17D
47482	1D	47547	19C	47612	2E	47680	5B
47483	1D	47548	19A	47614	12A	47681	87K
47484	33A			47615	6B		

Webb 0-4-2ST 1F

No.	Shed
47862	CW

Beyer-Garratt 2-6-6-2T

No.	Shed	No.	Shed
47967	18A	47984	18A
47968	18C	47985	18A
47969	18A	47986	18C
47970	18A	47987	18A
47971	18A	47988	18A
47972	18A	47989	18A
47973	18C	47990	18A
47974	18A	47991	18A
47975	18A	47992	18C
47976	18C	47993	18C
47977	18C	47994	18A
47978	18A	47995	18A
47979	18C	47996	18A
47980	18C	47997	18C
47981	18A	47998	18A
47982	18C	47999	18A
47983	18C		

Stanier 2-8-0 8F

No.	Shed
48000	16C
48001	16D
48002	17B
48003	16C
48004	16C
48005	20B
48006	16C
48007	18A
48008	15A
48009	16C
48010	15A
48011	19C
48012	2C
48016	2B
48017	8D
48018	2C
48020	2B
48024	16D
48026	19C
48027	15C
48029	16C
48033	18D
48035	15B
48036	1A
48037	18A
48039	8C

Number	Shed	Number	Shed
48927	2B	49116	8D
48930	3A	49117	87K
48932	8A	49119	8B
48940	3B	49120	2B
48942	8C	49121	86K
48943	3C	49122	1A
48944	8C	49125	3A
48945	84G	49126	8D
48950	3A	49129	10A
48951	1E	49130	11A
48952	1E	49132	9D
48953	1E	49134	8C
48964	3A	49137	8A
49002	2B	49139	1A
49005	1E		

LNWR G1 class 0-8-0 6F

Number	Shed
49140	CW

(continuing)

Number	Shed	Number	Shed
49007	10A		
49008	8B		
49009	3A		

LNWR G2a class 0-8-0 7F

Number	Shed
49010	9B
49018	10A
49020	3C
49021	3A
49023	10A
49024	2C
49025	10A
49027	10C
49028	85C
49033	87K
49034	10C
49035	87K
49037	3B
49044	3B
49045	3A
49046	85C
49047	5C
49048	3C
49049	1E
49051	85C
49057	9D
49061	1E
49063	3A
49064	86K
49066	3C
49068	2B
49070	1A
49073	8D
49077	3A
49078	1A
49079	8D
49081	8D
49082	8A
49087	10C
49088	1A
49093	8B
49094	10C
49099	3A
49104	10B
49105	2E
49106	3A
49108	3C
49109	11A
49112	2B
49113	86K
49114	2A
49115	5C
49141	10B
49142	2B
49143	8C
49144	10A
49145	1C
49146	85C
49147	10C
49148	87K
49149	10C
49150	10B
49153	8C
49154	10A
49155	10A
49157	84G
49158	5C
49160	10A
49161	86K
49164	1A
49167	3B
49168	85C
49172	2B
49173	8A
49174	86K
49177	87K
49180	1A
49181	2B
49186	3D
49189	3D
49191	10B
49196	10B
49198	3C
49199	10C
49200	8A
49202	3A
49203	10A
49209	10C
49210	9D
49212	2B
49214	9D
49216	3A
49223	3A
49224	8A
49226	85C
49228	10A
49229	5C
49230	5B
49234	10C
49239	10E
49240	3B
49243	84G
49245	2A
49246	3A
49247	3B
49249	8B
49252	11A
49254	10C
49260	84G
49262	10E
49266	8C
49267	10B
49268	10A
49270	2E
49271	3C
49275	1A
49276	84G
49277	1A
49278	3D
49281	10E
49287	1E
49288	10E
49289	1E
49293	2B
49301	3C
49304	9G
49306	10A
49308	3A
49310	1E
49311	10A
49313	3A
49314	8A
49315	10A
49316	86K
49318	10E
49321	2E
49322	10A
49323	1C
49327	3A
49328	3A
49330	2B
49335	10C
49340	10C
49341	10A
49342	2B
49343	8D
49344	1A
49345	84G
49348	9D
49350	2B
49352	10A
49354	3C
49355	8A
49357	2E
49358	87K
49361	3A
49366	2E
49367	3A
49368	8C
49373	3C
49375	8A
49376	87K
49377	10E
49378	10A
49381	10A
49382	10B
49385	10A
49386	10C
49387	9D
49390	10B
49391	10B
49392	8A
49393	10A
49394	8A

LNWR G2 class 0-8-0 7F

Number	Shed
49395	8C
49396	10B
49397	2A
49398	8C
49399	8A
49400	10C
49401	10A
49402	10A
49403	86G
49404	8A
49405	9G
49406	8C
49407	5B
49408	10A
49409	86K
49410	5C
49411	2D
49412	8A
49413	2A
49414	2B
49415	2D
49416	8D
49417	2A
49418	9B
49419	8A
49420	8C
49421	10C
49422	86G
49423	8A
49424	2B
49425	2D
49426	10C
49427	8A
49428	9A
49429	8A
49430	2B
49431	2A
49432	2B
49433	2A
49434	8A
49435	9G
49436	10A
49437	8A
49438	11A
49439	9A
49440	84G
49441	2D
49442	2D
49443	1E
49444	2A
49445	8A
49446	2A
49447	2A
49448	5B
49449	11A
49450	1E
49451	8C
49452	2A
49453	9B
49454	5B

Fowler 0-8-0 7F

Number	Shed
49505	27B
49508	26A
49509	26F
49511	27B
49515	27B
49532	26C
49536	26F
49538	26C
49544	26C
49545	27B
49547	27B
49552	27B
49554	25E
49555	26B
49557	26A
49560	26A
49566	27B
49570	26A
49578	26F
49582	27B
49586	27B
49592	27D
49598	27D
49603	26B
49618	26F
49620	27B
49624	25E
49627	26B
49637	27D
49638	27D
49640	27B
49648	25E
49657	25E
49659	27B
49662	26F
49664	27B
49666	26A
49667	26A
49668	26F
49672	27B
49674	25E

Aspinall 2-4-2T 2P

Number	Shed
50636	20E
50643	8B
50644	8B
50646	20C
50647	26D
50648	24B
50650	20C
50651	24B
50652	24B
50653	24B
50655	24B
50656	26C

The Stanier 8F 2-8-0 was the successful heavy freight engine the LMS had been waiting for when it was introduced in 1935. This is No 48007, which entered traffic in September 1935 at Willesden shed after being built at Crewe, and here seen at Harrow in September 1954. This was one of the original 12 locomotives fitted with a domeless straight throatplate boiler. At Nationalisation it was allocated to Kirkby in Ashfield and then started a number of moves to Wellingborough, Rose Grove, Sheffield Grimesthorpe and, during the week ended 28 May 1949, to Toton, where it stayed until March 1955, when it went to Leicester Midland. Then in March 1960 it started its wanderings again, going to Wellingborough, Kettering, Cricklewood, Toton, Saltley, Annesley, Woodford Halse, Willesden and finally Bescot in September 1964 from where it was withdrawn during the week ended 9 January 1965. *G. W. Sharpe*

Shrewsbury shed in June 1955 sees Manchester Longsight-based 'G2' 0-8-0 No 49439. Dating from July 1922, it had moved to 9A from Nuneaton during the week ended 8 July 1950 and moved on to Carnforth in May 1959 and Crewe South the following July. September 1960 found it at Bletchley and the following November a return to Nuneaton was made. Buxton acquired the engine in January 1962 where it stayed until withdrawn during the week ended 8 December the same year. *G. W. Sharpe*

Derby shed on Thursday 6 May 1954 has an interesting visitor in the shape of Fowler 0-8-0 No 49554 allocated to Sowerby Bridge. Built in 1929, this was a less than successful design with high maintenance costs and poor availability due to problems with the chassis and bearings. Nicknamed 'Austin 7s', scrapping started in 1949 and the last to go was No 49508 during the week ended 20 January 1962. No 49554 was withdrawn from Sowerby Bridge during the week ended 27 August 1955. *Initial Photographics/R. J. Buckley*

50660	26C
50686	20E
50705	8B
50712	27C
50715	25E
50721	27C
50725	25B
50731	26C
50746	27C
50752	25E
50757	25E
50764	25F
50777	25E
50781	27C
50788	24F
50795	20E
50807	25F
50818	25E
50829	26D
50831	25B
50850	26C
50855	26C
50865	25B
50869	25F
50887	26D

Aspinall 0-4-0ST 0F

51202	22A
51204	5B
51206	27A
51207	26B
51212	22A
51216	27A
51217	17A
51218	5B
51221	5B
51222	25C
51227	27A
51229	27A
51230	26B
51231	27A
51232	27A
51234	27A
51235	17A
51237	27A
51240	25C
51241	25C
51244	25C
51246	27A
51253	27A

Aspinall Rebuilt 0-6-0ST 2F

51307	27A
51313	8A
51316	10E
51319	10E
51321	24F
51323	25C
51336	26A
51338	27E
51343	27B
51345	24C
51353	8A
51358	25D

51361	25C
51371	27A
51376	26D
51379	25C
51381	25E
51390	24A
51396	27A
51397	10E
51404	25F
51408	25B
51412	CW
51413	27B
51415	24D
51419	26D
51423	24C
51424	25D
51425	27C
51429	HW
51432	25C
51436	26A
51439	8C
51441	10E
51444	CW
51445	8A
51446	CW
51447	26A
51453	25D
51457	26A
51458	26A
51462	27B
51464	24A
51470	26A
51472	26A
51474	27D
51477	24F
51479	25C
51481	24F
51484	26G
51486	26D
51488	25E
51491	10E
51496	26A
51497	24A
51498	24F
51499	24D
51500	26B
51503	25C
51504	26D
51506	24D
51510	26G
51511	26C
51512	26B
51513	26C
51516	25C
51521	25C
51524	25B
51526	24C
51530	27B

Aspinall 0-6-0T 1F

51535	27B
51537	27B
51544	27A
51546	27A

Barton Wright 0-6-0 2F

52016	10C
52021	10A
52044	25A
52045	10C
52051	10A
52053	25A

Aspinall 0-6-0 3F

52089	26A
52093	CW
52094	26D
52095	27D
52099	26F
52104	25D
52108	26A
52119	6H
52120	25A
52121	25C
52123	26C
52125	10E
52129	26D
52132	26C
52133	25A
52135	27B
52136	27B
52139	26C
52140	8A
52141	2B
52143	10A
52150	25A
52154	25A
52159	26A
52160	24D
52161	27C
52162	6K
52163	8C
52164	26D
52165	26A
52166	25F
52167	6K
52171	27B
52172	6K
52175	8C
52177	10E
52179	26D
52182	24C
52183	27C
52186	25A
52194	24D
52196	10E
52197	27D
52201	12D
52203	24C
52207	CW
52212	CW
52215	24E
52216	24D
52217	25E
52218	CW
52220	24D
52225	8B
52230	6H
52232	8C
52235	25A

52236	25D
52237	26D
52239	26D
52240	24E
52244	25A
52248	26F
52252	25C
52260	24D
52268	26D
52269	6H
52270	6C
52271	26A
52272	24C
52273	25C
52275	27D
52278	27B
52289	27D
52290	24C
52293	26B
52300	26A
52305	25C
52311	27B
52312	CW
52317	26A
52319	24B
52322	10A
52328	26A
52331	25C
52336	25D
52338	10E
52341	10A
52343	25F
52345	CW
52348	26C
52350	26C
52351	25E
52355	25F
52356	6K
52358	26A
52360	26A
52366	10A
52368	24C
52369	24B
52376	25A
52378	27B
52379	27B
52381	27B
52387	27D
52388	26F
52389	26A
52390	26A
52393	10E
52397	10E
52399	25E
52400	25E
52405	26D
52408	25E
52410	25E
52411	25A
52412	27B
52413	26C
52415	24E
52416	27B
52418	12D
52427	26F

52429	10E
52431	26C
52432	8B
52437	24E
52438	8C
52441	CW
52443	26D
52445	24C
52447	24D
52449	10A
52450	27D
52452	25D
52453	6K
52455	26A
52456	24C
52458	24C
52459	CW
52461	26A
52464	CW
52465	2B
52466	24E

Furness Railway Pettigrew 0-6-0 3F

52494	12D
52499	12D
52501	12D
52509	12D
52510	12D

Aspinall 0-6-0 3F

52515	25F
52517	CW
52521	25F
52522	24D
52523	24C
52526	24D
52527	24E
52529	24B

Hughes 0-6-0 3F

52551	10A
52561	25F
52569	26F
52575	26C
52576	25A
52582	27C
52608	6K

Fowler 2-8-0 7F

53800	71G
53801	71G
53802	71G
53803	71G
53804	71G
53805	71G
53806	71G
53807	71G
53808	71G
53809	71G
53810	71G

McIntosh 4-4-0 3P

54438	68B

Huddersfield shed in 1955 sees Aspinall 2-4-2T No 50725 on view. Built in March 1896 for the L&Y, this was one that retained its original fittings. Allocated to Blackpool at Nationalisation, it moved to Lostock Hall in June 1953 and then to Huddersfield in July 1954, from where it was withdrawn on 2 October 1958. Stored at Badnalls Wharf, it was cut up at Looms yard at Spondon in July 1959. *G. W. Sharpe*

Aspinall 2-4-2T No 50850 is seen at Bolton shed in August 1955. Built in October 1899, this was one of the class fitted with a Belpaire boiler in May 1911. No 50850 had been reallocated to Bolton from Fleetwood during the week ended 11 August 1951 and remained at 26C until 1960 when it returned to the seaside at Southport. Withdrawal was actioned during the week ended 28 October 1961.

G. W. Sharpe

Horwich Works in October 1957 sees L&Y 'Pug' 0-4-0ST No 51234. Built to an Aspinall design in February 1906, it was based at Liverpool Bank Hall after transfer from Manchester Newton Heath during the week ended 11 February 1950. No 51234 was withdrawn during the week ended 19 October 1957 and was awaiting scrapping when this scene was recorded. *G. W. Sharpe*

0-6-0ST No 51423 is seen at Lostock Hall shed in July 1955. Originally built in March 1881 by Barton Wright as an 0-6-0 tender engine, Aspinall had rebuilt it into this form in October 1895. Apart from a short stay at Fleetwood from 23 December 1950 to 24 February 1951, this was a Lostock Hall engine from before 1 January 1948 until withdrawal during the week ended 6 December 1958.

R. H. G. Simpson

Originally a class of 20 engines, the Aspinall 0-6-0Ts were built in 1897. This is No 51546 at Liverpool Bank Hall shed in September 1956. It was on allocation at Bank Hall from before 1948 to withdrawal during the week ended 17 January 1959.

P. H. Groom

Barton Wright 0-6-0 No 52021 stands at Wigan Springs Branch shed in August 1953. Built in 1887 at Vulcan Foundry, this was a 1955 withdrawal condemned during the week ended 27 August.

Photomatic/RAS Marketing

Above: Aspinall 0-6-0 No 52183 is ex-works at Horwich on Sunday 20 November 1955. Built in February 1893, it lasted until the week ended 21 November 1959, its last allocation being at Lees after transfer from Southport in March 1958.

Graham Kaye

Below: Manchester Patricroft shed is host to Aspinall 0-6-0 No 52201 in October 1957, shortly after the engine had been transferred from Nuneaton to Sutton Oak. It is fitted with a Belpaire boiler and extended smokebox, the conversion being completed in January 1912. Withdrawal was carried out during the week ended 4 February 1961 from Bury shed.

P. H. Groom

Above: Moor Row shed near Workington closed in July 1954 and its allocation transferred to Workington. This shot was recorded shortly before closure and shows ex-Furness Railway 0-6-0 No 52494, designed by Pettigrew. It still retained the original boiler and remained in service until the week ended 28 April 1956.

G. W. Sharpe

Below: Another view of an ex-Furness Railway Pettigrew 0-6-0, No 52509, but this time with an L&Y boiler, at Moor Row in 1954. It was withdrawn during the week ended 22 December 1956.

G. W. Sharpe

54439	60A		
54440	66D		
54441	66D		
54443	68B		
54446	64D		
54448	63A		
54450	63C		
54451	64C		
54452	64C		
54453	66D		
54454	63C		
54456	66D		
54457	66B		
54458	60A		
54460	66B		

Pickersgill 4-4-0 3P

54461	64D
54462	66B
54463	60A
54464	66B
54465	66B
54466	60B
54467	63A
54468	66D
54469	63A
54470	60C
54471	60E
54472	60E
54473	60E
54474	65B
54475	65B
54476	63A
54477	64D
54478	64C
54479	66D
54480	60C
54482	60E
54483	65F
54484	60A
54485	63A
54486	63C
54487	60A
54488	60B
54489	63A
54490	64D
54491	60D
54492	66D
54493	60A
54494	63A
54495	60C
54496	60A
54497	66D
54498	66D
54499	63A
54500	63A
54501	65B
54502	68B
54503	63A
54504	63B
54505	64D
54506	66D
54507	68B
54508	66D

P. Drummond 0-4-4T 0P

55051	60C
55053	60C

McIntosh 0-4-4T 2P

55124	68B
55125	68C
55126	63B
55141	66A
55145	63B

McIntosh 439 class 0-4-4T 2P

55160	60A
55162	62B
55164	68B
55165	64C
55167	66A
55168	65B
55169	62B
55173	62B
55174	60B
55176	63C
55177	64C
55178	60E
55182	66C
55185	61C
55187	67A
55189	66A
55193	63C
55194	63A
55195	63E
55196	63E
55198	63C
55199	60A
55200	63C
55201	66A
55202	64C
55203	67B
55204	65B
55206	67A
55207	66A
55208	63A
55209	63A
55210	64C
55211	67A
55212	63A
55213	63A
55214	65F
55215	63E
55216	60A
55217	62B
55218	63A
55219	67A
55220	68D
55221	61C
55222	63B
55223	62B
55224	66A
55225	67A
55226	63A
55227	62B
55228	66A
55229	64C
55230	63C

55231	67C
55232	68D
55233	64C
55234	68D
55235	67A
55236	60D

Pickersgill 431 class 0-4-4T 2P

55237	68D
55238	65F
55239	66A
55240	67C

McIntosh 439 class 0-4-4T 2P

55260	68D
55261	64D
55262	67C
55263	63E
55264	67B
55265	66A
55266	67A
55267	66D
55268	66A
55269	67A

Drummond 0-4-0ST 0F

56011	60A
56020	21C
56025	St Rollox Wks
56027	10B
56028	66D
56029	65D
56030	65G
56031	66D
56032	CW
56035	66D
56038	60A
56039	65G

McIntosh 0-6-0T 2F

56151	65B
56152	65F
56153	66A
56154	66A
56155	66A
56156	66D
56157	66D
56158	65G
56159	66A
56160	66A
56161	65G
56162	66A
56163	66D
56164	65F
56165	66D
56166	66D
56167	65D
56168	65G
56169	65B
56170	65G
56171	65D
56172	65E
56173	66D

McIntosh 0-6-0T 3F

56230	65F
56231	68A
56232	63B
56233	65B
56234	68C
56235	68A
56236	67B
56238	65G
56239	66A
56240	61B
56241	66B
56242	66C
56243	65F
56244	66A
56245	66B
56246	63A
56247	66B
56248	66A
56249	67A
56251	61B
56252	65B
56253	64C
56254	63B
56255	66C
56256	66C
56257	67C
56259	67D
56260	66A
56261	66A
56262	60A
56263	66A
56264	66B
56265	66B
56266	66A
56267	65F
56269	66B
56271	66B
56272	67C
56273	67C
56274	67C
56275	65F
56277	66B
56278	61B
56279	67D
56280	66A
56281	66A
56282	67D
56283	64C
56284	66C
56285	66B
56286	66C
56287	66C
56288	66D
56289	65B
56290	63C
56291	60A
56292	66A
56293	60A
56294	66A
56295	66A
56296	66C
56297	65G
56298	66A
56299	60A

56300	65D
56301	60E
56302	65D
56303	66C
56304	66A
56305	66A
56306	66A
56307	66A
56308	66A
56309	66C
56310	65B
56311	67D
56312	64C
56313	64C
56314	66A
56315	65G
56316	68A
56317	68A
56318	66A
56319	66C
56320	66C
56321	66C
56322	66A
56323	62B
56324	66A
56325	62B
56326	61B
56327	68B
56328	63A
56329	67A
56330	65B
56331	63A
56332	68A
56333	68A
56334	66B
56335	66B
56336	65F
56337	66B
56338	66B
56339	65G
56340	68A
56341	60A
56342	66A
56343	63B
56344	65D
56345	66B
56346	66A
56347	63A
56348	61B
56349	66A
56350	67A
56352	63A
56353	63A
56354	66B
56355	68A
56356	66B
56357	66B
56358	66B
56359	63A
56360	66C
56361	67A
56362	66C
56363	67C
56364	67D
56365	63B

Fowler's 1925-designed 2-8-0 for the S&D, No 53807, is ex-works at Derby shed on Monday 14 June 1954. All 11 class members were based at Bath Green Park and the first to be withdrawn was No 53800 in July 1959. No 53807 was the last to go in October 1964 and was cut up at Cashmore's in Newport. *Initial Photographics/R. J. Buckley*

Dumfries shed on Friday 4 June 1954 and in steam prepared for duty is McIntosh 4-4-0 No 54443. Built for the Caledonian Railway in July 1911, it lasted until 26 October 1955. Other engines recorded on shed with No 54443 were Nos 40576, 40577, 40902, 41129, 41135, 41179, 42915, 42919, 44199, 45480, 54502, 54507, 55124, 57362, 57600 and 57621. *K. C. H. Fairey*

Pickersgill Caledonian Railway '113' class 4-4-0 No 54467 is seen at Forfar shed in 1956. Built by the North British Loco Co in March 1916, it operated from Perth shed for most of its BR days, but was allocated to Forfar from November 1955 to November 1958. Withdrawal came on 20 October 1959. *R. H. G. Simpson*

Above: McIntosh '92' class 0-4-4T No 55126 is viewed in the carriage sidings at Stirling in September 1957. This design dated from 1897 and No 55126 survived until 1961, withdrawal coming on 19 July. It had been transferred to Oban from November 1958 and its last duties had been on the Ballachulish to Connel Ferry branch. It was the last of its class to remain on the active list.

P. H. Groom

Below: The McIntosh Caledonian Railway '439' class of 0-4-4T was a later version of the '92' class built between 1900 and 1914. No 55214, with condensing gear still fitted, is at Grangemouth station on a train to Larbert in September 1957. A Grangemouth engine from September 1953, after transfer from Beattock, it was still on allocation when withdrawn on 13 September 1961.

P. H. Groom

130

A Caledonian 'Pug' 0-4-0ST built in December 1908 to a design dating from 1885, No 56038 is on Inverness shed in July 1955. The combination of sprung buffers added to the original dumb buffers created a considerable overhang, which made them lively riders over points and indifferent track. This engine had been transferred to Inverness from Glasgow Dawsholm during the week ended 8 April 1950 and remained at 60A until withdrawn on 19 May 1959. *G. W. Sharpe*

McIntosh '498' class 2F 0-6-0T No 56172 is seen at Glasgow Kipps shed in September 1954. Built between 1911 and 1921, all 23 came into BR ownership at Nationalisation. Some retained original Caledonian chimneys, but No 56172 had a less attractive stovepipe. Withdrawals commenced in 1958 and the class had disappeared by the end of April 1962. No 56172 had been transferred to Kipps from Motherwell in January 1952 and in July 1959 went on to Glasgow Polmadie. In February 1960 transfer to Greenock was to be the last as withdrawal came on 2 September 1960. *Photomatic/RAS Marketing*

McIntosh standard shunting engine Class 782 0-6-0T No 56334 is seen at Motherwell shed in August 1957, still with an original Caledonian chimney. The design dated from 1905 and the last were built in 1922. No 56334 spent its entire BR allocation at Motherwell and was withdrawn on 17 January 1958. *P. H. Groom*

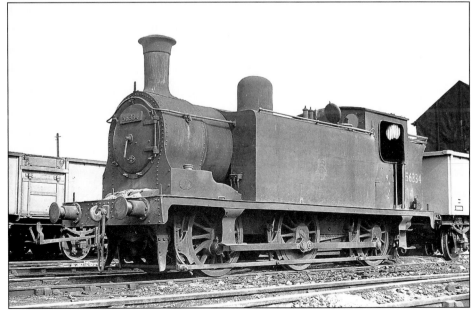

No.	Shed	No.	Shed	No.	Shed	No.	Shed	No.	Shed
56366	63B	57295	67C	57411	65B	57580	67A	57653	62B
56367	66B	57296	65D	57412	66A	57581	66A	57654	64C
56368	67B	57299	66B	57413	66C	57582	66B	57655	64D
56369	67A	57300	67A	57414	66B	57583	64D	57658	67C
56370	65B	57302	68B	57416	66B	57585	60D	57659	66B
56371	66C	57303	66B	57417	66B	57586	60B	57661	60A
56372	68C	57307	66C	57418	66B	57587	60C	57663	66C
56373	68A	57309	67A	57419	66B	57588	66B	57665	66C
56374	68A	57311	65B	57424	63E	57589	67A	57666	66B
56375	65F	57314	65D	57426	65B	57590	67D	57667	65F
56376	65F	57315	67C	57429	65D	57591	61C	57668	66B

Drummond 0-6-0 2F

No.	Shed	No.	Shed	No.	Shed	No.	Shed	No.	Shed
57230	66A	57317	66A	57430	66C	57592	65D	57669	67D
57232	63B	57319	66A	57431	66C	57593	66B	57670	64D
57233	63B	57320	66A	57432	66A	57594	67A	57671	67B
57234	67C	57321	66A	57434	65B	57595	66B	57672	67B
57235	67C	57324	63B	57435	66B	57596	67A	57673	67D
57236	67B	57325	66B	57436	66B	57597	60A	57674	66A
57237	66C	57326	66B	57437	66B	57599	66B	57679	64C
57238	66A	57328	66B	57441	63B	57600	68B	57681	66B
57239	66A	57329	68B	57443	66A	57601	68B	57682	66D
57240	65B	57331	67B	57444	66A	57602	68B	57684	67C
57241	67A	57335	66C	57445	68C	57603	66A	57686	65B
57242	66C	57336	65D	57446	66A	57604	64D	57688	67B
57243	63B	57338	65F	57447	66A	57605	65D	57689	65F
57244	66C	57339	63B	57448	66A	57607	65D	57690	66D
57245	65D	57340	68C	57451	64D	57608	64D	57691	65F
57246	63B	57341	65D	57456	65D	57609	66C		
57247	66B	57345	63A	57457	65B	57611	67C	**Johnson 0-4-4T 1P**	
57249	67A	57346	65D	57459	66A	57612	65D	58040	15A
57250	66C	57347	66A	57460	63B	57613	64D	58051	71J
57251	65B	57348	67D	57461	66B	57614	67C	58054	33A
57252	63B	57349	68B	57462	66B	57615	67C	58062	33A
57253	65B	57350	65B	57463	66A	57617	65B	58065	33A
57254	63E	57353	67B	57465	66A	57618	64D	58066	20C
57256	66B	57354	67C	57470	65D	57619	66A	58071	22B
57257	63B	57355	67D	57472	65D	57620	60E	58072	71J
57258	65B	57356	67D	57473	63A	57621	68B	58073	71J
57259	65G	57357	67D			57622	60A	58077	16A
57260	66C	57359	67A	**McIntosh 812 class**		57623	68B	58080	19B
57261	65B	57360	66A	**0-6-0 3F**		57625	60B	58083	9D
57262	67C	57361	66A	57550	64C	57626	64D	58084	9D
57263	67D	57362	68B	57552	66D	57627	67D	58085	16A
57264	63B	57363	66B	57553	66A	57628	67C	58086	71J
57265	65F	57364	67C	57554	65D			58087	33A
57266	67A	57365	66A	57555	66A	**McIntosh 652 class**		58091	33A
57267	66B	57366	65F	57556	66D	**0-6-0 3F**			
57268	66A	57367	66A	57557	65B	57630	66C	**Fowler 0-10-0**	
57269	65B	57368	63C	57558	65B	57631	65B	58100	21C
57270	66B	57369	66A	57559	64C	57632	60B		
57271	66A	57370	66A	57560	67A	57633	67C	**Johnson 0-6-0 2F**	
57273	65D	57373	65B	57562	67A	57634	61C	58114	19C
57274	67D	57375	68C	57563	66A	57635	64D	58115	11B
57275	66A	57377	66B	57564	66A	57637	67B	58116	11B
57276	67D	57378	68B	57565	64C	57638	66B	58117	3E
57278	66B	57383	67B	57566	67A	57640	67C	58118	2B
57279	67C	57384	66C	57568	62B	57642	60A	58119	3B
57282	67D	57385	64D	57569	67C	57643	67B	58120	11B
57284	67C	57386	64D	57570	67B	57644	67C	58121	11B
57285	65F	57389	66A	57571	67B	57645	64C	58122	3C
57287	65F	57392	67C	57572	67B			58123	3C
57288	66A	57396	63B	57573	67B	**Pickersgill 294 class**		58124	3E
57291	66B	57398	66C	57575	67A	**0-6-0 3F**		58125	3C
57292	66A	57404	66B	57576	64C	57650	67B	58126	21B
		57405	68B	57577	67D	57651	67B	58127	19C
		57407	66C	57579	67A	57652	65D	58128	26G

Dugald Drummond's 0-6-0 'Jumbo' class '294' was numerically the largest on the Caledonian, the first entering traffic in November 1883. This example, No 57275, dated from December 1885 and is seen at Glasgow Polmadie shed in work-worn condition in August 1955. It remained on 66A's allocation throughout its BR days and was withdrawn on 2 April 1962. *G. W. Sharpe*

McIntosh '812' class 0-6-0 No 57597 is seen at Inverness shed on a foggy day in November 1955. Originally a class of 79 locomotives and built between May 1899 and September 1900, the first was withdrawn in October 1946. No 57597 had been transferred to Inverness from Aviemore during the week ended 22 April 1950 and returned there in March 1959. In May 1961 it went to Glasgow Polmadie where its official withdrawal date was 2 April 1962. *G. W. Sharpe*

The Pickersgill 0-6-0s for the Caledonian Railway were built from January 1918 to February 1920. Basically the same as the McIntosh design, there were detail differences such as larger piston valves and shorter front end overhang. All 43 engines were built at Glasgow St Rollox Works and, under the LMS, superheaters were fitted. This is No 57691 at Grangemouth shed in September 1954. Later moves were to Glasgow Dawsholm in October 1960 and to Hurlford in May 1962, with withdrawal on 16 July 1962.

Photomatic/RAS Marketing

Derby shed on Tuesday 2 March 1954 sees ex-Midland Railway Johnson 0-4-4T No 58085 after a works visit. The design dated from 1881 and this example had been rebuilt with a Belpaire boiler. A Leicester Midland-based engine at Nationalisation, it moved to Wellingborough during the week ended 7 May 1949. From here it was transferred to Nottingham Midland in March 1953 and was sub-shedded at Southwell for working the branch. When this sub-shed closed in January 1955, No 58085 was moved to Newark which was a sub-shed to Retford after the Southwell branch duties had become Newark's responsibility. When Newark closed on 5 January 1959, instead of the duties going to Retford they went to Lincoln and with them went No 58085 and sister engine No 58065. Withdrawal for No 58085 came on 8 April 1959.
Initial Photographics/R. J. Buckley

'Big Bertha' as it was affectionately known was the unique 0-10-0 Lickey banking engine. No 58100 is seen here at Derby Works in September 1956 awaiting cutting up after being withdrawn during the week ended 19 May. Appearing from Derby Works in December 1919 it remained on banking duties throughout, although in 1925 it was recorded on tests between Toton and Brent as a possible design for a heavy freight locomotive.
P. H. Groom

Midland Railway Johnson 2F 0-6-0 No 58204 is ex-works on Derby shed on Saturday 15 May 1954. Built by Robert Stephenson & Co in 1880, it was later rebuilt with a Type G6 Belpaire boiler and new cab as seen here. Allocated to Canklow at the time of this photograph, it moved to Wolverhampton Bushbury in January 1956. Withdrawal came while still based at 3B during the week ended 16 May 1959.
Initial Photographics/R. J. Buckley

58129	33A
58130	17B
58131	14B
58132	17A
58133	16A
58135	2A
58136	20B
58137	16A
58138	21B
58139	11B
58140	19A
58142	15C
58143	21B
58144	17A
58146	18A
58148	17A
58152	3B
58153	18C
58154	20C
58156	11B
58157	3C
58158	17A
58159	18A
58160	17B
58162	84G
58163	17C
58164	15C
58165	19A
58166	18B
58167	21A
58168	18B
58169	3A
58170	19C
58171	18A
58173	18A
58174	3A
58175	19A
58176	18C
58177	11B
58178	3E
58179	3E
58181	2A
58182	3D
58183	3B
58184	33A
58185	3E
58186	17B
58187	11B
58188	20C
58189	17D
58190	19A
58191	33A
58192	19A
58193	15C
58194	84G
58196	5B
58197	18A
58198	19C
58199	11B
58203	84G
58204	19C
58206	22B
58207	84G
58209	17C
58212	20C
58213	84G
58214	15B
58215	14B
58216	19B
58217	2D
58218	2A
58219	17A
58220	19A
58221	11B
58224	17D
58225	19A
58228	17D
58230	21A
58233	19C
58236	17B
58238	19C
58241	84G
58246	17A
58247	17C
58257	11B
58260	20C
58261	21A
58269	2A
58271	5B
58273	11B
58276	19A
58277	3A
58279	3C
58281	2B
58283	3C
58286	3E
58287	11B
58288	3C
58291	11B
58293	2D
58295	3D
58298	15C
58299	11B
58300	15C
58305	15D
58306	2D
58308	2A
58309	11B
58310	33B

Webb 18" Goods 0-6-0 2F

58375	8D
58376	8D
58394	6H
58409	12C
58412	12A
58427	8D
58430	8D

North London Railway 0-6-0T 2F

58850	17D
58851	1D
58852	1D
58854	1D
58855	1D
58856	17D
58857	1D
58859	1D
58860	17D
58862	17D

Webb 0-6-2T 2F

58887	1E
58891	86K
58904	84G
58925	86K
58926	86K

A4 class 4-6-2 8P6F

60001*	52A
60002*	52A
60003*	34A
60004*	64B
60005*	52A
60006*	34A
60007*	34A
60008*	34A
60009*	64B
60010*	34A
60011*	64B
60012*	64B
60013*	34A
60014*	34A
60015*	34A
60016*	52A
60017*	34A
60018*	52A
60019*	52A
60020*	52A
60021*	34A
60022*	34A
60023*	52A
60024*	64B
60025*	34A
60026*	34A
60027*	64B
60028*	34A
60029*	34A
60030*	34A
60031*	64B
60032*	34A
60033*	34A
60034*	34A

A3 class 4-6-2 7P6F

60035*	64B
60036*	50B
60037*	64B
60038*	52A
60039*	35B
60040*	52A
60041*	64B
60042*	52A
60043*	64B
60044*	38C
60045*	52A
60046*	36A
60047*	35B
60048*	36A
60049*	38C
60050*	34E
60051*	37B
60052*	38C
60053*	37B
60054*	38C
60055*	36A
60056*	35B
60057*	64B
60058*	37B
60059*	38C
60060*	52A
60061*	35B
60062*	34A
60063*	34E
60064*	36A
60065*	35B
60066*	36A
60067*	36A
60068*	68E
60069*	52B
60070*	52A
60071*	51A
60072*	52B
60073*	52B
60074*	50B
60075*	51A
60076*	52A
60077*	52B
60078*	52A
60079*	68E
60080*	52B
60081*	50B
60082*	52A
60083*	52B
60084*	50B
60085*	52B
60086*	50B
60087*	64B
60088*	52B
60089*	64B
60090*	64B
60091*	52B
60092*	52B
60093*	68E
60094*	64B
60095*	68E
60096*	64B
60097*	64B
60098*	64B
60099*	64B
60100*	64B
60101*	64B
60102*	38C
60103*	35B
60104*	38C
60105*	35B
60106*	37B
60107*	38C
60108*	34E
60109*	36A
60110*	35B
60111*	34E
60112*	36A

A1 class 4-6-2 8P6F

60113*	35B
60114*	35B
60115*	52A
60116*	52B
60117*	37B
60118*	37B
60119*	37B
60120*	37B
60121*	50A
60122*	37B
60123*	37A
60124*	52A
60125*	35B
60126*	52B
60127*	52B
60128*	35B
60129*	52A
60130*	37A
60131*	37B
60132*	52A
60133*	37B
60134*	37B
60135*	52A
60136*	35B
60137*	52A
60138*	50A
60139*	37B
60140*	50A
60141*	37B
60142*	52A
60143*	52A
60144*	35B
60145*	52A
60146*	50A
60147*	52A
60148*	35B
60149*	35B
60150*	52A
60151*	52A
60152*	64B
60153*	50A
60154*	52A
60155*	52A
60156*	35B
60157*	35B
60158*	35B
60159*	64B
60160*	64B
60161*	64B
60162*	64B

A2 class 4-6-2 8P7F

60500*	35A
60501*	50A
60502*	50A
60503*	50A
60504*	35A
60505*	35A
60506*	35A
60507*	64B
60508*	35A
60509*	64B
60510*	64B
60511*	52B
60512*	50A
60513*	35A
60514*	35A
60515*	50A

Not all the Johnson 0-6-0s received Belpaire boilers, and No 58246 was one, seen at Derby shed on Friday 23 April 1954 after surviving a works visit. Built at Derby in 1887, it retained its original round-topped boiler and short cab throughout. It had been transferred to Coalville during the two weeks ended 13 March 1954, but returned to Derby on release from the works. Coalville had it back again, but not until November 1958, from where it was withdrawn during the week ended 13 June 1959 and stored at Coalville for a further two years, no doubt supplying spare parts for other class members based there for working the Leicester West Bridge line through Glenfield Tunnel. Scrapping was carried out at Derby Works. *Initial Photographics/R. J. Buckley*

North London Railway 0-6-0T No 58862, a long way from its original home, is seen at Cromford Wharf at the lower end of the Cromford and High Peak line in June 1953. Built at Bow Works in August 1901, two of the class were successfully tried on the C&HP in 1932 and No 58862, then numbered 7530, was transferred to Rowsley shortly afterwards. Withdrawal came during the week ended 10 March 1956. *G. W. Sharpe*

The Webb 'Coal Tanks' dated from 1882 and 300 of these 0-6-2Ts were built. Only one survived at the end of 1955. This scene is at Birmingham New Street on Tuesday 1 June 1954 with No 58903, a Monument Lane engine. The working is the SLS New Street Centenary Special. This was an evening tour departing at 6.55pm with a run round Birmingham including Perry Barr, Handsworth, Smethwick, Old Hill, Halesowen, Longbridge, to Camp Hill and Saltley with a reversal to New Street — all for a fare of 6s (30p). No 58903 did not last into 1955, being withdrawn 18 days after this tour. *Initial Photographics/R. J. Buckley*

'A4' 4-6-2 No 60009 *Union of South Africa* is being serviced at Edinburgh Haymarket shed in July 1955. The engine entered traffic on 29 June 1937 and was allocated to Haymarket, where it remained until 20 May 1962 when Aberdeen Ferryhill added it to its allocation. After making a distinguished impact running on the 3hr Glasgow express workings, it bowed out on 1 June 1966 to be saved for preservation. *G. W. Sharpe*

An 'A4' in action: No 60015 *Quicksilver* storms up Holloway Bank on its way out of London with a relief to the 'Flying Scotsman' in June 1955. Entering traffic at King's Cross shed on 21 September 1935, it operated from Gateshead and Grantham sheds, but was back at King's Cross when withdrawn on 25 April 1963. *P. H. Groom*

'A3' class 4-6-2 No 60085 *Manna* is seen at Grantham on a northbound express in July 1954. Entering traffic on 22 February 1930, it went to Gateshead. When this scene was recorded it was a Heaton engine, moving back to Gateshead in June 1963, from where it was removed from traffic on 12 October 1964. *P. H. Groom*

'A3' class 4-6-2 No 60097 *Humorist* seen at Edinburgh Haymarket shed in 1955 with large smoke deflectors fitted in May 1947. Entering traffic on 7 March 1929, it was withdrawn on 23 July 1963. Its allocations included Doncaster, Grantham and King's Cross and it arrived in Scotland at Haymarket in July 1950. In 1954 it spent January and February at Carlisle Canal and then returned to Haymarket, moving across the city to St Margarets in December 1961, its final base.

Photomatic/RAS Marketing

'A1/1' class 4-6-2 No 60113 *Great Northern*, the Thompson 1945 rebuild from the Gresley Pacific, is seen approaching York in 1955 on an express from the south. Allocated to Grantham at the time, it went to King's Cross for a short stay in September 1957, and on to Doncaster from where it was withdrawn on 19 November 1962.

G. W. Sharpe

Peppercorn 'A1' class 4-6-2 No 60114 *W. P. Allen* is seen in charge of a London-bound express at Little Ponton just south of Grantham in September 1955. Added to stock on 26 October 1948 at King's Cross, by the date of the photograph it was a Grantham engine. Transferred to Doncaster on 22 September 1957, it continued to give useful service until condemned on 26 December 1964.

P. H. Groom

No.	Shed
60516*	52A
60517*	52B
60518*	52A
60519*	64B
60520*	35A
60521*	52A
60522*	50A
60523*	35A
60524*	50A
60525*	61B
60526*	50A
60527*	62B
60528*	62B
60529*	64B
60530*	64B
60531*	61B
60532*	61B
60533*	35B
60534*	64B
60535*	64B
60536*	64B
60537*	64B
60538*	52A
60539*	52B

W1 class 4-6-4 8P7F

No.	Shed
60700	36A

V2 class 2-6-2 7P6F

No.	Shed
60800*	34A
60801	52B
60802	52A
60803	31B
60804	62B
60805	52D
60806	52B
60807	52A
60808	52D
60809*	52A
60810	52B
60811	52B
60812	52B
60813	64A
60814	34A
60815	36A
60816	64B
60817	38E
60818	64A
60819	61B
60820	38C
60821	34A
60822	62B
60823	64A
60824	61B
60825	64A
60826	37A
60827	61B
60828	34A
60829	35A
60830	31B
60831	38E
60832	35A
60833	52B
60834	62B
60835*	52B

No.	Shed
60836	64A
60837	50A
60838	62B
60839	50A
60840	64A
60841	35A
60842	35A
60843	50A
60844	62B
60845	35A
60846	37A
60847*	50A
60848	64A
60849	36A
60850	35A
60851	61B
60852	36A
60853	35A
60854	35A
60855	34A
60856	50A
60857	36A
60858	31B
60859	37B
60860*	52D
60861	37A
60862	34A
60863	38C
60864	50A
60865	37B
60866	35A
60867	36A
60868	52A
60869	35A
60870	36A
60871	38E
60872*	36A
60873*	64A
60874	35A
60875	36A
60876	34A
60877	36A
60878	38C
60879	38E
60880	36A
60881	36A
60882	64A
60883	52A
60884	52D
60885	52B
60886	52B
60887	52B
60888	61B
60889	36A
60890	38E
60891	52B
60892	64A
60893	35A
60894	64A
60895	50A
60896	36A
60897	35A
60898	61B
60899	31B
60900	64A

No.	Shed
60901	50A
60902	36A
60903	34A
60904	50A
60905	35A
60906	35A
60907	50A
60908	35A
60909	34A
60910	52B
60911	35A
60912	35A
60913	37B
60914	34A
60915	38E
60916	35A
60917	36A
60918	50A
60919	61B
60920	62B
60921	36A
60922	64A
60923	52A
60924	35A
60925	50A
60926	52D
60927	64B
60928	36A
60929	50A
60930	36A
60931	62B
60932	52D
60933	64A
60934	50A
60935	36A
60936	35A
60937	62B
60938	31B
60939	52B
60940	52A
60941	50A
60942	52B
60943	36A
60944	52B
60945	52B
60946	50A
60947	52A
60948	31B
60949	52A
60950	35A
60951	64B
60952	52B
60953	64A
60954	50A
60955	61B
60956	36A
60957	52A
60958	62B
60959	64B
60960	50A
60961	50A
60962	50A
60963	50A
60964	52A
60965	64A

No.	Shed
60966	35A
60967	52A
60968	50A
60969	62B
60970	61B
60971	62B
60972	62B
60973	61B
60974	50A
60975	50A
60976	50A
60977	50A
60978	50A
60979	50A
60980	64A
60981	50A
60982	50A
60983	34A

B1 class 4-6-0 5MT

No.	Shed
61000*	30A
61001*	34E
61002*	50A
61003*	30F
61004*	30F
61005*	30F
61006*	30F
61007*	64B
61008*	30A
61009*	34E
61010*	53B
61011*	52A
61012*	52A
61013*	52A
61014*	52D
61015*	50A
61016*	50A
61017*	50B
61018*	51E
61019*	52A
61020*	50A
61021*	51A
61022*	52A
61023*	51A
61024*	51A
61025*	52D
61026*	36A
61027*	34D
61028*	34E
61029*	64A
61030*	51E
61031*	37C
61032*	51E
61033*	31A
61034*	51E
61035*	50B
61036*	36A
61037*	51E
61038*	50A
61039*	51A
61040*	51A
61041	39B
61042	32A
61043	32A
61044	39B

No.	Shed
61045	32A
61046	32A
61047	35A
61048	32A
61049	51A
61050	32A
61051	32A
61052	32B
61053	50A
61054	32B
61055	32B
61056	38A
61058	32B
61059	32B
61060	53A
61061	51A
61062	50B
61063	38B
61064	65A
61065	50B
61066	38B
61067	65C
61068	53B
61069	50B
61070	35A
61071	50A
61072	62A
61073	35A
61074	53A
61075	34A
61076	64B
61077	34E
61078	38E
61079	40B
61080	53A
61081	64B
61082	40B
61083	34E
61084	50A
61085	35A
61086	50B
61087	36A
61088	38C
61089	30A
61090	34D
61091	34D
61092	38A
61093	34D
61094	34D
61095	35A
61096	39B
61097	34D
61098	40B
61099	64A
61100	52A
61101	62B
61102	62B
61103	62A
61104	30A
61105	34D
61106	38A
61107	36A
61108	64A
61109	30A
61110	37A

'A2/2' class 4-6-2 No 60503 *Lord President* seen at York shed in May 1955. Rebuilt from the 'P2' class 2-8-2 No 2003 by Thompson, it entered traffic on 17 December 1944 and served from a number of depots in England and Scotland until 17 December 1950 when it settled at York. It was withdrawn on 27 November 1959.

Real Photographs

The four 'A2/1' class 4-6-2s were introduced by Thompson in 1944 and were a development of the 'A2/2' using a 'V2' class 2-6-2 boiler. One of the four, No 60509 *Waverley*, is at Edinburgh Haymarket shed in September 1955 where it had been allocated since 25 September 1949. Condemned on 15 August 1960, it was cut up at Doncaster Works.   *Photomatic/RAS Marketing*

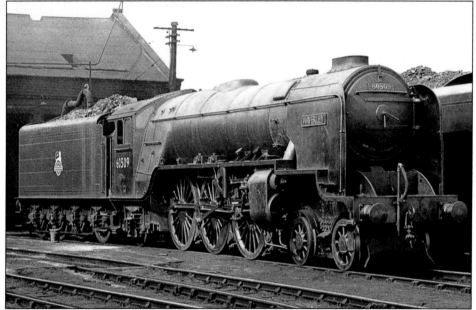

On Thompson's retirement, A. H. Peppercorn brought his own version of the 'A2' into service and this example, No 60527 *Sun Chariot*, is secured on film with a single-chimney at Dundee West shed in September 1955. Starting at Gateshead on 30 January 1948, it was reallocated to Dundee on 26 June 1949 and served from Perth for just one month in 1960, then on to Aberdeen Ferryhill on 28 May and Glasgow Polmadie on 15 September 1963. Withdrawn on 24 April 1965, it was scrapped at the Motherwell Machinery yard.

Photomatic/RAS Marketing

A superb period scene at Newcastle station in June 1955 shows Haymarket-based 'A2' No 60537 *Bachelors Button* entering on the southbound 'Queen of Scots' Pullman express. Transferred to Edinburgh St Margarets on 13 November 1961, withdrawal came on 29 December 1962.

G. W. Sharpe

The unique 'W1' class 4-6-4 No 60700 at Doncaster shed in October 1957. This was the rebuild from Gresley's high-pressure engine No 10000. Coming to Doncaster shed on 25 October 1953 from King's Cross, it remained at 36A until withdrawn on 1 June 1959.   *G. W. Sharpe*

Ex-works at Doncaster shed on Sunday 13 May 1956 is King's Cross-based Gresley 'V2' class 2-6-2 No 60876. Released new from Doncaster Works on 30 May 1940, its first allocation was to Peterborough New England. The final operating base was York, where the engine had been transferred from New England in November 1958. Withdrawal came on 19 October 1965 and Cashmore's at Great Bridge reduced the engine to scrap metal in January 1966.

L. Hanson

No.	Shed	No.	Shed	No.	Shed	No.	Shed	No.	Shed
61111	38A	61176	50A	61241*	52D	61306	53B	61371	40A
61112	36B	61177	40A	61242*	61C	61307	61C	61372	30A
61113	35A	61178	64B	61243*	65A	61308	61C	61373	30A
61114	36A	61179	39B	61244*	64B	61309	37B	61374	40B
61115	50A	61180	65A	61245*	64B	61310	37A	61375	30A
61116	34E	61181	39B	61246*	64A	61311	40A	61376	38A
61117	65A	61182	40B	61247*	36A	61312	32A	61377	37A
61118	62A	61183	39B	61248*	40A	61313	39B	61378	30A
61119	30A	61184	64A	61249*	30A	61314	39B	61379*	40B
61120	36A	61185	38C	61250*	36A	61315	39B	61380	38C
61121	31A	61186	38A	61251*	34D	61316	39B	61381	38E
61122	35A	61187	34E	61252	32B	61317	32A	61382	37A
61123	37A	61188	38A	61253	32B	61318	40B	61383	37A
61124	36A	61189*	51E	61254	32B	61319	54C	61384	30A
61125	36A	61190	40B	61255	51A	61320	54C	61385	37A
61126	36E	61191	64A	61256	50B	61321	54C	61386	37B
61127	36A	61192	38E	61257	50B	61322	52D	61387	37B
61128	36A	61193	36A	61258	40A	61323	61A	61388	37B
61129	37B	61194	36B	61259	50B	61324	61A	61389	35A
61130	40B	61195	40B	61260	65A	61325	40B	61390	40B
61131	37A	61196	36A	61261	65A	61326	36A	61391	35A
61132	62B	61197	65A	61262	62A	61327	39B	61392	35A
61133	65A	61198	51A	61263	62B	61328	40B	61393	34A
61134	65A	61199	52A	61264	30F	61329	30A	61394	34A
61135	30F	61200	34A	61265	39A	61330	64D	61395	68E
61136	34E	61201	38C	61266	36A	61331	34A	61396	65A
61137	36A	61202	40A	61267	37C	61332	64A	61397	64A
61138	35A	61203	34A	61268	37C	61333	61A	61398	64D
61139	34A	61204	35A	61269	38A	61334	31A	61399	30A
61140	65A	61205	35A	61270	32A	61335	30A	61400	61A
61141	38C	61206	34E	61271	38A	61336	30A	61401	61A
61142	40B	61207	35A	61272	38C	61337	50A	61402	62B
61143	35A	61208	36E	61273	51A	61338	50A	61403	62B
61144	40B	61209	38B	61274	51A	61339	50A	61404	64B
61145	36A	61210	35A	61275	51C	61340	65A	61405	40A
61146	62A	61211	36E	61276	51A	61341	64A	61406	40B
61147	62A	61212	36E	61277	65A	61342	65A	61407	64A
61148	62A	61213	36E	61278	62B	61343	61A	61408	40B
61149	30F	61214	51E	61279	40A	61344	65A	61409	40B
61150	39B	61215*	53B	61280	30A	61345	61A		
61151	39B	61216	50B	61281	40A	61346	61A	**B16 class 4-6-0 5MT**	
61152	39B	61217	68E	61282	35A	61347	61A	61410	50B
61153	39B	61218	50B	61283	38E	61348	61A	61411	50B
61154	39B	61219	68E	61284	40B	61349	61A	61412	50B
61155	36A	61220	51E	61285	31A	61350	61A	61413	50B
61156	39B	61221*	64B	61286	31A	61351	61A	61414	50B
61157	36A	61222	68E	61287	31A	61352	61A	61415	50B
61158	36A	61223	31A	61288	50A	61353	51A	61416	50A
61159	40B	61224	50A	61289	51A	61354	64A	61417	50A
61160	31A	61225	39B	61290	68E	61355	64B	61418	50A
61161	39A	61226	30F	61291	51A	61356	64A	61419	50A
61162	36A	61227	30A	61292	62B	61357	64A	61420	50A
61163	38A	61228	32B	61293	62B	61358	64A	61421	50A
61164	34E	61229	37C	61294	61A	61359	64A	61422	50C
61165	36B	61230	37C	61295	37A	61360	30A	61423	50A
61166	36B	61231	36E	61296	37C	61361	30A	61424	50A
61167	36B	61232	30F	61297	37A	61362	30A	61425	50B
61168	40B	61233	30A	61298	38C	61363	30A	61426	50A
61169	39B	61234	30A	61299	38C	61364	35A	61427	50B
61170	36A	61235	30A	61300	31A	61365	36A	61428	50B
61171	36A	61236	30A	61301	31A	61366	40B	61429	50B
61172	65A	61237*	50B	61302	31A	61367	38A	61430	50A
61173	51E	61238*	52A	61303	51E	61368	38E	61431	50B
61174	39B	61239	68E	61304	53B	61369	38C	61432	50B
61175	40B	61240*	50B	61305	53B	61370	30A	61433	50B

142

The successful Thompson 'B1' 4-6-0 was first introduced in December 1942. This example, No 61273, is passing Beningbrough north of York on a freight in 1954. Allocated new to Darlington on 30 December 1947, this was the last 'B1' to enter traffic under the LNER. It was one of a batch built by the North British Loco Co and remained at Darlington until transfer to York on 14 June 1959, from where it was withdrawn on 7 May 1963.

G. W. Sharpe

'B16/1' class 4-6-0 No 61416 is seen on a freight working at Pilmoor between Tollerton and Thirsk in 1955 with a northbound freight. Built in 1921 to a design by Raven, most of the class was allocated to Leeds Neville Hill or York. After a lengthy stay at York, No 61416 went to Mirfield in December 1960 to work its final months, withdrawal coming on 12 May 1961.

G. W. Sharpe

Gresley rebuilt seven of the 'B16' class with Walschaerts valve gear and derived motion including No 61438, seen at Leeds City station in September 1955. A long-time resident of York, in December 1962 transfer to Hull Dairycoates was ordered and withdrawal followed on 29 June 1964.

G. W. Sharpe

61434 50A
61435 50A
61436 50A
61437 50A
61438 50A
61439 50A
61440 50B
61441 50A
61442 50D
61443 50A
61444 50A
61445 50E
61446 50B
61447 50B
61448 50A
61449 50A
61450 50A
61451 50A
61452 50A
61453 50A
61454 50A
61455 50A
61456 50A
61457 50A
61458 50A
61459 50A
61460 50A
61461 50A
61462 50A
61463 50A
61464 50A
61465 50A
61466 50A
61467 50A
61468 50A
61469 50B
61470 50B
61471 50B
61472 50A
61473 50A
61474 50A
61475 50A
61476 50A
61477 50A
61478 50B

B12/3 class 4-6-0 4P3F
61512 30A
61514 32D
61516 30A
61519 30A
61520 32F
61523 30A
61530 32F
61533 32D
61535 32B
61537 32B
61538 35B
61540 32A
61541 35B
61542 32D
61545 32A
61546 30A
61547 32A
61549 30A

61550 30A
61553 35B
61554 35B
61555 30A
61556 30A
61557 30A
61558 30A
61561 32B
61562 32B
61564 32B
61565 35B
61566 32B
61567 35B
61568 32A
61569 32B
61570 32B
61571 32B
61572 32B
61573 30A
61574 35B
61575 30A
61576 30A
61577 32B
61578 30A
61579 30A
61580 35B

B17 class 4-6-0 5P4F
61600* 30A
61601* 30A
61602* 30A

B2 class 4-6-0 5P
61603* 30E

B17 class 4-6-0 5P4F
61605* 30A
61606* 30A

B2 class 4-6-0 5P
61607* 30E

B17 class 4-6-0 5P4F
61608* 30A
61609* 30A
61610* 30A
61611* 30A
61612* 30A
61613* 30A

B2 class 4-6-0 5P
61614* 30E
61615* 30E
61616* 30E
61617* 31A

B17 class 4-6-0 5P4F
61618* 32B
61619* 31B
61620* 31B
61621* 31B
61622* 32D
61623* 31A
61625* 32B
61626* 31B

61627* 31B
61629* 32A
61630* 30A
61631* 32B

B2 class 4-6-0 5P
61632* 30E

B17 class 4-6-0 5P4F
61633* 31B
61634* 30A
61635* 31B
61636* 31A
61637* 32B
61638* 31B

B2 class 4-6-0 5P
61639* 30E

B17 class 4-6-0 5P4F
61640* 31A
61641* 31B
61642* 31A
61643* 31B

B2 class 4-6-0 5P
61644* 30E

B17 class 4-6-0 5P4F
61645* 30E
61646* 30E
61647* 32B
61648* 30A
61649* 32B
61650* 30E
61651* 30E
61652* 31A
61653* 31A
61654* 30A
61655* 30A
61656* 32A
61657* 31A
61658* 31B
61659* 32D
61660* 30A
61661* 30A
61662* 30E
61663* 30A
61664* 32A
61665* 32A
61666* 30E
61667* 30E
61668* 30A
61669* 32B
61670* 32D

B2 class 4-6-0 5P
61671* 31A

B17 class 4-6-0 5P4F
61672* 30A

V4 class 2-6-2 4MT
61700* 61B
61701 61B

K2 class 2-6-0 4MT
61720 40B
61721 62C
61722 65C
61723 38A
61724 40B
61725 40F
61726 38A
61727 40B
61728 40F
61729 38A
61730 40B
61731 40F
61732 38A
61733 65C
61734 61C
61735 65C
61736 40B
61737 38A
61738 38A
61739 40B
61740 40B
61741 62A
61742 40F
61743 40A
61744 40F
61745 40F
61746 40A
61747 38A
61748 40A
61749 38A
61750 40F
61751 38A
61752 38A
61753 38A
61754 38A
61755 62A
61756 40F
61757 40F
61758 62C
61759 38A
61760 40F
61761 40A
61762 40F
61763 38A
61764* 65A
61765 40A
61766 40F
61767 40F
61768 38A
61769 65C
61770 62C
61771 38A
61772* 65C
61773 38A
61774* 65A
61775* 65A
61776 65A
61777 38A
61778 40A
61779 61C
61780 38A
61781* 65A
61782* 61C
61783* 61A

61784 65A
61785 65A
61786 65A
61787* 63D
61788* 63D
61789* 65A
61790* 61A
61791* 63D
61792 61C
61793 61C
61794* 65A

K3 class 2-6-0 5P6F
61800 40B
61801 30A
61802 40B
61803 40B
61804 31B
61805 30A
61806 40B
61807 40A
61808 39A
61809 38A
61810 30A
61811 31B
61812 40A
61813 53A
61814 53A
61815 30A
61816 31B
61817 30A
61818 52B
61819 53A
61820 30A
61821 38A
61822 31B
61823 64A
61824 38A
61825 40B
61826 31B
61827 31B
61828 40A
61829 40A
61830 30A
61831 30A
61832 39A
61833 38A
61834 30A
61835 31B
61836 40B
61837 40B
61838 40B
61839 40B
61840 30A
61841 31B
61842 31B
61843 31B
61844 53A
61845 31B
61846 53A
61847 53A
61848 40A
61849 30A
61850 31B
61851 68E

'B12/3' class 4-6-0 No 61558 is seen at Stratford shed in May 1955. Built by William Beadmore & Co in March 1921 to an S. D. Holden design for the Great Eastern Railway, it was rebuilt in November 1935 under Gresley with a larger round-topped boiler and long-travel valves. Allocated to Stratford, No 61558 moved to Colchester on 28 October 1956. Further moves to Peterborough Spital Bridge and King's Lynn occurred, and on 24 November 1957 it moved to Cambridge where it was condemned on 13 April 1959. Stratford Works carried out the cutting up. *R. H. G. Simpson*

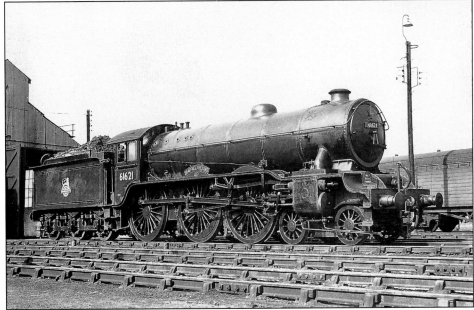

'B17/1' class 4-6-0 No 61621 *Hatfield House* seen at March shed in September 1956 paired with a Great Eastern-type tender. A Gresley design from 1928, No 61621 spent its BR days at various sheds including Stratford, Cambridge, Ipswich and finally March from February 1954 where it was removed from traffic on 10 November 1958. *P. H. Groom*

'B2' class 4-6-0 No 61671 *Royal Sovereign* is seen at Cambridge station in August 1954 in its usual immaculate condition for working Royal trains to Sandringham. Built in June 1937 as a 'B17/4', conversion to a 'B2' came in August 1945 which included two cylinders and a 'B1'-type boiler. Allocated to Cambridge throughout its BR career, it was withdrawn on 22 September 1958 and scrapped at Stratford Works. *P. H. Groom*

Gresley two-cylinder 'K2' class 2-6-0 No 61773 is seen at Nottingham Colwick shed on Sunday 10 July 1955. Built by Kitson & Co in June 1921, this engine retained its rather spartan cab throughout. Allocated to Colwick in 1948, it moved to Boston in October 1958, then to Immingham in February 1959, returning to Colwick in September 1960 to be withdrawn three months later on 23 December. *K. C. H. Fairey*

The Scottish 'K2s' were fitted with side-window cabs and acquired names associated with their workings on the West Highland line. Built by Kitson & Co in August 1921, No 61788 *Loch Rannoch* is at Glasgow Eastfield shed in September 1956 after a visit to Cowlairs Works. It was allocated alternatively between Eastfield and Fort William and was withdrawn on 26 June 1961 during a time at Eastfield.

Photomatic/RAS Marketing

The Gresley 'K3' with three cylinders was a more powerful 2-6-0 than the 'K2'. This example, No 61818, was built at Darlington in October 1924 and first allocated to Blaydon. This view is at Doncaster shed after a works visit in December 1955 when allocated to Heaton. The official withdrawal date was 5 March 1962 when allocated to Hull Dairycoates. *G. W. Sharpe*

No.	Shed
61852	40A
61853	31B
61854	68E
61855	64A
61856	38A
61857	64A
61858	68E
61859	40A
61860	31B
61861	31B
61862	30A

K5 class 2-6-0 5P6F

No.	Shed
61863	30A

K3 class 2-6-0 5P6F

No.	Shed
61864	31B
61865	39A
61866	31B
61867	31B
61868	31B
61869	53A
61870	38A
61871	53A
61872	53A
61873	31B
61874	53A
61875	52B
61876	64A
61877	32A
61878	64A
61879	64A
61880	30A
61881	64A
61882	68E
61883	53A
61884	53A
61885	64A
61886	31B
61887	31B
61888	31B
61889	40A
61890	31B
61891	40B
61892	53A
61893	53A
61894	40A
61895	31B
61896	38A
61897	64A
61898	68E
61899	52D
61900	64A
61901	52D
61902	53A
61903	53A
61904	52B
61905	40B
61906	52B
61907	31B
61908	32A
61909	64A
61910	39A
61911	64A
61912	40B
61913	39A
61914	38A
61915	31B
61916	68E
61917	52D
61918	32A
61919	40A
61920	53A
61921	30A
61922	53A
61923	53A
61924	
61925	
61926	32C
61927	52B
61928	64A
61929	31B
61930	52D
61931	64A
61932	52B
61933	64A
61934	53A
61935	53A
61936	68E
61937	68E
61938	31B
61939	32A
61940	31B
61941	53A
61942	30A
61943	31B
61944	40A
61945	53A
61946	31B
61947	31B
61948	31B
61949	32C
61950	40A
61951	30A
61952	52D
61953	32A
61954	31B
61955	64A
61956	40B
61957	32A
61958	32C
61959	32C
61960	40A
61961	31B
61962	52D
61963	30A
61964	40A
61965	53A
61966	39A
61967	31B
61968	64A
61969	52D
61970	32A
61971	32A
61972	31B
61973	32C
61974	38B
61975	38B
61976	31B
61977	30A
61978	31B
61979	31B
61980	38B
61981	32A
61982	31B
61983	64A
61984	52B
61985	52D
61986	52B
61987	52B
61988	64A
61989	32A
61990	64A
61991	64A
61992	64A

K4 class 2-6-0 5P6F

No.	Shed
61993*	65A
61994*	65A
61995*	65A
61996*	65A

K1/1 class 2-6-0 5P6F

No.	Shed
61997*	63D

K4 class 2-6-0 5P6F

No.	Shed
61998*	65A

K1 class 2-6-0 5P6F

No.	Shed
62001	51A
62002	52C
62003	51A
62004	51A
62005	51A
62006	52C
62007	51A
62008	51A
62009	51A
62010	52C
62011	63D
62012	63D
62013	31B
62014	31B
62015	31B
62016	31B
62017	31B
62018	31B
62019	31B
62020	31B
62021	52C
62022	52C
62023	52C
62024	52C
62025	52C
62026	52C
62027	52C
62028	52C
62029	52C
62030	52C
62031	63D
62032	31B
62033	31B
62034	63D
62035	31B
62036	31B
62037	31B
62038	31B
62039	31B
62040	31B
62041	51E
62042	51E
62043	51E
62044	51J
62045	51A
62046	51A
62047	51A
62048	51G
62049	51A
62050	51G
62051	31B
62052	63D
62053	31B
62054	31B
62055	31B
62056	51G
62057	51G
62058	51G
62059	51G
62060	51E
62061	51G
62062	51A
62063	51A
62064	51E
62065	51E
62066	31B
62067	31B
62068	31B
62069	31B
62070	31B

D40 class 4-4-0 1P

No.	Shed
62262	61C
62264	61C
62265	61C
62267	61C
62268	61C
62269	61C
62271	61C
62272	61C
62273*	61C
62274*	61A
62275*	61C
62276*	61A
62277*	61C
62278*	61A
62279*	61A

D20 class 4-4-0 2P

No.	Shed
62343	50C
62345	50A
62349	52C
62355	52D
62359	51J
62360	52D
62372	51C
62375	52D
62378	50C
62381	50C
62383	52D
62384	50C
62386	50C
62387	52B
62395	50C
62396	52D
62397	50B

D30 class 4-4-0 3P

No.	Shed
62418*	62A
62419*	62A
62420*	64G
62421*	64A
62422*	64G
62423*	64G
62424*	64A
62425*	64G
62426*	63B
62427*	62C
62428*	64G
62429*	62A
62430*	62A
62431*	62A
62432*	64G
62434*	62B
62435*	64G
62436*	62C
62437*	64B
62438*	62B
62439*	64F
62440*	64G
62441*	62C
62442*	62A

D34 class 4-4-0 3P

No.	Shed
62467*	62A
62468*	62A
62469*	61A
62470*	63A
62471*	64A
62472*	65A
62474*	65A
62475*	62A
62477*	65A
62478*	62A
62479*	61A
62480*	61A
62482*	61A
62483*	64A
62484*	63A
62485*	62B
62487*	64A
62488*	64A
62489*	61A
62490*	64A
62492*	62A
62493*	61A
62494*	64A
62495*	64F
62496*	65A
62497*	61A
62498*	61A

D16 class 4-4-0 3P1F

No.	Shed
62510	32A
62511	32E
62513	31E

The unique 'K5' class 2-6-0 No 61863 is seen at Stratford shed in April 1955. Originally built as a 'K3' at Darlington in September 1925 and first allocated to Gorton, it was rebuilt by Thompson in June 1945 with two 'B1'-type cylinders and larger capacity boiler. Peterborough New England operated it for a time until November 1952 when it went to Stratford, to remain based in London until withdrawn on 6 June 1960. *G. W. Sharpe*

Gresley three-cylinder 'K4' class 2-6-0 No 61994 *The Great Marquess* is pictured at Glasgow Eastfield shed in June 1955. Built at Darlington in July 1938 for use on the West Highland line, it had smaller wheels than the 'K3s' but with a higher tractive effort. All five members of the class were transferred to Thornton Junction in 1959, from where No 61994 was withdrawn on 18 December 1961 — the last to go. Rescued from oblivion, the *Marquess* lives on in preservation. *G. W. Sharpe*

'K1/1' class 2-6-0 No 61997 *MacCailin Mor* takes the single-line token on leaving Fort William for Mallaig in June 1954. Originally built as a 'K4' in January 1939, Thompson rebuilt it in December 1945 as the prototype for the two-cylinder 'K1'. A resident at Fort William shed for many years, it was withdrawn on 12 June 1961.

Photomatic/RAS Marketing

Rather strangely, when the Thompson 'K1' class 2-6-0s were built none went to Scotland, being allocated in blocks to Darlington, Gorton, Blaydon and March. During the week ended 10 February 1952 five 'K1s' — Nos 62011, 62012, 62031, 62034 and 62052 — were transferred from March to Glasgow Eastfield. Nos 62011 and 62012 went to Fort William in June 1952 and were joined by the other three in June 1954. Nos 62011 and 62012 were transferred to the North Eastern Region to Tweedmouth in December 1962 and became regular performers on the Alnmouth Branch. The other three remained at Fort William until withdrawn in February 1963, but in reality had been stored at Bo'ness since December 1961. This is No 62052, one of the November 1949 build, at Lochailort on a Mallaig to Fort William train in June 1954. *Photomatic/RAS Marketing*

The graceful lines of 'D40' class 4-4-0 No 62264 can be seen at Lossiemouth, northeast Scotland, on Wednesday 7 April 1954. Built in October 1899 by Neilson Reid & Co, this was a Pickersgill design for the Great North of Scotland Railway and had the advantage of adequate cabs for the crew's comfort against the rigours of the weather. No 62264 was withdrawn from Keith Junction on 5 March 1957. *G. W. Sharpe*

'D20/2' class 4-4-0 No 62349 is seen at Blaydon shed in August 1955. This was a 1936 rebuild with long-travel valves of the original W. Worsdell's 1899 design. The frames were also raised, the cab improved, the tender rebuilt and the right-hand drive gave way to standard left-hand. Although others were modified, No 62349 remained unique in its appearance and was withdrawn on 2 February 1956. *G. W. Sharpe*

An original 'D20' 4-4-0, No 62378, allocated to Selby, is pictured at Monkton Moor between Knaresborough and York on a passenger working in May 1955. It was withdrawn on 5 November 1956, still at Selby shed.
G. W. Sharpe

'D30' class 4-4-0 No 62441 *Black Duncan* is seen at Dunfermline shed in August 1955. This was a Reid 'Superheated Scott' Class J for the North British Railway and was built in November 1920. It was allocated to Dunfermline throughout its BR days until withdrawal on 14 August 1958.
R. H. G. Simpson

'D16/3' class 4-4-0 No 62572 leaves March on a local in September 1956. Built as a 'D15' 'Claud Hamilton' class to a design by J. Holden, in May 1933 Gresley rebuilt the engine with a larger round-topped boiler and modified footplating. After service at Cambridge shed it was withdrawn on 28 July 1958.
P. H. Groom

62514	31C	62592	32A	**D49/1 'Shire' class 4-4-0 4P**		62754*	53B	63364	51D
62515	32G	62593	32A	62700*	53B	62755*	50D	63365	54D
62516	31C	62596	32A	62701*	53D	62756*	50E	63366	54C
62517	32E	62597	32D	62702*	50A	62757*	53B	63367	51G
62518	31C	62599	35C	62703*	53D	62758*	50D	63368	51D
62519	32G	62601	31C	62704*	62A	62759*	50D	63369	51D
62521	31A	62604	32D	62705*	64B	62760*	50A	63370	51B
62522	32A	62605	31B	62706*	64B	62761*	50D	63371	51B
62523	32A	62606	31C	62707*	53D	62762*	50D	63372	54D
62524	32E	62607	31A	62708*	62A	62763*	50D	63373	51D
62525	31A	62608	32A	62709*	64B	62764*	50B	63374	51G
62526	31B	62609	35C	62710*	53D	62765*	50D	63375	51D
62529	31B	62610	32A	62711*	64A	62766*	53D	63376	52C
62530	31A	62611	32E	62712*	64A	62767*	53B	63377	54C
62531	31A	62612	32B	62713*	62A	62769*	50E	63378	50C
62532	31A	62613	32E	62714*	63B	62770*	50E	63379	54D
62533	32G	62614	31C	62715*	64A	62771*	52C	63380	51D
62534	31C	62615	31E	62716*	62A	62772*	50D	63381	52C
62535	35C	62617	32G	62717*	53B	62773*	50D	63382	50C
62536	35C	62618	31A	62718*	64A	62774*	50D	63383	51C
62539	31B	62619	32A	62719*	64B	62775*	50B	63384	54C
62540	32A	62620	32G	62720*	53B			63385	52C
62541	31A			62721*	64A	**E4 class 2-4-0 1MT**		63386	54C
62542	31B	**D10 class 4-4-0 3P**		62722*	53B	62780	31A	63387	54B
62543	31E	62653*	9G	62723*	53B	62781	31A	63388	51B
62544	32D	62656*	9G	62724*	53B	62784	31A	63389	51B
62545	31A	62658*	9G	62725*	63B	62785	34D	63390	52C
62546*	32D					62786	31A	63391	52C
62548	31B	**D11 class 4-4-0 3P2F**		**D49/2 'Hunt' class 4-4-0 4P**		62787	32A	63392	51C
62549	31A	62660*	40A	62726*	50E	62788	32A	63393	51D
62551	35C	62661*	9E	62727*	50D	62789	32A	63394	52C
62552	32B	62662*	9E			62790	31A	63395	50C
62553	32A	62663*	40A	**D49/1 'Shire' class 4-4-0 4P**		62791	31A	63396	51C
62554	32A	62664*	9E	62728*	62B	62792	32A	63397	51C
62555	32A	62665*	9G	62729*	62A	62793	32A	63398	52C
62556	32A	62666*	40A	62730*	50A	62794	31A	63399	52C
62557	31A	62667*	40A	62731*	50A	62795	31A	63400	54C
62558	31A	62668*	9E	62732*	68E	62796	32A	63401	51D
62559	31C	62669*	9G	62733*	64B	62797	32C	63402	54C
62561	32A	62670*	40B	62734*	68E			63403	52C
62562	31B	62671*	65A	62735*	50E	**Q6 class 0-8-0 6F**		63404	54D
62564	32G	62672*	65A			63340	51D	63405	51D
62565	31C	62673*	65A	**D49/2 'Hunt' class 4-4-0 4P**		63341	51B	63406	50C
62566	31E	62674*	65A	62736*	50D	63342	54C	63407	51G
62567	31A	62675*	65A	62737*	53B	63343	51B	63408	54C
62568	35C	62676*	65A	62738*	50D	63344	51B	63409	51D
62569	31C	62677*	64B	62739*	50E	63345	51B	63410	51C
62570	31A	62678*	64B	62740*	50D	63346	54D	63411	51D
62571	31A	62679*	64B	62741*	53B	63347	51B	63412	52C
62572	31B	62680*	65A	62742*	50B	63348	50B	63413	52C
62573	31C	62681*	65A	62743*	64B	63349	51D	63414	51C
62574	31A	62682*	65A	62744*	62B	63350	54C	63415	51C
62575	31C	62683*	64B	62745*	50D	63351	51F	63416	51G
62576	31E	62684*	65A	62746*	50D	63352	54B	63417	51D
62577	32A	62685*	64B	62747*	52C	63353	52C	63418	54D
62578	32G	62686*	65A	62748*	50B	63354	54C	63419	51C
62579	31C	62687*	65A	62749*	50D	63355	51D	63420	51D
62580	32E	62688*	65A	62750*	53D	63356	52C	63421	51C
62582	31C	62689*	65A	62751*	50E	63357	54D	63422	51C
62584	32A	62690*	64B	62752*	50D	63358	54C	63423	50C
62585	31A	62691*	64B	62753*	50D	63359	54B	63424	51C
62586	32E	62692*	64B			63360	51B	63425	50C
62587	35C	62693*	64B			63361	54D	63426	51B
62588	31E	62694*	64B			63362	54B	63427	54D
62589	31B					63363	52C	63428	52C

Robinson 'Improved Director' class 'D11' 4-4-0 No 62667 *Somme* is seen at Derby Midland station after arrival from Lincoln on Monday 9 August 1956. Built in November 1922 for the Great Central Railway, the last to be withdrawn, No 62666, went in December 1960. No 62667 was withdrawn five months earlier on 12 August from Sheffield Darnall where it had been transferred from Lincoln in April 1957. *Ken Hunt*

In 1924 a further batch of 24 'D11s' was built for the Scottish section of the LNER and classified 'D11/2'. These were produced when Gresley was in office and to conform with the North British Railway loading gauge had lower cab and boiler mountings and were without a water scoop. The most obvious outward difference was the squat flowerpot chimney which gave these locomotives a more robust look than their English sisters. Some were also fitted with round instead of oval buffers as shown on this example, No 62678 *Luckie Mucklebackit* at Edinburgh Haymarket shed ex-works in 1955. All were allocated either to Eastfield or Haymarket and withdrawals started in September 1958, many spending long periods in store towards the end. No 62678 was condemned on 3 March 1959 after transfer to Thornton Junction in May 1957. *Photomatic/RAS Marketing*

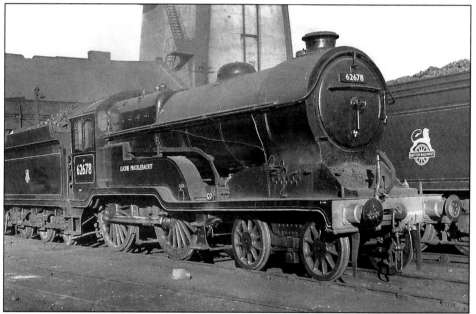

'D49/1' 'Shire' class 4-4-0 No 62720 *Cambridgeshire* is seen at Hull Botanic Gardens shed in September 1956 paired with a Great Central-type tender. Built in May 1928 and first allocated to Leeds Neville Hill, this example was fitted with Walschaerts valve gear and derived motion. After operating from various sheds in the northeast its final allocation was Hull Dairycoates when withdrawn on 6 October 1959. *P. H. Groom*

Pounding over the crossing at Wormald Green on the Ripon to Harrogate line is 'D49/2' 'Hunt' class 4-4-0 No 62736 *The Bramham Moor* in July 1955. Placed in service in April 1932 at Leeds Neville Hill, it was a development of the 'D49/1' with Lentz rotary cam poppet valves. It was withdrawn from Starbeck shed on 19 June 1958. *G. W. Sharpe*

Built in July 1902 by W. Holden for the Great Eastern Railway, 'E4' class 2-4-0 No 62796 is captured on film at Cambridge station on Friday 19 August 1955 shortly after transfer to 31A from Norwich. It remained at Cambridge until withdrawal on 13 May 1957. *G. W. Sharpe*

Raven North Eastern Railway-design 'Q6' class 0-8-0 No 63363 is seen on a mineral working near Blaydon in 1955. Built at Darlington Works in June 1913, it lasted until 4 September 1966 when allocated at Tyne Dock. *G. W. Sharpe*

63429	50C
63430	51B
63431	54C
63432	52C
63433	54D
63434	54C
63435	51D
63436	50B
63437	54B
63438	51C
63439	54D
63440	50C
63441	52C
63442	51D
63443	51G
63444	54C
63445	51B
63446	51G
63447	51B
63448	50C
63449	50C
63450	50C
63451	50C
63452	51D
63453	54B
63454	51C
63455	54D
63456	54C
63457	51C
63458	54C
63459	51F

Q7 class 0-8-0 8F

63460	54B
63461	54B
63462	54B
63463	54B
63464	54B
63465	54B
63466	54B
63467	54B
63468	54B
63469	54B
63470	54B
63471	54B
63472	54B
63473	54B
63474	54B

04 class 2-8-0 7F

63570	37A

01 class 2-8-0 8F

63571	38B

04 class 2-8-0 7F

63572	36C
63573	39A
63574	39B
63575	39A
63576	36C
63577	40E

01 class 2-8-0 8F

63578	38B

63579	38B

04 class 2-8-0 7F

63581	39B
63582	39A
63583	39B
63584	37A
63585	40E
63586	36B
63587	38D
63588	37A

01 class 2-8-0 8F

63589	38B
63590	38B
63591	38B
63592	38B

04 class 2-8-0 7F

63593	36B

01 class 2-8-0 8F

63594	38B

04 class 2-8-0 7F

63595	36C

01 class 2-8-0 8F

63596	38B

04 class 2-8-0 7F

63597	40E
63598	39A
63599	39B
63600	39A
63601	36C
63602	38A
63603	39A
63604	39B
63605	37A
63606	36C
63607	39B
63608	36E
63609	39B

01 class 2-8-0 8F

63610	38B

04 class 2-8-0 7F

63611	36B
63612	36B
63613	38A
63614	38A
63615	40E
63616	40B
63617	36C
63618	38A

01 class 2-8-0 8F

63619	38B

04 class 2-8-0 7F

63620	39B
63621	39B
63622	39B

63623	36D
63624	39B
63625	36D
63626	36C
63628	38A
63629	39B

01 class 2-8-0 8F

63630	38B

04 class 2-8-0 7F

63631	39A
63632	40E
63633	37A
63634	40E
63635	39B
63636	40E
63637	36E
63638	38A
63639	38A
63640	39B
63641	39A
63642	36C
63643	40E
63644	40E
63645	39B

01 class 2-8-0 8F

63646	38B

04 class 2-8-0 7F

63647	38A
63648	38D
63649	39A

01 class 2-8-0 8F

63650	38B

04 class 2-8-0 7F

63651	40B

01 class 2-8-0 8F

63652	38B

04 class 2-8-0 7F

63653	36C
63654	36E
63655	36C
63656	36D
63657	38A
63658	39B
63659	36C
63660	36C
63661	39B
63662	36C

01 class 2-8-0 8F

63663	38B

04 class 2-8-0 7F

63664	40E
63665	40E
63666	36B
63667	40E

63668	36B
63669	36D

01 class 2-8-0 8F

63670	38B

04 class 2-8-0 7F

63671	36C
63672	36B
63673	38A
63674	38A
63675	38D

01 class 2-8-0 8F

63676	38B

04 class 2-8-0 7F

63677	37A

01 class 2-8-0 8F

63678	38B

04 class 2-8-0 7F

63679	40E
63680	39B
63681	39A
63682	39B
63683	40E
63684	38A
63685	39B
63686	39A

01 class 2-8-0 8F

63687	38B

04 class 2-8-0 7F

63688	36E

01 class 2-8-0 8F

63689	38B

04 class 2-8-0 7F

63690	36C
63691	39B
63692	40B
63693	36B
63694	38D
63695	39B
63696	36C
63697	36D
63698	36B
63699	38A
63700	39A
63701	36B
63702	38D
63703	40E
63704	36B
63705	38D
63706	38A
63707	40E
63708	39B
63709	39A
63710	39B

01 class 2-8-0 8F

63711	38B
63712	54B

04 class 2-8-0 7F

63713	39A
63714	39B
63715	40E
63716	39A
63717	40E
63718	36D
63719	39A
63720	38D
63721	39A
63722	39B
63723	38A
63724	37A

01 class 2-8-0 8F

63725	38B

04 class 2-8-0 7F

63726	36D
63727	36D
63728	36C
63729	38A
63730	36B
63731	36D
63732	40E
63733	39B
63734	39B
63735	38D
63736	36E
63737	39B
63738	40B
63739	39A

01 class 2-8-0 8F

63740	38B

04 class 2-8-0 7F

63741	36C
63742	39B
63743	39A
63744	36C
63745	38A

01 class 2-8-0 8F

63746	38B

04 class 2-8-0 7F

63747	36C
63748	39B
63749	38D
63750	40E
63751	38A

01 class 2-8-0 8F

63752	38B

04 class 2-8-0 7F

63753	36A
63754	38A

The Raven 'T3' class three-cylinder 0-8-0s, later designated 'Q7' by the LNER, were all built at Darlington and totalled only 15. The first five were built at the end of 1919, and the remaining 10 in 1924. All were allocated to Tyne Dock when the complete class was withdrawn at the end of 1962, with No 63460 saved for preservation. This is No 63465, the first of the 1924 batch, at Darlington shed in 1955 showing the Westinghouse pump for operating the doors of the special iron ore wagons on the Tyne Dock to Consett workings.

G. W. Sharpe

The Robinson '04' class 2-8-0s built for the Great Central Railway were somewhat unique in that the class was subdivided into seven parts by various rebuilds, with an eighth becoming a new class, the '01'. This is '04/1' No 63625 making a rare sight on the Calder Valley line near Sowerby Bridge on a coal working on Saturday 12 May 1956, when allocated to Barnsley. Built in June 1912, this was one that escaped rebuilding and retained its smaller Belpaire boiler. It was withdrawn on 16 April 1959, still allocated to Barnsley.

G. W. Sharpe

'04/7' 2-8-0 No 63634 is seen at Peterborough New England shed in March 1955. First built in September 1912, it was rebuilt in January 1940 with a shortened '02'-type boiler and retaining the GC smokebox. It was withdrawn from Immingham on 23 September 1962.

G. W. Sharpe

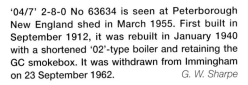

01 class 2-8-0 8F
63755 54B

04 class 2-8-0 7F
63756 38A
63757 36B
63758 40E
63759 40E

01 class 2-8-0 8F
63760 54B

04 class 2-8-0 7F
63761 36C
63762 38D
63763 36D
63764 36A
63765 40E
63766 39A
63767 39A

01 class 2-8-0 8F
63768 38B

04 class 2-8-0 7F
63769 36A
63770 40B
63771 39B
63772 38D

01 class 2-8-0 8F
63773 38B

04 class 2-8-0 7F
63774 36B
63775 36B
63776 40E

01 class 2-8-0 8F
63777 38B

04 class 2-8-0 7F
63779 36B

01 class 2-8-0 8F
63780 38B

04 class 2-8-0 7F
63781 38A
63782 36E
63783 39B

01 class 2-8-0 8F
63784 38B

04 class 2-8-0 7F
63785 36E

01 class 2-8-0 8F
63786 38B

04 class 2-8-0 7F
63787 38D
63788 36C

01 class 2-8-0 8F
63789 38B

04 class 2-8-0 7F
63790 39B
63791 36B

01 class 2-8-0 8F
63792 38B

04 class 2-8-0 7F
63793 36C
63794 39A

01 class 2-8-0 8F
63795 38B
63796 38B

04 class 2-8-0 7F
63797 39B
63798 38A
63799 36C
63800 40E
63801 38D
63802 40B

01 class 2-8-0 8F
63803 38B

04 class 2-8-0 7F
63804 38D
63805 39A

01 class 2-8-0 8F
63806 38B

04 class 2-8-0 7F
63807 36C

01 class 2-8-0 8F
63808 38B

04 class 2-8-0 7F
63812 38A
63813 36B
63816 38A

01 class 2-8-0 8F
63817 38B

04 class 2-8-0 7F
63818 36C
63819 40B
63821 39B
63822 39B
63823 37A
63824 36D
63827 38D
63828 36B
63829 38A
63832 38A
63833 40E
63835 38A
63836 40B
63837 40E

01 class 2-8-0 8F
63838 38B

04 class 2-8-0 7F
63839 38A
63840 40E
63841 38A
63842 40E
63843 36B
63845 38A
63846 39B
63847 38D
63848 39A
63850 39B
63851 38A
63852 39B
63853 36C

01 class 2-8-0 8F
63854 38B

04 class 2-8-0 7F
63855 36A

01 class 2-8-0 8F
63856 54B

04 class 2-8-0 7F
63857 37A
63858 36A
63859 38A
63860 39B
63861 40E
63862 39A

01 class 2-8-0 8F
63863 38B

04 class 2-8-0 7F
63864 37A

01 class 2-8-0 8F
63865 38B
63867 38B
63868 38B
63869 38B

04 class 2-8-0 7F
63870 40E

01 class 2-8-0 8F
63872 38B

04 class 2-8-0 7F
63873 38A

01 class 2-8-0 8F
63874 54B

04 class 2-8-0 7F
63876 38A
63877 38A
63878 40B

01 class 2-8-0 8F
63879 38B

04 class 2-8-0 7F
63880 36C
63881 39B
63882 39B
63883 36D
63884 38D
63885 37A

01 class 2-8-0 8F
63886 38B
63887 38B

04 class 2-8-0 7F
63888 39B
63889 39B

01 class 2-8-0 8F
63890 38B

04 class 2-8-0 7F
63891 38A
63893 40E
63894 38A
63895 39A
63897 36B
63898 36B
63899 38D
63900 40B

01 class 2-8-0 8F
63901 38B

04 class 2-8-0 7F
63902 40E
63904 36D
63905 36E
63906 36C
63907 36D
63908 38A
63911 36C
63912 39B
63913 36D
63914 36E
63915 40E
63917 36C
63920 37C

02 class 2-8-0 8F
63922 36A
63923 35B
63924 36E
63925 36E
63926 36E
63927 36E
63928 36A
63929 35B
63930 35B
63931 35B
63932 35B
63933 35B
63934 36A
63935 36A
63936 35B
63937 36E
63938 35B
63939 36A
63940 35B
63941 36A
63942 36A
63943 36A
63944 36A
63945 36E
63946 35B
63947 36A
63948 35B
63949 36E
63950 35B
63951 36A
63952 36A
63953 36A
63954 36A
63955 36A
63956 36A
63957 36A
63958 36A
63959 36A
63960 35B
63961 36E
63962 36A
63963 36A
63964 36A
63965 36E
63966 35B
63967 36A
63968 36A
63969 36A
63970 36E
63971 36A
63972 36E
63973 36A
63974 36A
63975 36A
63976 36E
63977 36A
63978 36A
63979 36E
63980 36E
63981 36A
63982 36E
63983 36A
63984 36A
63985 36A
63986 36E
63987 36E

J6 class 0-6-0 2P3F
64170 37C
64171 35A
64172 35A
64173 37B
64174 37A
64175 34D
64176 35A
64177 35A
64178 35B
64179 36A
64180 40F

'01' class 2-8-0 No 63773 trundles into Sheffield from the north with a train of mineral wagons in 1955. Built in August 1912, in April 1946 it was rebuilt by Thompson with a 100A boiler, Walschaerts valve gear and new cylinders. It was withdrawn on 18 October 1964 from Staveley Great Central shed. *G. W. Sharpe*

'04/6' class 2-8-0 No 63917 is seen at Grantham shed in August 1956, when allocated to Frodingham. Built in December 1920 as a Class 05, rebuilding was carried out in June 1935 and the engine retained the higher cab with side-windows. It was withdrawn on 5 June 1962, still on Frodingham's books. *G. W. Sharpe*

The Gresley design of 2-8-0, the '02', is represented by No 63981 resident at its home shed Doncaster in June 1955. Built in December 1942, it was withdrawn from Retford shed on 3 November 1963 after transfer there the previous month and was one of the last five to survive, all of which were at Retford. *R. H. G. Simpson*

64181	35A	64246	35A	64309	36A	64377	36B	64442	36D
64182	37A	64247	40F	64310	40E	64378	39A	64443	39B
64183	38A	64248	40F	64311	39A	64379	40E	64444	38D
64184	35A	64249	38A	64312	40B	64380	36E	64445	39B
64185	36A	64250	40F	64313	38D	64381	40A	64446	40B
64186	34D	64251	34D	64314	40B	64382	39A	64447	39B
64187	35B	64252	36E	64315	40A	64383	38D	64448	36D
64188	36E	64253	34B	64316	39A	64384	36E	64449	36B
64189	35A	64254	35A	64317	38D	64385	38D	64450	39A
64190	40F	64255	36A	64318	38B	64386	39B	64451	36E
64191	35A	64256	34B	64319	36C	64387	38E	64452	36D
64192	35A	64257	38A	64320	40C	64388	40E	64453	38A
64193	36A	64258	36A	64321	36E	64389	38A	**J35 class 0-6-0 3F**	
64194	38A	64259	35A	64322	39A	64390	36D	64460	65E
64195	36A	64260	40F	64323	40B	64391	40D	64461	65C
64196	34B	64261	36A	64324	38E	64392	36E	64462	64A
64197	34D	64262	37A	64325	40B	64393	39B	64463	64G
64198	35A	64263	36A	64326	39A	64394	36C	64464	62A
64199	38A	64264	36A	64327	38E	64395	38D	64466	62A
64200	38A	64265	35A	64328	40C	64396	38A	64468	64F
64201	40F	64266	34B	64329	39B	64397	36D	64470	65E
64202	38A	64267	37A	64330	38E	64398	36D	64471	66A
64203	37C	64268	37C	64331	38E	64399	36B	64472	65E
64204	40F	64269	38A	64332	39A	64400	39A	64473	65E
64205	37C	64270	36A	64333	39A	64401	36E	64474	62A
64206	34D	64271	37A	64334	36A	64402	36E	64475	62C
64207	35A	64272	35A	64336	38D	64403	36A	64476	62C
64208	37A	64273	38A	64337	40E	64404	38B	64477	62A
64209	36A	64274	37A	64338	38A	64405	36C	64478	68E
64210	35A	64275	35A	64340	36E	64406	40E	64479	64A
64211	35A	64276	37B	64341	36E	64407	39A	64480	62C
64212	38A	64277	37B	64342	39A	64408	36E	64482	61A
64213	38A	64278	35A	64343	36D	64409	36A	64483	61B
64214	40F	64279	35A	64344	40D	64410	36A	64484	64F
64215	38A			64345	38D	64411	40A	64485	61B
64216	35A	**J11 class 0-6-0 2P3F**		64346	39A	64412	40A	64486	64A
64217	35A	64280	36E	64347	36E	64413	36B	64487	62C
64218	38A	64281	40E	64348	36A	64414	40D	64488	62A
64219	35A	64282	36E	64349	36A	64415	38B	64489	64A
64220	35A	64283	36B	64350	40A	64416	36B	64490	64E
64221	34B	64284	40B	64351	40A	64417	39A	64491	64F
64222	34B	64285	36A	64352	36B	64418	36E	64492	64A
64223	34B	64286	39B	64353	40D	64419	36A	64493	62C
64224	35A	64287	36E	64354	38B	64420	36A	64494	64G
64225	38A	64288	38A	64355	40B	64421	40A	64495	64C
64226	37C	64289	40E	64356	36B	64422	36E	64496	62C
64227	35B	64290	36D	64357	39A	64423	36E	64497	63B
64228	35A	64291	39B	64358	40E	64424	40D	64498	65E
64229	40F	64292	38B	64359	40A	64425	36D	64499	68E
64230	38A	64293	40E	64360	39B	64426	39A	64500	64C
64231	35A	64294	39A	64361	38B	64427	40E	64501	63B
64232	36A	64295	36E	64362	36D	64428	38E	64502	64E
64233	34B	64296	36A	64363	39A	64429	36C	64504	64F
64234	36E	64297	40E	64364	38E	64430	40A	64505	62C
64235	38A	64298	39A	64365	40A	64431	38B	64506	64A
64236	36A	64299	40D	64366	36D	64432	36B	64507	65E
64237	34D	64300	38B	64368	39A	64433	38D	64509	64G
64238	38A	64301	38A	64369	38A	64434	39A	64510	64F
64239	34B	64302	36D	64370	38B	64435	39A	64511	68E
64240	34D	64303	40A	64371	40A	64436	36D	64512	64F
64241	36E	64304	39A	64372	40B	64437	39A	64513	62C
64242	34B	64305	40B	64373	39B	64438	38C	64514	65C
64243	36A	64306	39A	64374	36B	64439	40B	64515	64A
64244	40F	64307	40B	64375	38C	64440	39A	64516	62A
64245	36E	64308	36C	64376	36A	64441	39B		

Above: 'J6' class 0-6-0 No 64173 is seen at its home shed Leeds Copley Hill in May 1955. This was a Gresley design dating from 1911 and the last three were withdrawn in June 1962. No 64173 lasted until 11 January 1961 and was last operated by Ardsley shed after it transferred there from Leeds in November 1960.

G. W. Sharpe

Below: 'J11' class 0-6-0 No 64419 at Sheffield Midland station in June 1954 is seen on a passenger working. This was a Robinson design for the Great Central and was introduced in 1901. No 64419 was a Sheffield Darnall engine throughout its BR period and was withdrawn on 10 August 1962.

G. W. Sharpe

Above: Carlisle Canal shed in July 1956 sees 'J35' class 0-6-0 No 64526. Introduced in 1908 for the North British Railway, this was a Reid design with the last examples withdrawn in December 1962. No 64526 was another engine that was never transferred under BR and was allocated to Canal. It was withdrawn on 22 March 1958 and cut up at Inverurie Works

G. W. Sharpe

Below: Another NBR Reid design, the 'J37' class 0-6-0, No 64540 stands at Thornton Junction shed in June 1955. This was a superheated development of the 'J35' with a higher tractive effort. No 64540 was another 'non-mover' from January 1948, allocated to Glasgow Eastfield until withdrawal on 29 December 1962. It was then stored at Glasgow Parkhead shed for a further year before scrapping at Arnott Young's yard at Old Kilpatrick.

R. H. G. Simpson

64517	64C	64580	65A	64643	31B	64704	52A	64769	30A
64518	64A	64581	65A	64644	32A	64705	52C	64770	30F
64519	64A	64582	64A	64645	30E	64706	50D	64771	30A
64520	65D	64583	64F	64646	31D	64707	54C	64772	30A
64521	62A	64584	65C	64647	30E	64708	30A	64773	30F
64522	62A	64585	63B	64648	31B	64709	53A	64774	30A
64523	64A	64586	64A	64649	30E	64710	54C	64775	30A
64524	64A	64587	62B	64650	30E	64711	52D	64776	30A
64525	62C	64588	64E	64651	30E	64712	40D	64777	30F
64526	68E	64589	64E	64652	30E	64713	54C	64778	51F
64527	64C	64590	64A	64653	30E	64714	40A	64779	30A
64528	64E	64591	64C	64654	31A	64715	40A	64780	30A
64529	64F	64592	64E	64655	31B	64716	38A	64781	30A
64530	62B	64593	64E	64656	30A	64717	39A	64782	30A
64531	65E	64594	64A	64657	30A	64718	39A	64783	30A
64532	64A	64595	64A	64658	31A	64719	35C	64784	30A
64533	64A	64596	62A	64659	30E	64720	37A	64785	32B
64534	65E	64597	64A	64660	30E	64721	36A	64786	62B
64535	64A	64598	62B	64661	31B	64722	40A	64787	30F
		64599	64A	64662	30A	64723	35C	64788	30F
J37 class 0-6-0 5F		64600	62A	64663	30A	64724	32A	64789	35C
64536	64C	64601	64A	64664	30A	64725	50C	64790	62B
64537	64E	64602	62A	64665	30A	64726	32B	64791	50B
64538	64A	64603	64A	64666	30E	64727	68E	64792	62B
64539	64G	64604	62C	64667	30E	64728	40A	64793	32B
64540	65A	64605	64A	64668	31B	64729	40D	64794	64A
64541	65A	64606	64A	64669	31B	64730	50C	64795	61B
64542	63B	64607	64A	64670	30A	64731	32A	64796	37A
64543	64A	64608	64A	64671	31B	64732	37A	64797	32A
64544	63B	64609	65C	64672	31B	64733	68E	64798	38A
64545	62C	64610	65H	64673	31A	64734	40A	64799	40D
64546	62A	64611	65A	64674	32A	64735	40D	64800	32B
64547	64A	64612	62A			64736	40A	64801	37A
64548	65E	64613	64A	**J20 class 0-6-0 5F**		64737	36A	64802	32A
64549	62A	64614	64A	64675	30A	64738	39B	64803	30A
64550	62A	64615	62B	64676	30A	64739	38A	64804	40A
64551	64E	64616	62A	64677	30A	64740	39A	64805	40D
64552	64A	64617	62C	64678	31B	64741	40A	64806	37A
64553	64F	64618	62A	64679	31B	64742	39A	64807	40D
64554	62C	64619	62B	64680	30A	64743	39A	64808	39B
64555	64A	64620	62B	64681	30A	64744	39B	64809	39B
64556	62C	64621	65C	64682	30A	64745	39A	64810	30A
64557	64A	64622	65A	64683	31A	64746	39B	64811	37A
64558	65A	64623	65A	64684	31B	64747	38A	64812	52C
64559	65C	64624	64A	64685	30A	64748	39A	64813	52D
64560	62C	64625	64A	64686	30A	64749	37A	64814	52C
64561	62C	64626	65C	64687	31B	64750	40D	64815	52D
64562	64A	64627	62B	64688	31A	64751	40D	64816	52C
64563	65C	64628	65A	64689	31A	64752	32B	64817	51J
64564	62A	64629	62A	64690	31B	64753	39B	64818	50D
64565	62A	64630	62C	64691	31B	64754	37A	64819	53A
64566	64A	64631	62B	64692	31B	64755	40A	64820	37A
64567	62C	64632	65A	64693	31A	64756	51D	64821	50D
64568	62C	64633	65A	64694	31A	64757	37A	64822	62B
64569	63B	64634	62B	64695	31B	64758	50B	64823	38A
64570	64E	64635	62A	64696	31A	64759	36E	64824	39B
64571	64E	64636	64E	64697	31B	64760	37A	64825	37A
64572	64A	64637	64A	64698	31B	64761	32A	64826	32B
64573	65C	64638	65A	64699	31B	64762	38A	64827	38A
64574	62C	64639	65A			64763	40D	64828	40D
64575	62B			**J39 class 0-6-0 4P5F**		64764	30A	64829	32B
64576	64A	**J19 class 0-6-0 3P5F**		64700	54C	64765	30A	64830	36E
64577	64A	64640	31B	64701	52A	64766	30A	64831	37A
64578	65A	64641	31B	64702	40A	64767	30A	64832	38A
64579	65E	64642	31B	64703	52B	64768	30A	64833	37A

161

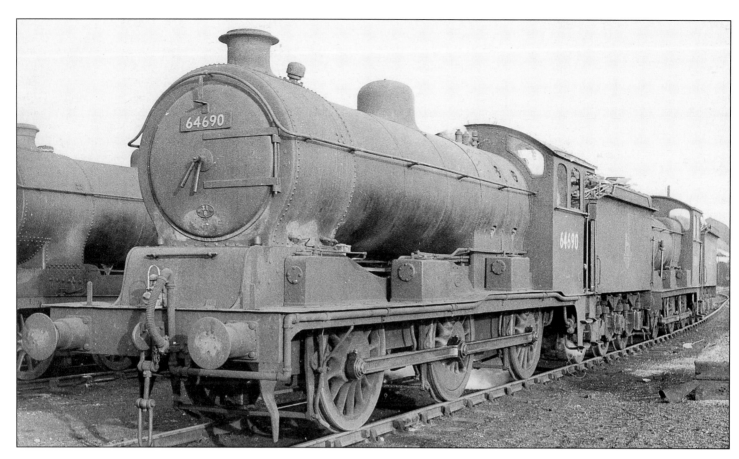

Above: Class J20 0-6-0 No 64690 is seen at March shed in April 1955. Introduced in 1920 to a design by A.J. Hill, a rebuild with a 'B12/1'-type round-topped boiler was actioned in 1943. Withdrawal came on 16 September 1962 after being on March's allocation since January 1954.   *R. H. G. Simpson*

Below: Class J39 0-6-0 No 64818, allocated to Starbeck, disturbs the peace of the cutting at Wormald Green on a goods train on Saturday 20 February 1954. Designed by Gresley and built at Darlington, No 64818 entered traffic on 30 January 1930 as LNER 1489. Withdrawal came on 3 December 1962 from Ardsley shed.

G. W. Sharpe

64834	32B	64899	68E	64964	68E	65162	10A	65251	64A
64835	50B	64900	32G	64965	35C	65165	9G	65252	62A
64836	37A	64901	35C	64966	37A	65166	8E	65253*	62C
64837	37A	64902	35C	64967	36A	65167	9E	65257	64E
64838	40D	64903	37C	64968	32A	65169	9G	65258	64A
64839	37A	64904	50C	64969	37A	65170	9E	65259	64G
64840	37A	64905	32B	64970	36E	65171	9E	65260	65E
64841	32B	64906	36E	64971	53A	65173	10A	65261	64F
64842	52C	64907	37C	64972	37A	65175	10A	65265	64F
64843	52D	64908	36E	64973	30A	65176	10A	65266	65E
64844	52D	64909	36A	64974	38A	65177	27E	65267	64A
64845	50D	64910	51J	64975	61B	65178	9F	65268*	64F
64846	54C	64911	37B	64976	40D	65180	27E	65270	65A
64847	50D	64912	68E	64977	40A	65181	9E	65273	65A
64848	51D	64913	32A	64978	51J	65182	8E	65275	64E
64849	52C	64914	53A	64979	37A	65184	9E	65276	64F
64850	50C	64915	52B	64980	38A	65185	8E	65277	64F
64851	54C	64916	52B	64981	35C	65186	9E	65280	64F
64852	52A	64917	52D	64982	51F	65187	9E	65281	62C
64853	52B	64918	37A	64983	38A	65191	9E	65282	64F
64854	54C	64919	54A	64984	40A	65192	27E	65285	65E
64855	50D	64920	50B	64985	30A	65194	9F	65287	65E
64856	52B	64921	54C	64986	64A	65196	8E	65288	64A
64857	50D	64922	50C	64987	36A	65197	9E	65290	64E
64858	52C	64923	52B	64988	38A	65198	8D	65293	68E
64859	50D	64924	52D			65199	10A	65295	65C
64860	50B	64925	52D	**J21 class 0-6-0 2F**		65200	9F	65296	65A
64861	50D	64926	54C	65033	52F	65202	9G	65297	61B
64862	51C	64927	54C	65035	52B	65203	10A	65300	63D
64863	50B	64928	50F	65039	52B	65205	9E	65303	64F
64864	53A	64929	52A	65061	51A	65208	6D	65304	68E
64865	52A	64930	68E	65064	51J	65209	9E	65305	64A
64866	50D	64931	54C	65070	51A			65306	64E
64867	50F	64932	68E	65078	51A	**J36 class 0-6-0 2F**		65307	62C
64868	52D	64933	50B	65082	52D	65210	65E	65309	62B
64869	52A	64934	50B	65088	52C	65211	64F	65310	64A
64870	52C	64935	50B	65090	52C	65213	61A	65311	64A
64871	52A	64936	54C	65091	52D	65214	65E	65312	68E
64872	37A	64937	40A	65099	52F	65216*	68E	65313	63D
64873	30F	64938	50F	65103	52C	65217*	65E	65314	64F
64874	30F	64939	54A	65110	52B	65218	62A	65315	65A
64875	68E	64940	51F	65117	51A	65221	65A	65316	64G
64876	30A	64941	52D			65222*	64E	65317	64G
64877	68E	64942	50D	**J10 class 0-6-0 2F**		65224*	64A	65318	64F
64878	39B	64943	50B	65131	9G	65225	64F	65319	62B
64879	37A	64944	50D	65132	9F	65227	65I	65320	62C
64880	68E	64945	52B	65133	27E	65228	65A	65321	68E
64881	40A	64946	64A	65134	9G	65229	64F	65323	62C
64882	32A	64947	50F	65135	9F	65230	64F	65324	65C
64883	35C	64948	68E	65138	8D	65232	64G	65325	65E
64884	68E	64949	53A	65139	9G	65233*	64E	65327	64A
64885	36A	64950	62B	65140	6D	65234	64F	65329	64A
64886	50B	64951	35C	65142	8E	65235*	64B	65330	62B
64887	40A	64952	36A	65143	6D	65236*	65E	65331	64G
64888	68E	64953	30F	65144	9E	65237	63D	65333	62B
64889	32A	64954	35C	65145	8E	65239	62C	65334	64A
64890	30A	64955	38A	65146	9E	65241	64E	65335	65H
64891	35C	64956	36A	65147	8E	65242	64A	65338	64E
64892	68E	64957	32B	65148	10A	65243*	64B	65339	65A
64893	36E	64958	30A	65153	9E	65244	64E	65341	64F
64894	32B	64959	40A	65156	9E	65246	64E	65342	64F
64895	68E	64960	40A	65157	9E	65247	61A	65343	65E
64896	35C	64961	36E	65158	9G	65248	64F	65344	64F
64897	52D	64962	39B	65159	10A	65249	65E	65345	62A
64898	36E	64963	64A	65160	9F	65250	64F	65346	64F

Above: The 'J21' class 0-6-0 was a design by Worsdell for the North Eastern Railway, with 201 engines being built between 1886 and 1894. This is Darlington-allocated No 65061 which was withdrawn on 12 May 1958 from Tweedmouth shed. The photograph was taken on Sunday 4 September 1955 and the 'J21' is paired with Ivatt 2-6-0 No 46478 at Kirkby Stephen working the SLS Northern Dales Railtour. Run jointly with the Manchester Locomotive Society, the eight-coach train left Manchester Victoria at 9.23am with LMS 4-4-0 No 41102 in charge running through to Tebay via Hellifield and the Ingleton line. At Tebay Nos 65061 and 46478 took over and the tour participants visited the shed at Kirkby Stephen which contained Nos 43038, 43055, 43122, 43124, 43128, 43130, 46470, 46472, 78017, 78019, 82026 and 82027. Then followed a run over Stainmore Summit to Darlington where a visit to the works had been arranged. 'A8' 4-6-2T No 69855 took over for the run to Northallerton where 'D20' 4-4-0 No 62360 came on and both engines worked through to Hawes where No 41102 was waiting for the run to Garsdale and back to Manchester. The cost of the trip was 30s 6d (£1.52p). *G. W. Sharpe*

Below: Wigan North Western station on Saturday 19 March 1955 sees Springs Branch-allocated 'J10' 0-6-0 No 65159. This was T. Parker's design for the Manchester, Sheffield & Lincolnshire Railway, 124 engines being built between 1892 and 1902. No 65159 was withdrawn from Wigan on 21 December 1957, the last class members lasting until August 1961. *G. W. Sharpe*

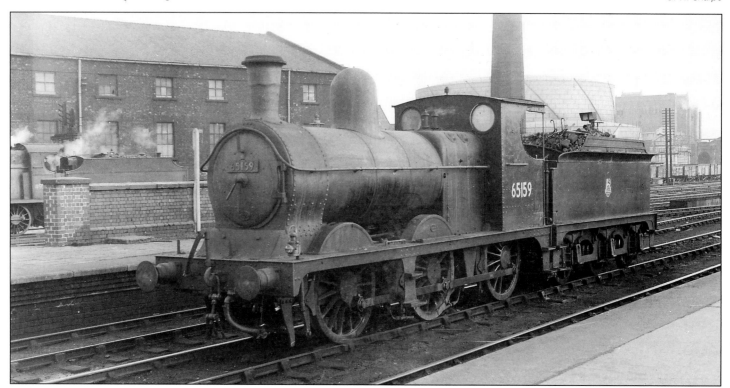

No.	Shed
65849	50A
65850	54A
65851	52F
65852	52E
65853	51G
65854	54A
65855	51G
65856	54A
65857	50A
65858	52E
65859	51G
65860	51B
65861	50C
65862	52F
65863	52F
65864	52F
65865	51C
65866	51C
65867	52F
65868	51E
65869	52B
65870	52F
65871	54A
65872	54A
65873	52B
65874	50A
65875	50C
65876	52F
65877	52F
65878	54A
65879	52F
65880	52F
65881	50C
65882	52B
65883	50A
65884	51D
65885	50C
65886	52F
65887	50A
65888	50C
65889	52F
65890	50A
65891	50C
65892	52B
65893	52B
65894	50A

J38 class 0-6-0 6F

No.	Shed
65900	62C
65901	62A
65902	62A
65903	62A
65904	62A
65905	62C
65906	64A
65907	62A
65908	62A
65909	64E
65910	62A
65911	62A
65912	64A
65913	62A
65914	64A
65915	64A
65916	64A
65917	64E
65918	64A
65919	64A
65920	64A
65921	62A
65922	64A
65923	62C
65924	62C
65925	62A
65926	62C
65927	64A
65928	62C
65929	64A
65930	62C
65931	62A
65932	62A
65933	62C
65934	64A

F4 class 2-4-2T 1MT

No.	Shed
67157	61A
67162	32E
67187	32C

F5 class 2-4-2T 1MT

No.	Shed
67188	30A
67189	30E
67190	32C
67191	30E
67192	30A
67193	30A
67194	30A
67195	32C
67196	30E
67197	30A
67198	30A
67199	32D
67200	30A
67201	32C
67202	30A
67203	30A
67204	32C
67205	30A
67206	32C
67207	32C
67208	30A
67209	30A
67210	30A
67211	30A
67212	30A
67213	30A
67214	32C
67215	30A
67216	32C
67217	30E
67218	32D
67219	30A

F6 class 2-4-2T 1MT

No.	Shed
67220	32B
67221	31A
67222	31E
67223	32C
67224	32G
67225	32G
67226	32C
67227	31A
67228	32G
67229	32C
67230	32B
67231	32C
67232	32C
67233	32C
67234	32C
67235	32D
67236	31E
67237	31E
67238	31A
67239	32B

G5 class 0-4-4T 1MT

No.	Shed
67240	50G
67241	52C
67243	54A
67246	52F
67248	52C
67249	52C
67250	50C
67251	54A
67253	53B
67254	53B
67256	53B
67258	54A
67259	52C
67261	53B
67262	50B
67263	54A
67265	52A
67266	50B
67268	52D
67269	31A
67270	52C
67271	51E
67273	53B
67274	50B
67277	52F
67278	51J
67279	31A
67280	53B
67281	51E
67282	53B
67284	51A
67286	50C
67289	50F
67290	50B
67293	50F
67294	54A
67296	52F
67297	54A
67298	54A
67300	54A
67301	53B
67302	50G
67304	52C
67305	51A
67307	54A
67308	50F
67309	52C
67310	54A
67311	53B
67312	51A
67314	51C
67315	54A
67316	52C
67318	51A
67319	50B
67320	52A
67321	53B
67322	31A
67323	52F
67324	51C
67325	52C
67326	52F
67327	61A
67328	54A
67329	52C
67332	50F
67333	51C
67334	52F
67336	54A
67337	53B
67338	51C
67339	52F
67340	52F
67341	51J
67342	51C
67343	54A
67344	54A
67345	51E
67346	52F
67347	52F

C12 class 4-4-2T 1MT

No.	Shed
67350	35A
67352	53B
67353	53B
67357	35A
67360	31C
67361	35A
67362	35B
67363	38B
67364	40C
67365	35A
67366	35C
67367	31C
67368	35C
67371	53B
67374	31C
67375	31E
67376	35A
67379	40C
67380	35C
67382	35B
67383	40C
67384	40C
67385	31E
67386	31C
67387	32D
67389	35A
67391	53B
67392	
67394	53B
67395	53B
67397	
67398	40C

C13 class 4-4-2T 2P1F

No.	Shed
67400	6D
67401	39A
67403	39A
67405	39A
67407	39A
67409	36D
67411	36D
67413	6D
67414	6E
67415	39A
67416	34E
67417	39A
67418	34E
67419	38D
67420	34E
67421	39A
67423	39A
67424	39B
67425	39A
67427	40E
67428	6E
67430	6E
67431	39A
67433	6D
67434	36D
67436	6D
67437	40E
67438	37B
67439	39B

C14 class 4-4-2T 2P1F

No.	Shed
67440	39A
67441	39A
67442	6E
67443	37A
67444	39A
67445	39A
67446	37A
67447	39A
67448	39A
67449	6E
67450	39A
67451	39A

C15 class 4-4-2T 2P

No.	Shed
67452	62A
67455	61A
67457	64G
67458	68E
67459	64E
67460	65A
67463	64E
67466	62C
67467	65E
67472	64G
67474	65A
67478	61C
67480	65A
67481	68E

C16 class 4-4-2T 2P

No.	Shed
67482	65C
67483	62B
67484	62B

Above: Class J27 0-6-0 No 65885 passes Beningbrough on a van train in May 1954 when allocated to York. This was a development of the 'J26' class with superheaters and piston valves. No 65885 moved to Selby in June 1954 and Malton in August 1959, then back to York in September 1960. A year later Sunderland was its home until withdrawal on 7 June 1967.

G. W. Sharpe

Below: Gresley's design of powerful freight engines, the 'J38' class 0-6-0s, first appeared in January 1926 with all 35 being built at Darlington. The last to come into traffic on 28 May 1926 was No 65934, seen here at Thornton Junction shed in June 1954 when allocated to Dunfermline. Subsequent moves were to St Margarets on 10 November 1954, Thornton Junction on 29 December 1962, and back to Dunfermline on 7 January 1963, to be taken out of traffic on 31 December 1966.

G. W. Sharpe

Above: 'F6' class 2-4-2T No 67228 is seen at Stratford shed in June 1956. This was an S. D. Holden design and a development of the earlier 'F4' class designed by Wilson Worsdell. This example was built at Stratford in June 1911 and was withdrawn on 21 April 1958, still allocated to 30A. *P. H. Groom*

Below: Worsdell-designed 'G5' class 0-4-4T No 67286 is seen fitted for push-pull operation at its home shed Selby in July 1956. The type was introduced between 1894 and 1901 and No 67286 remained in service at Selby until withdrawal on 8 October 1956. *P. H. Groom*

'C12' class 4-4-2T No 67382 is seen at Grantham shed on Sunday 3 April 1955. An Ivatt design for the Great Northern, originally 60 engines were built between 1898 and 1907. No 67382 had a 'paper only' transfer to Hull Botanic Gardens at the beginning of April from Grantham, but was withdrawn immediately on the 6th, and is unlikely to have got there, which is perhaps confirmed by the date of this photograph.

InitialPhotographics/B. K. B. Green

Robinson's '9K' class 4-4-2T for the Great Central, classified 'C13' under the LNER, No 67420 is seen at Chesham on Saturday 8 May 1954, fitted with push-pull equipment. It was about to depart for Chalfont & Latimer with the train formed of ex-Metropolitan Railway electric stock converted for push-pull working. No 67420 was built at Gorton Works in August 1904, and was superheated in May 1930. Withdrawal came on 13 December 1958 from Neasden. *G. W. Sharpe*

Another Robinson GC design was the '9L' class 4-4-2T, later known as the 'C14'. Only 12 were built, and this is No 67450 at Gorton shed in June 1955. Built by Beyer Peacock in June 1907, it had a superheater added in January 1931. Withdrawn from Gorton on 23 January 1960, it was the last of the class to remain in the active list. *G. W. Sharpe*

67485	65A
67486	62B
67487	65C
67488	65A
67489	62B
67490	62B
67491	62B
67492	64A
67493	62B
67494	64E
67495	64A
67496	61B
67497	64A
67498	62B
67499	62B
67500	65C
67501	61B
67502	62B

V1 class 2-6-2T 3MT

67600	65A
67601	65I
67602	65I
67603	65A

V3 class 2-6-2T 4MT

67604	65H
67605	64A
67606	64A

V1 class 2-6-2T 3MT

67607	64A
67608	64A

V3 class 2-6-2T 4MT

67609	64A

V1 class 2-6-2T 3MT

67610	64B

V3 class 2-6-2T 4MT

67611	65C
67612	65C

V1 class 2-6-2T 3MT

67613	65H
67614	65H

V3 class 2-6-2T 4MT

67615	64B

V1 class 2-6-2T 3MT

67616	65C
67617	64A
67618	65E
67619	65H

V3 class 2-6-2T 4MT

67620	64B

V1 class 2-6-2T 3MT

67621	65C
67622	65H
67623	65C

V3 class 2-6-2T 4MT

67624	64A
67625	65H
67626	65C
67627	65E

V1 class 2-6-2T 3MT

67628	65H
67629	64A
67630	64A
67631	65C
67632	65C
67633	65H

V3 class 2-6-2T 4MT

67634	52A

V1 class 2-6-2T 3MT

67635	52B

V3 class 2-6-2T 4MT

67636	52C

V1 class 2-6-2T 3MT

67637	52B
67638	51D
67639	52C
67640	52B
67641	52B
67642	52B
67643	65C
67644	65A
67645	52B
67646	52B
67647	52B
67648	65C
67649	64A
67650	63B
67651	52B

V3 class 2-6-2T 4MT

67652	52B
67653	52C
67654	52B

V1 class 2-6-2T 3MT

67655	65C

V3 class 2-6-2T 4MT

67656	52C

V1 class 2-6-2T 3MT

67657	52C
67658	52C
67659	64A
67660	65E
67661	65C
67662	65C
67663	51D
67664	65A
67665	65E
67666	64A
67667	65A

V3 class 2-6-2T 4MT

67668	64A
67669	62C

V1 class 2-6-2T 3MT

67670	64A
67671	65A

V3 class 2-6-2T 4MT

67672	62C

V1 class 2-6-2T 3MT

67673	52B
67674	65E

V3 class 2-6-2T 4MT

67675	63B

V1 class 2-6-2T 3MT

67676	65C
67677	51D
67678	65C

V3 class 2-6-2T 4MT

67679	65C

V1 class 2-6-2T 3MT

67680	65A
67681	65C

V3 class 2-6-2T 4MT

67682	52A
67683	52A
67684	51D
67685	51D
67686	51D
67687	52C
67688	52A
67689	52A
67690	52A
67691	51D

L1 class 2-6-4T 4MT

67701	30A
67702	32B
67703	32B
67704	32C
67705	32B
67706	32B
67707	32A
67708	32B
67709	32B
67710	32B
67711	32B
67712	30A
67713	30A
67714	32C
67715	32B
67716	32B
67717	32C
67718	34D
67719	32B
67720	34A
67721	30A
67722	30A
67723	30A
67724	30A
67725	30A
67726	30A
67727	30A
67728	30A
67729	30A
67730	30A
67731	30A
67732	30A
67733	30A
67734	30A
67735	30A
67736	30A
67737	30A
67738	30A
67739	32A
67740	34E
67741	34D
67742	51A
67743	34D
67744	34D
67745	34D
67746	34D
67747	34E
67748	34E
67749	34E
67750	51A
67751	34A
67752	34E
67753	34E
67754	53B
67755	53B
67756	34A
67757	34A
67758	34E
67759	53B
67760	34E
67761	34E
67762	34E
67763	53B
67764	53B
67765	53B
67766	34E
67767	34E
67768	34E
67769	34E
67770	34E
67771	34E
67772	34E
67773	34E
67774	34E
67775	34A
67776	34E
67777	51A
67778	34E
67779	34A
67780	34E
67781	34A
67782	34E
67783	34E
67784	34A
67785	34D
67786	34E
67787	34E
67788	34E
67789	34E
67790	34D
67791	34D
67792	34A
67793	34A
67794	34E
67795	34A
67796	34E
67797	34A
67798	34E
67799	34A
67800	34A

J94 class 0-6-0ST 4F

68006	6F
68007	51B
68008	51A
68009	40B
68010	52C
68011	51B
68012	39A
68013	6F
68014	52B
68015	51A
68016	54A
68017	54A
68018	40B
68019	54D
68020	40B
68021	52B
68022	40B
68023	51B
68024	54A
68025	51A
68026	40B
68027	51A
68028	40B
68029	50A
68030	6F
68031	50A
68032	50A
68033	40B
68034	6F
68035	52C
68036	52C
68037	51B
68038	52C
68039	51A
68040	50A
68041	54A
68042	50A
68043	51A
68044	50A
68045	51A
68046	50A
68047	51A
68048	54A
68049	51B
68050	51A
68051	50A
68052	51A
68053	51C
68054	51C
68055	51C

Above: 'C15' class saturated 4-4-2T No 67474, with push-pull equipment fitted, is photographed here at Tarbet in June 1956 on the shuttle service between Craigendoran and Arrochar. It shared the service with sister engine No 67460. Built in August 1913 by Yorkshire Engine Co to a design by W. P. Reid for the North British Railway, it was the last in traffic when withdrawn from Glasgow Eastfield on 12 April 1960. No 67460 had been condemned on the first of the same month.

G. W. Sharpe

Below: The 'C16' 4-4-2T was a superheated version of the 'C15'. This is No 67494 at Bo'ness in May 1955 waiting to run the four miles along the branch to Manuel, which was closed to passenger traffic on Thursday 3 May 1956. Freight continued until Monday 19 July 1965. No 67494 was built by the North British Locomotive Co in April 1916 and was withdrawn from Polmont shed on 15 February 1961. It was outlived by one other member of the class, No 67485, which was withdrawn from Glasgow Eastfield seven weeks later.

G. W. Sharpe

Above: Gresley 'V1' class No 67600 was the first of the type to enter traffic, on 6 September 1930, at Glasgow Eastfield shed in May 1955. Note the 'slip-coupling' apparatus, which was a steel wire attached to the front of the engine and allowed the crew to unhook from the train they were banking out of Glasgow Queen Street station without stopping. This was a unique arrangement for Eastfield engines on these duties, and was a result of the recommendations from a previous accident report. This engine was converted to a 'V3' in November 1956 with a higher boiler pressure. Withdrawn from 65A on 29 December 1962, it was stored at Glasgow Parkhead until September 1963 when it made its last journey to Darlington Works for scrapping. *G. W. Sharpe*

Below: The Thompson 'L1' class 2-6-4T was not without its problems and was a relatively short-lived design. No 67725 entered traffic from Darlington Works at Neasden on 25 June 1948 and is seen at Liverpool Street station in September 1954. It had moved to Stratford shed on 13 February 1949 where it remained until withdrawal on 4 December 1960, being cut up at the adjacent works. *P. H. Groom*

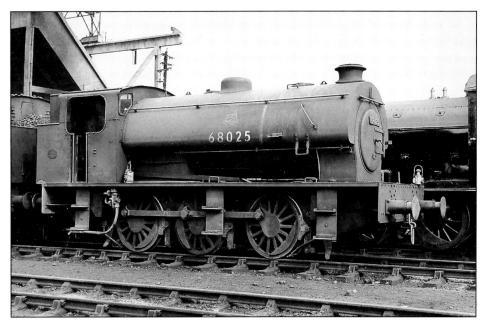

The Class J94 0-6-0ST was a product of the Ministry of Supply when a large number were produced between 1943 and 1945. The LNER purchased 75 in 1946 and all passed into British Railways hands. This is No 68025 at its home shed, Darlington, in July 1954, where it was based until withdrawal on 14 October 1963.

Real Photographs

North British Railway 'Pug' 0-4-0ST 'Y9' class No 68100 was built at Cowlairs Works in January 1896. This view is at Dundee Tay Bridge shed in July 1954. No 68100 was permanently attached to its wooden tender and is fitted with a spark arrestor over the chimney for working in the timber yards at the docks. After a long stay at Dundee it moved to Glasgow Kipps in September 1957 and was withdrawn on 5 May 1960.   *P. H. Groom*

'Y4' class 0-4-0T No 68127 was one of five engines built for the Great Eastern Railway when A. J. Hill was locomotive superintendent and it was introduced in 1913. All were allocated to Stratford; one survived in service stock until 1962, but the other four had gone by 1957. No 68127 is seen at Stratford in 1954 with 'British Railways' in tiny lettering on the tank side. It was withdrawn on 23 April 1956.   *G. W. Sharpe*

68056	51C	68149	51F	68266	54B	68349	65A	68450	64A
68057	51C	68150	50C	68267	52C	68350	64E	68451	62A
68058	54A			68269	51F	68351	62C	68452	62B
68059	52C	**Y3 Sentinel 0-4-0T**		68270	52A	68352	64A	68453	62A
68060	51B	68155	53D	68272	52A	68353	62A	68454	64A
68061	50A	68158	50C	68273	52C	68354	64E	68455	62B
68062	51B	68159	52A	68275	50A			68456	62A
68063	6F	68160	52A	68276	51C	**J73 class 0-6-0T 3F**		68457	64B
68064	39A	68162	6E	68278	52B	68355	51C	68458	62A
68065	6F	68164	6E	68279	51A	68356	50C	68459	62A
68066	6F	68169	39A	68280	50A	68357	50C	68460	64B
68067	40B	68180	50C	68283	52A	68358	51C	68461	65E
68068	40B	68182	53A	68284	53A	68359	51J	68463	64A
68069	40B	68183	53A	68287	54C	68360	53C	68464	64A
68070	40B	68185	40B	68289	54C	68361	53C	68465	62B
68071	40B			68290		68362	50C	68466	62B
68072	40B	**Z4 class 0-4-2T 0F**		68291	51C	68363	53B	68467	62A
68073	40B	68190	61A	68293	50A	68364	51C	68468	65A
68074	40B	68191	61A	68294	20D			68469	64A
68075	40B			68295	51C	**J66 class 0-6-0T 2F**		68470	62B
68076	40B	**Z5 class 0-4-2T 0F**		68296	53A	68383	38D	68471	64E
68077	40B	68192	61A	68297	50A			68472	64A
68078	40B	68193	61A	68298	53A	**J77 class 0-6-0T 2F**		68473	64B
68079	39A			68300	51A	68391	51F	68474	64A
68080	40B	**J63 class 0-6-0T**		68301	51C	68392	50D	68475	65A
		68204	40B	68303	51D	68393	50D	68476	65A
Y9 class 0-4-0ST 0F		68205	40B	68305	51E	68395	50B	68477	64A
68093	64A	68206	40B	68306	51C	68397	52F	68478	64B
68094	65E	68207	40B	68307	51D	68399	52F	68479	65A
68095	64A	68209	6E	68308	51A	68402	52D	68480	65A
68097	64A	68210	40B	68309	52A	68405	52F	68481	64B
68099	64A			68312	51D	68406	50C		
68100	62B	**J65 class 0-6-0T 1F**		68313	50A	68407	51E	**J69 class 0-6-0T 2F**	
68101	62C	68214	32F	68314	52A	68408	51A	68490	31C
68102	64A			68316	54C	68409	51D	68491	31A
68104	64E	**J70 class Tram Engine**				68410	51A		
68105	64A	68222	32B	**J88 class 0-6-0T 0F**		68412	51E	**J67 class 0-6-0T 2F**	
68106	65E	68223	32E	68320	64A	68414	51D	68492	64A
68108	62B	68225	32B	68321	62A	68417	52F		
68110	62B	68226	30E	68322	62A	68420	51E	**J69 class 0-6-0T 2F**	
68112	65G			68323	62A	68423	51A	68494	31D
68113	64E	**J71 class 0-6-0T**		68324	64E	68424	52F	68495	31C
68114	62B	68230	50A	68325	64A	68425	51D		
68115	64A	68232	53A	68326	65A	68426	52F	**J67 class 0-6-0T 2F**	
68116	65E	68233	51C	68327	65A	68427	52F	68496	35A
68117	65E	68235	51A	68328	64B	68428	52B		
68118	65G	68236	51A	68329	65E	68429	50C	**J69 class 0-6-0T 2F**	
68119	64A	68238	20D	68330	65A	68430	52F	68497	31E
68120	65E	68239	51A	68331	65E	68431	52F	68498	31C
68121	65E	68240	50A	68332	62A	68432	51A	68499	40F
68122	64A	68242	53A	68333	65D	68434	50D	68500	30F
68123	62B	68244	51C	68334	62A	68435	50A	68501	40F
68124	65A	68245	52B	68335	62A	68436	52D	68502	31C
		68246	50A	68336	65E	68437	52D	68503	65C
Y4 class 0-4-0T		68250	50A	68337	62A	68438	50C	68504	62A
68125	30A	68251	52B	68338	64A			68507	30A
68126	30A	68252	53A	68339	64B	**J83 class 0-6-0T 2F**		68508	30E
68127	30A	68253	50A	68340	64A	68442	65E	68510	30A
68128	30A	68254	51F	68342	64A	68443	65E		
		68259	51A	68343	65E	68444	65E	**J67 class 0-6-0T 2F**	
Y1 Sentinel 0-4-0T		68260	51D	68344	66B	68445	65E	68511	64A
68138	64G	68262	52B	68345	62C	68446	62B		
68142	51E	68263	52B	68346	62C	68447	65A	**J69 class 0-6-0T 2F**	
68145	51F	68264	52B	68347	65A	68448	64A	68512	40A
68148	53A	68265	54B	68348	64A	68449	64A	68513	30A

177

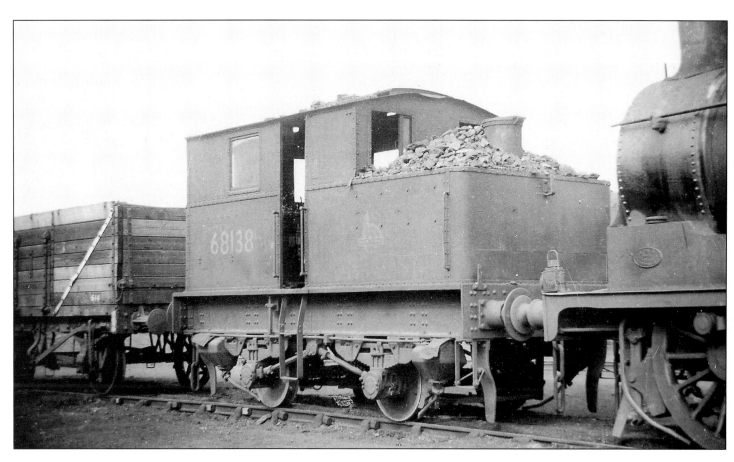

Above: Class Y1 Sentinel 0-4-0T No 68138 is seen at Ayr shed on Saturday 19 May 1956. Entering traffic in December 1927, this had a single-speed gearbox and spent many years at Kelso, a sub-shed to Hawick. Moving to Ayr on 4 August 1955 when Kelso closed, it was withdrawn on 5 January 1959. *Ken Hunt*

Below: The 'Z5' class 0-4-2T was a slightly larger version of the 'Z4' and this is No 68192 at Aberdeen Kittybrewster shed in July 1955. Built by Manning Wardle of Leeds in 1915 for dock shunting at Aberdeen, both the two 'Z4s' and two 'Z5s' were based at Kittybrewster. No 68192 was withdrawn on 28 April 1960, sister engine No 68193 having been condemned much earlier on 24 April 1956. *G. W. Sharpe*

Above: The last of its kind: 'J65' class 0-6-0T No 68214. Originally a class of 20 engines for the Great Eastern Railway, and to a design by J. Holden, all had been built at Stratford Works. This last survivor was produced in March 1893 and is seen at Stratford shed in December 1956. It had already been withdrawn on 22 October after its last journey from Yarmouth Beach.
P. H. Groom

Below: Another last survivor at Stratford awaiting breaking up is 'J70' tram engine No 68226 on Monday 1 August 1955. The last four were all withdrawn during 1955, and this was No 68226's last day on the active list as its official withdrawal was the next day. Built for the Wisbech & Upwell Tramway, it dated from 1921.
Initial Photographics/B. K. B. Green

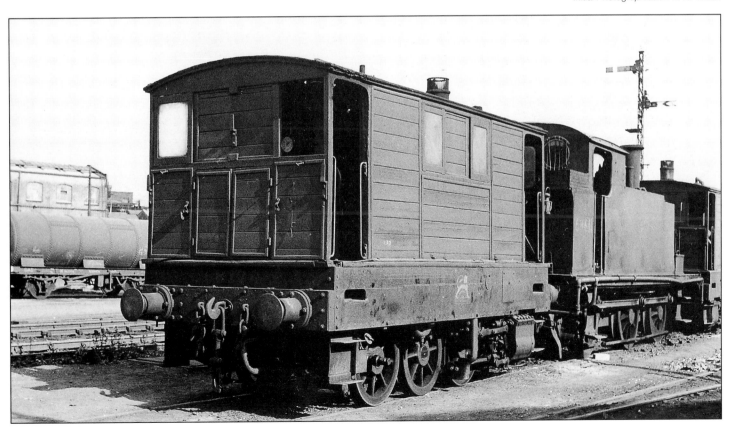

Above: 'J88' class 0-6-0T No 68321 is seen at Thornton Junction shed in August 1955. Introduced in 1904 to a design by W. P. Reid for the North British Railway, the class had a short wheelbase for shunting in yards and docks with tight curves. No 68321 was allocated to 62A for its entire BR career and bowed out to diesel shunters on 20 June 1958.
G. W. Sharpe

Below: 'J66' class 0-6-0T No 68383 is photographed at Staveley Great Central shed on Wednesday 26 May 1954. Built at Stratford Works in November 1888 and designed by J. Holden, it was one of a class of 50 engines. This was the last in capital stock, another three being departmental engines. Based at March at Nationalisation, it moved to Cambridge during the week ended 27 November 1948 and on to Staveley during the week ended 1 August 1953. Here it remained until it was withdrawn on 17 October 1955.
Initial Photographics/B. K. B. Green

Above: Heading a line-up of tank engines, which includes No 47162 and a 'Y9', is 'J83' class 0-6-0T No 68477. This is Edinburgh St Margarets shed in August 1956 on the opposite side of the line to the main shed building. The 'J83' class originally consisted of 40 engines built for the North British Railway in 1900 and 1901. No 68477 remained loyal to 64A throughout its British Railways days and was withdrawn on 29 December 1962. It then served at the shed as a stationary boiler for a further nine months.

G. W. Sharpe

Below: 'J67' class 0-6-0T No 68536, with a white-painted cab roof, is seen at Cambridge shed in May 1955 while allocated to Melton Constable. Another J. Holden type, it was built at Stratford in April 1892 and was originally classified as an 'R24'. It remained at Melton Constable until withdrawn on 21 February 1958 and returned to its birthplace for scrapping.

G. W. Sharpe

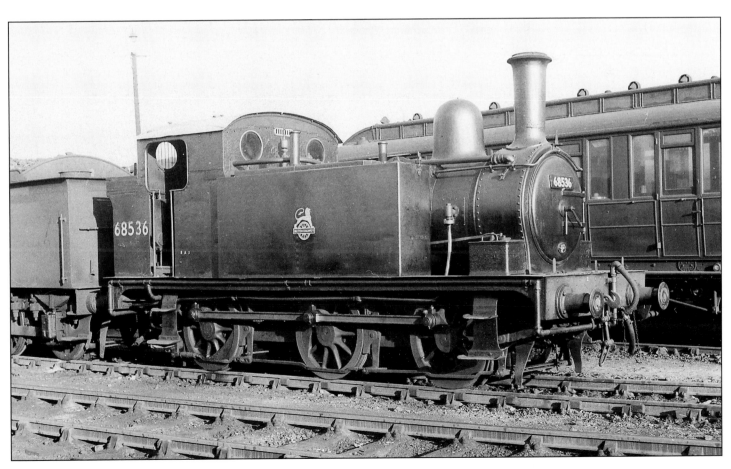

J67 class 0-6-0T 2F

Number	Shed
68514	32A
68515	32G
68516	32A
68517	30A
68518	32B

J69 class 0-6-0T 2F

Number	Shed
68519	30A
68520	36B

J67 class 0-6-0T 2F

Number	Shed
68521	32B

J69 class 0-6-0T 2F

Number	Shed
68522	30E

J67 class 0-6-0T 2F

Number	Shed
68523	32A

J69 class 0-6-0T 2F

Number	Shed
68524	64E
68526	30A
68527	30A
68528	40A
68529	30A
68530	31A

J67 class 0-6-0T 2F

Number	Shed
68531	6E

J69 class 0-6-0T 2F

Number	Shed
68532	30A
68535	62B

J67 class 0-6-0T 2F

Number	Shed
68536	32G

J69 class 0-6-0T 2F

Number	Shed
68537	40A
68538	30A

J67 class 0-6-0T 2F

Number	Shed
68540	34D

J69 class 0-6-0T 2F

Number	Shed
68541	40A
68542	31D
68543	40F
68544	64E
68545	31C
68546	30A

J67 class 0-6-0T 2F

Number	Shed
68547	8E

J69 class 0-6-0T 2F

Number	Shed
68549	30A
68550	30A
68551	62B
68552	30A
68553	40A
68554	30A
68555	31D
68556	30A
68557	40F
68558	40A
68559	6E
68560	40F
68561	30A
68562	68B
68563	30A
68565	30A
68566	31D
68567	31A
68568	30A
68569	40A
68570	40F
68571	30A
68573	30A
68574	30A
68575	30A
68576	30A
68577	30A
68578	30E
68579	30A
68581	40F

J67 class 0-6-0T 2F

Number	Shed
68583	9E
68584	6E

J69 class 0-6-0T 2F

Number	Shed
68585	27E

J67 class 0-6-0T 2F

Number	Shed
68586	32B

J69 class 0-6-0T 2F

Number	Shed
68587	40A
68588	30A

J67 class 0-6-0T 2F

Number	Shed
68589	38D
68590	30A

J69 class 0-6-0T 2F

Number	Shed
68591	30A

J67 class 0-6-0T 2F

Number	Shed
68592	32A
68593	32B
68594	32B
68595	6E

J69 class 0-6-0T 2F

Number	Shed
68596	30A

J67 class 0-6-0T 2F

Number	Shed
68597	32A

J69 class 0-6-0T 2F

Number	Shed
68598	8E
68599	40A
68600	31A
68601	30A
68602	40F
68603	31B
68605	40A

J67 class 0-6-0T 2F

Number	Shed
68606	32B

J69 class 0-6-0T 2F

Number	Shed
68607	30A

J67 class 0-6-0T 2F

Number	Shed
68608	32A

J69 class 0-6-0T 2F

Number	Shed
68609	31A

J67 class 0-6-0T 2F

Number	Shed
68610	34D
68611	32C

J69 class 0-6-0T 2F

Number	Shed
68612	30A
68613	30A

J67 class 0-6-0T 2F

Number	Shed
68616	32A

J69 class 0-6-0T 2F

Number	Shed
68617	30A
68618	40A
68619	30A
68621	30A
68623	31D
68625	31E
68626	30A

J67 class 0-6-0T 2F

Number	Shed
68628	32E

J69 class 0-6-0T 2F

Number	Shed
68629	30A
68630	30A
68631	30A
68632	30A
68633	30A
68635	31C
68636	30E

J68 class 0-6-0T 2F

Number	Shed
68638	30E
68639	30A
68640	32C
68641	32A
68642	30A
68643	30F
68644	30A
68645	32A
68646	30A
68647	30A
68648	30A
68649	30A
68650	30A
68651	32F
68652	30A
68653	30A
68654	30A
68655	30A
68656	32D
68657	30A
68658	30A
68659	30A
68660	30A
68661	30A
68662	30A
68663	30A
68664	32A
68665	30A
68666	30A

J72 class 0-6-0T 2F

Number	Shed
68670	53A
68671	6E
68672	50B
68673	53C
68674	52A
68675	52A
68676	53C
68677	50A
68678	54A
68679	51A
68680	52A
68681	50B
68682	52B
68683	51C
68684	51C
68685	51C
68686	50A
68687	54B
68688	51D
68689	51D
68690	51D
68691	51F
68692	51F
68693	52A
68694	54C
68695	50A
68696	51F
68697	54C
68698	54A
68699	50A
68700	61A
68701	20D
68702	52B
68703	51C
68704	54A
68705	54C
68706	54B
68707	51F
68708	52B
68709	65A
68710	61A
68711	51C
68712	51D
68713	51D
68714	6C
68715	51C
68716	51C
68717	61A
68718	53A
68719	61A
68720	52A
68721	51D
68722	50A
68723	52A
68724	50A
68725	52B
68726	50A
68727	6E
68728	54C
68729	54B
68730	54C
68731	52C
68732	52A
68733	65A
68734	51C
68735	50A
68736	54C
68737	54C
68738	52B
68739	50A
68740	51D
68741	53A
68742	52B
68743	54B
68744	52A
68745	53C
68746	53C
68747	52B
68748	51A
68749	61A
68750	61A
68751	53A
68752	53C
68753	53A
68754	51D

J52 class 0-6-0ST 3F

Number	Shed
68758	38A
68759	35C
68761	36A
68765	35A
68768	38A
68769	36A
68771	35A
68778	36A
68783	35C
68784	36A
68785	36A
68787	38A
68790	37A
68793	35A
68795	36A
68796	36A
68797	35C
68800	36A
68804	36A
68805	34A
68806	36A
68807	38A
68808	34B
68809	35C
68810	38A
68811	36A
68812	38A
68813	36A
68814	38A
68815	35B
68817	35A
68818	34A

Above: A scene at Elsenham sees 'J68' class 0-6-0T No 68645, a Cambridge engine, about to work a local along the line to Thaxted in the week before the line closed, which came on 15 September 1952. No 68645 was built at Stratford Works in September 1912, and was transferred to Norwich during the week ended 1 August 1953 and withdrawn from 32A on 6 November 1959.

G. W. Sharpe

Below: 'J52' class 0-6-0ST No 68838 is photographed at King's Cross shed in May 1956. Introduced in 1897 by H. A. Ivatt as the standard Great Northern Railway saddle tank, the last three, Nos 68869, 68875 and 68890, lasted in service until 20 March 1961, allocated to Ardsley. No 68838 was on 34A's allocation throughout its BR ownership and was withdrawn on 7 August 1956.

P. H. Groom

No.	Shed	No.	Shed	No.	Shed
68819	34D	**J50 class 0-6-0T 4F**		68954	65A
68820	35A	68890	37A	68955	65A
68821	38A	68891	34B	68956	65A
68822	34A	68892	37C	68957	65A
68823	35A	68893	40B	68958	65A
68824	34B	68894	34B	68959	37C
68826	35A	68895	37C	68960	36C
68827	34A	68896	38B	68961	34B
68828	35A	68897	37C	68962	36C
68829	34A	68898	37C	68963	30A
68830	34A	68899	32A	68964	36C
68831	35B	68900	37A	68965	30A
68832	34A	68901	37A	68966	37A
68833	36B	68902	37A	68967	30A
68834	34B	68903	34B	68968	34B
68835	36A	68904	37A	68969	37C
68836	36A	68905	32A	68970	36C
68837	37A	68906	34B	68971	34B
68838	34A	68907	34B	68972	34B
68839	38C	68908	37C	68973	36C
68840	35A	68909	37A	68974	36A
68841	36A	68910	37A	68975	38B
68842	36A	68911	37B	68976	38B
68843	36A	68912	37C	68977	30A
68846	35A	68913	37B	68978	37B
68847	36A	68914	37A	68979	40B
68848	37A	68915	37A	68980	36C
68849	36A	68916	37A	68981	34B
68851	38A	68917	34B	68982	34B
68852	35A	68918	34B	68983	34B
68853	36A	68919	37A	68984	37B
68855	34A	68920	34B	68985	34B
68856	36A	68921	34B	68986	34B
68857	37A	68922	37C	68987	37B
68858	36A	68923	37C	68988	34B
68860	36A	68924	32A	68989	34B
68861	34A	68925	37B	68990	34B
68862	34A	68926	40B	68991	34B
68863	38A	68927	38B		
68864	34A	68928	34B	**J72 class 0-6-0T 2F**	
68865	36A	68929	34B	69001	53C
68866	34B	68930	34B	69002	54A
68867	34C	68931	34B	69003	53C
68868	37A	68932	37C	69004	51A
68869	36A	68933	37C	69005	52A
68870	36A	68934	37C	69006	51D
68871	37A	68935	37A	69007	54A
68872	37A	68936	34B	69008	54B
68873	38A	68937	37B	69009	53C
68874	34A	68938	37A	69010	53C
68875	37A	68939	37A	69011	53C
68876	38A	68940	37C	69012	62A
68877	35B	68941	37A	69013	62A
68878	34A	68942	37C	69014	64A
68879	35A	68943	37C	69015	65C
68880	38A	68944	37C	69016	50E
68881	34A	68945	34B	69017	54C
68882	38A	68946	40B	69018	51F
68883	34B	68947	37A	69019	51D
68884	35A	68948	37A	69020	50A
68885	34C	68949	34B	69021	51A
68886	36A	68950	30A	69022	51A
68887	38A	68951	37A	69023	52C
68888	34A	68952	65A	69024	52C
68889	35C	68953	65A	69025	52C

No.	Shed	No.	Shed
69026	52C	69154	62C
69027	52B	69155	68E
69028	52B	69156	64F
		69157	65C
L3 class 2-6-4T 5F		69158	64F
69050	38E	69159	64F
69064	36C	69160	62C
69069	38E	69161	65C
		69162	64E
N10 class 0-6-2T 3F		69163	65A
69090	52A	69164	62C
69091	52A	69165	65C
69092	52A	69166	65C
69093	53A	69167	64A
69094	53A	69168	64A
69095	52A	69169	64B
69096	53A	69170	65A
69097	52A	69171	65A
69098	53A	69172	64A
69099	53A	69173	64A
69100	52A	69174	68E
69101	54A	69175	64A
69102	53A	69176	65D
69104	53A	69177	65D
69105	54B	69178	65A
69106	53A	69179	65A
69107	53A	69180	65A
69108	53A	69181	65A
69109	52A	69182	65A
		69183	65A
N13 class 0-6-2T 3F		69184	65D
69114	50B	69185	64A
69115	50B	69186	64A
69117	50B	69187	64C
69119	50B	69188	65A
		69189	65A
N15 class 0-6-2T 3MT		69190	65C
69126	65A	69191	65A
69127	65A	69192	62C
69128	61B	69193	65C
69129	61B	69194	65C
69130	64A	69195	65C
69131	65A	69196	65E
69132	62A	69197	65A
69133	64A	69198	65C
69134	64A	69199	65C
69135	62C	69200	64E
69136	62C	69201	61B
69137	64E	69202	62C
69138	65A	69203	65D
69139	68E	69204	62C
69140	64A	69205	65D
69141	64A	69206	65E
69142	64F	69207	65E
69143	62A	69208	65D
69144	64A	69209	65C
69145	65E	69210	65C
69146	64A	69211	62A
69147	64A	69212	65C
69148	64A	69213	65C
69149	64A	69214	65A
69150	62A	69215	68E
69151	65C	69216	64F
69152	64A	69217	65C
69153	62A	69218	65A

184

Above: 'J50' class 0-6-0T No 68917 passes through Hornsey on Sunday 18 September 1955 on an empty coaching stock working to Wood Green. This was a Gresley rebuild from the smaller 'J51' class. No 68917 had come to Hornsey shed from Doncaster during October 1952 and remained on allocation until July 1961 when it transferred back to Doncaster. It was moved into Departmental stock as DM12 in September 1962 and was withdrawn in May 1965.

Initial Photographics/B. K. B. Green

Below: At Gorton Works on Sunday 24 April 1955 'L3' class 2-6-4T No 69050 has arrived from Woodford Halse and been marked by a painted cross for scrapping. The official withdrawal date was 12 March and behind, awaiting a similar fate, is 'J11' 0-6-0 No 64342. The 'L3' was a Robinson design for freight work and 20 were built between 1914 and 1917. The first withdrawals took place in 1947, and 1955 saw the last examples scrapped.

Initial Photographics/B. K. B. Green

Gateshead shed in March 1955 sees 'N10' class 0-6-2T No 69100 in the yard. Introduced in 1902 by Wilson Worsdell, the last three, Nos 69097, 69101 and 69109, lasted until April 1962. No 69100 was withdrawn on 25 November 1957 and cut up at Darlington Works. *G. W. Sharpe*

The last Hull & Barnsley Railway locomotive to operate on British Railways, 'N13' class No 69114 is here shunting near Leeds Neville Hill in September 1956. Introduced in 1913, it was designed by M. Stirling. Neville Hill shed operated the engine until withdrawal on 22 October 1956. *P. H. Groom*

'N5' class 0-6-2T No 69315 is seen in Gorton Works yard on Sunday 14 November 1954 awaiting return to Neasden. This was a design by T. Parker for the Manchester, Sheffield & Lincolnshire Railway, No 69315 being built at Gorton in April 1898. It moved from Neasden to Barnsley in October 1956, from where it was withdrawn on 3 June 1958. Gorton carried out the scrapping. *Initial Photographics/B. K. B. Green*

69219	64A	69310	38A	69392	54A	69503	61B	69568	34A
69220	64B	69312	39B	69394	54B	69504	34C	69569	34A
69221	62C	69313	36E			69505	34B	69570	34A
69222	64A	69314	36E	**N9 class 0-6-2T 2MT**		69506	34A	69571	34A
69223	62A	69315	34E	69424	54B	69507	65C	69572	34A
69224	62A	69316	39B	69427	54B	69508	65C	69573	34A
		69317	9F	69429	54B	69509	65D	69574	34A
N5 class 0-6-2T 2MT		69318	34E			69510	65C	69575	34A
69250	39A	69319	40E	**N1 class 0-6-2T 2MT**		69511	65D	69576	34A
69253	39B	69320	36D	69430	37B	69512	34A	69577	34A
69254	8E	69321	36E	69431	37A	69513	34B	69578	34A
69255	9E	69322	40C	69434	37C	69514	65C	69579	34A
69256	40F	69323	39B	69435	34B	69515	34D	69580	34C
69257	34E	69325	36D	69436	37C	69516	34C	69581	34A
69258	8E	69326	9E	69439	37C	69517	34A	69582	34C
69259	39B	69327	40C	69440	37A	69518	65E	69583	34A
69260	39A	69328	39A	69441	38A	69519	34A	69584	34A
69261	40F	69329	6E	69443	37C	69520	34A	69585	34A
69262	9F	69330	6E	69444	37B	69521	34A	69586	34C
69263	38D	69331	9F	69445	34B	69522	34B	69587	34B
69264	36B	69332	6D	69447	37C	69523	34A	69588	34C
69265	27E	69333	39A	69449	37C	69524	34A	69589	34A
69266	39B	69334	36D	69450	37B	69525	34A	69590	34A
69267	6E	69335	9E	69451	38A	69526	34A	69591	34A
69268	36D	69337	39B	69452	37A	69527	34A	69592	34A
69269	38D	69338	39A	69453	38A	69528	34A	69593	34A
69270	39A	69339	6F	69454	37C	69529	34A	69594	34B
69271	38A	69340	6E	69455	34B	69530	34B	69595	65C
69272	8E	69341	34E	69457	38A	69531	34B	69596	65E
69273	34E	69342	6D	69458	34B	69532	34A		
69274	6D	69343	9E	69459	37C	69533	34B	**N7 class 0-6-2T 3MT**	
69275	40A	69344	27E	69460	34B	69534	34C	69600	30A
69276	9F	69345	36D	69462	34C	69535	34A	69601	30A
69277	36E	69346	6E	69463	37A	69536	34A	69602	30A
69278	36D	69347	9E	69464	37C	69537	34B	69603	30A
69279	38D	69348	39B	69465	34B	69538	34A	69604	30A
69280	36B	69349	6E	69466	34B	69539	34A	69605	30A
69281	6D	69350	34E	69467	38A	69540	34A	69606	30A
69282	36E	69351	38D	69469	38A	69541	34A	69607	30A
69283	36E	69352	6E	69470	34B	69542	34A	69608	30A
69284	40E	69353	39A	69471	37C	69543	34A	69609	30A
69285	39B	69354	34E	69472	37A	69544	34A	69610	30A
69286	38A	69355	36D	69474	37C	69545	34A	69611	30A
69287	39B	69356	27E	69475	34C	69546	34A	69612	30A
69288	6E	69357	36B	69476	38A	69547	34B	69613	30A
69290	6E	69358	9E	69477	34C	69548	34A	69614	30A
69291	36D	69359	9F	69478	37C	69549	34A	69615	30A
69292	39B	69360	38A	69481	38A	69550	30A	69616	30A
69293	6D	69361	9E	69483	37B	69551	30F	69617	30A
69294	39B	69362	6E	69484	37A	69552	30F	69618	30A
69295	39B	69363	38D			69553	65D	69619	30A
69296	39B	69364	9E	**N2 class 0-6-2T 3P2F**		69554	34C	69620	30A
69297	36B	69365	36D	69490	34A	69555	30E	69621	30A
69298	27E	69366	6E	69491	34A	69556	34B	69622	30A
69299	9F	69367	36D	69492	34A	69557	34D	69623	30A
69300	36E	69368	36D	69493	34A	69558	30E	69624	30A
69301	38D	69369	39B	69494	34C	69559	30A	69625	30A
69302	39B	69370	9E	69495	34A	69560	34B	69626	30A
69303	36D			69496	34A	69561	30F	69627	30A
69304	9E	**N8 class 0-6-2T 2MT**		69497	34A	69562	65C	69628	30A
69305	40B	69377	52B	69498	34A	69563	65C	69629	30A
69306	36B	69378	53D	69499	34A	69564	65C	69630	30A
69307	39A	69381	53A	69500	65C	69565	65C	69631	34C
69308	39A	69386	53A	69501	34B	69566	30F	69632	34C
69309	40C	69390	54A	69502	30F	69567	34B	69633	30A

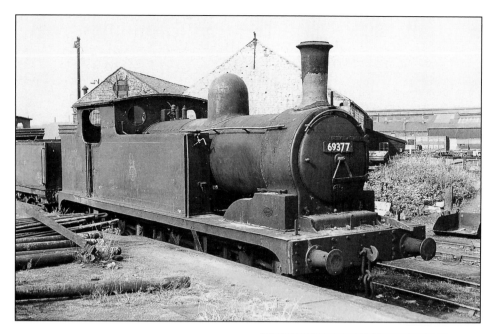

'N8' class 0-6-2T No 69377 in Darlington Works scrapyard on Sunday 4 September 1955 is awaiting cutting up after withdrawal on 28 June from Heaton shed. The class originally consisted of 62 engines to a T. W. Worsdell design built from 1886 to 1890. The locomotives were first constructed as Worsdell-Von Borries two-cylinder compounds, but were later converted to 'simples' and rebuilt with superheater, Stephenson valve gear, and piston valves.

Initial Photographics/B. K. B. Green

H. A. Ivatt-designed 'N1' class 0-6-2T No 69430 was built for the Great Northern Railway. This engine was the pioneer of the class and was constructed at Doncaster in April 1907. Its appearance was different from other members of the class as it was fitted with longer side-tanks. This view was recorded at Leeds Copley Hill shed in June 1955 where the engine was based for many years until withdrawal on 10 December 1956.   *Photomatic/RAS Marketing*

The A. J. Hill 'L77' class, more familiarly known as the 'N7', is shown here with No 69614 at Stratford shed in pristine condition on Sunday 16 September 1956. Built at Stratford Works in December 1923, it had had a round-topped firebox fitted in February 1940. A London-based engine for most of its working life, it was withdrawn on 4 December 1960 and cut up at Stratford.

G. W. Sharpe

Above: Sir Vincent Raven's North Eastern Railway 'Y' class 4-6-2T, later to become LNER class 'A7', No 69778 is seen at Hull Springhead shed on Sunday 3 October 1954. Built at Darlington Works in February 1911 for freight work, a superheater was later fitted and boiler pressure reduced. Withdrawal came on 3 May 1955 for No 69778 and the last three, Nos 69772, 69782 and 69786, were all withdrawn on 16 December 1957. *Initial Photographics/B. K. B. Green*

Below: J. G. Robinson's '9N' class for the Great Central Railway, LNER Class A5 4-6-2T No 69826 in ex-works condition, leaves Manchester London Road on the 12.59pm to Macclesfield on Wednesday 2 June 1954. Built at Gorton Works in May 1923, No 69826 was allocated to Norwich when this photograph was recorded, and this was almost certainly a running-in turn. It had been moved from Colwick to Norwich in June 1952 and in January 1956 went on to Lowestoft. Immingham became its base from February 1957 until withdrawal on 2 June 1958. *Initial Photographics/B. K. B. Green*

Above: 'A8' class 4-6-2T No 69858 is seen at its home shed, Hull Botanic Gardens, in July 1956. Built at Darlington in December 1913 as a 4-4-4T to a design by Sir Vincent Raven, it was rebuilt as a 4-6-2T in June 1936. Moving on to Middlesbrough in June 1957 and Sunderland three months later, it was withdrawn on 10 May 1960.

P. H. Groom

Below: 'S1' class 0-8-4T No 69904 is seen at its home shed, Mexborough, in October 1953 at a time when all six class members were allocated to 36B. Built in 1908 to a Robinson design for shunting in the nearby Wath marshalling yard, in November 1953 a start was made in splitting the class by transfer to other depots. By the end of January 1954 all had gone from Mexborough, with Sheffield Darnall receiving No 69900, Doncaster Nos 69901, 69902, 69905, and Immingham Nos 69903 and 69904. By the end of March 1954 all had come together again at Doncaster except for No 69903 which was withdrawn on 8 March. Doncaster found little work for the class and they spent long periods in storage. Withdrawal dates were 6 January 1956 for Nos 69900 and 69904; 13 January 1956 for No 69902, and 1 January 1957 for Nos 69901 and 69905.

Photomatic/RAS Marketing

Above: 'T1' class 4-8-0T No 69915 at Selby shed in July 1956 is seen shortly after transfer from York. This was a T. W. Worsdell design and No 69915 had been built at Gateshead Works in February 1910. Originally a class of 15 engines, two had been scrapped in 1937. In 1948 No 69915 was at Hull Dairycoates and moved to Newport during the week ended 21 July 1951. York added it to its allocation in September 1955. Withdrawal came on 19 March 1959 when it was still on Selby's roster.

P. H. Groom

Below: 'Q1' class 0-8-0T No 69932 , with 'J11' 0-6-0 No 64297 behind, is seen at Gorton shed on Sunday 24 April 1955. The 13 engines that made up the class were Thompson rebuilds from Robinson 0-8-0s. No 69932 was withdrawn from Frodingham shed on 12 November 1958 and cut up at Darlington Works.

Initial Photographics/B. K. B. Green

69634	30A	69699	30A
69635	34C	69700	30A
69636	30A	69701	30A
69637	34C	69702	30A
69638	34C	69703	30A
69639	34C	69704	34C
69640	34C	69705	30A
69641	30A	69706	32A
69642	30A	69707	32A
69643	30A	69708	32D
69644	34C	69709	34C
69645	30A	69710	30A
69646	30A	69711	30A
69647	30A	69712	30A
69648	34C	69713	30A
69649	34C	69714	30A
69650	34C	69715	30A
69651	38B	69716	30A
69652	30A	69717	30A
69653	30A	69718	30A
69654	34C	69719	30A
69655	30A	69720	30E
69656	30A	69721	30A
69657	30A	69722	30A
69658	30A	69723	30A
69659	30A	69724	30A
69660	30A	69725	30A
69661	30A	69726	30A
69662	30A	69727	30A
69663	30A	69728	30A
69664	30A	69729	30A
69665	30A	69730	30A
69666	30A	69731	30A
69667	30A	69732	30E
69668	30A	69733	30A
69669	30A		
69670	30A		

A7 class 4-6-2T 3F

69671	30A	69772	53A
69672	30E	69773	53A
69673	30E	69778	53C
69674	30A	69781	53C
69675	30A	69782	53A
69676	30A	69783	53C
69677	30A	69784	53C
69678	34C	69785	53C
69679	32A	69786	53A
69680	30A	69788	53A
69681	30A		

A5 class 4-6-2T 3MT

69682	30A	69800	40B
69683	30A	69801	38A
69684	30A	69802	53B
69685	30A	69803	40F
69686	30A	69804	40A
69687	30A	69805	39A
69688	30A	69806	39A
69689	38B	69807	38A
69690	32A	69808	40F
69691	37B	69809	38A
69692	38B	69810	38A
69693	30A	69811	53B
69694	37B	69812	40A
69695	37B	69813	40B
69696	37B	69814	35B
69697	30A	69815	40B
69698	32A		

69816	40F
69817	39A
69818	38A
69819	40F
69820	40B
69821	40A
69822	38A
69823	39A
69824	32A
69825	38A
69826	32A
69827	35B
69828	40A
69829	39A
69830	51A
69831	51A
69832	51A
69833	51A
69834	51A
69835	53B
69836	53B
69837	53B
69838	51A
69839	51A
69840	51A
69841	51A
69842	51A

A8 class 4-6-2T 3MT

69850	54A
69851	51F
69852	51K
69853	54A
69854	51D
69855	51K
69856	51F
69857	54A
69858	50B
69859	51K
69860	50G
69861	50G
69862	51D
69863	54A
69864	50G
69865	50G
69866	51K
69867	50E
69868	51F
69869	51K
69870	51F
69871	51C
69872	51F
69873	51D
69874	54A
69875	51F
69876	51D
69877	50F
69878	51D
69879	50E
69880	51K
69881	50B
69882	50B
69883	51C
69884	51K
69885	50E

69886	50E
69887	54A
69888	50G
69889	51D
69890	50G
69891	51D
69892	51K
69893	51C
69894	51K

S1 class 0-8-4T 6F

69900	36A
69901	36A
69902	36A
69904	36A
69905	36A

T1 class 4-8-0T 5F

69910	51B
69911	51B
69912	51E
69913	51B
69914	54B
69915	51B
69916	51B
69917	51B
69918	51E
69919	51E
69920	54B
69921	51B
69922	51B

Q1 class 0-8-0T 5F

69926	36C
69927	65A
69928	40E
69929	40E
69930	36C
69931	50C
69932	36C
69933	50C
69934	36C
69935	36C
69936	36C
69937	36C

U1 class Beyer-Garratt 2-8-8-2T

69999	36B

Standard 'Britannia' class 4-6-2 7MT

70000*	30A
70001*	30A
70002*	30A
70003*	30A
70004*	73A
70005*	30A
70006*	32A
70007*	32A
70008*	32A
70009*	32A
70010*	32A
70011*	32A
70012*	32A
70013*	32A
70014*	73A
70015*	81A
70016*	83D
70017*	81A
70018*	81A
70019*	83D
70020*	81A
70021*	83D
70022*	83A
70023*	81A
70024*	83D
70025*	86C
70026*	86C
70027*	86C
70028*	86C
70029*	86C
70030*	32A
70031*	9A
70032*	9A
70033*	9A
70034*	30A
70035*	32A
70036*	30A
70037*	30A
70038*	30A
70039*	30A
70040*	30A
70041*	30A
70042*	30A
70043*	9A
70044*	9A
70045	6J
70046	6J
70047	6J
70048	6J
70049	6J
70050*	66A
70051*	66A
70052*	66A
70053*	66A
70054*	66A

Standard 4-6-2 8P

71000*	5A

Standard 'Clan' class 4-6-2 6MT

72000*	66A
72001*	66A
72002*	66A
72003*	66A
72004*	66A
72005*	68A
72006*	68A
72007*	68A
72008*	68A
72009*	68A

Standard 4-6-0 5MT

73000	16A
73001	17A
73002	16A
73003	15C
73004	15C

Above: 'U1' class 2-8-8-2T No 69999 at Newton on the Manchester to Sheffield Woodhead route on a trial run on Saturday 12 February 1955 after a period in storage. This was the LNER's lone Garratt built with Gresley's intervention in 1925 to make it a virtual double '02'. Used on the Worsbrough Branch for banking duties, it was displaced by electrification. Converted to an oil burner at Gorton in August 1952, in 1955 it was sent to Bromsgrove to be tried on Lickey banking duties and left Gorton on 29 June but developed a hot box on the way. It was examined at Saltley and had to be sent to Burton shed to use the wheel drop, as Saltley did not possess the equipment. The wheels were removed and sent back to Gorton. It eventually left Burton on Sunday 7 August and ran light to Bromsgrove via the Camp Hill line, the journey taking four hours to complete at an average speed of just above 10mph. It made its first banking trip at 3.45pm the following day, working up the incline in reverse. It was not a success, and left Bromsgrove on Friday 16 September to return to Gorton and withdrawal followed three months later on 23 December. *Initial Photographics/B. K. B. Green*

Below: A view of No 69999 at Gorton Works on Sunday 24 April 1955 showing the headlamp fitted to the rear bunker, supplied from a generator fitted on the right-hand side at the front of the engine, in readiness for its ill-fated month on the Lickey. *Initial Photographics/B. K. B. Green*

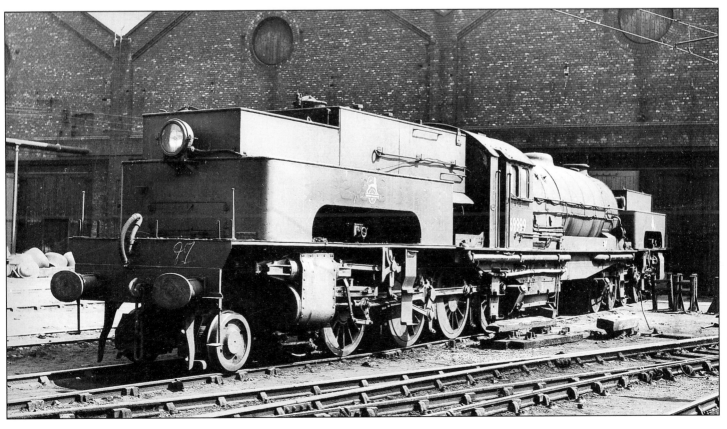

Above: Standard 'Britannia' class 4-6-2 No 70004 *William Shakespeare* is seen on the London-bound 'Golden Arrow' at Folkestone Junction on Sunday 26 June 1955. Built at Crewe Works, it entered traffic on 30 March 1951 at Stratford and moved across London to Stewarts Lane during the week ended 6 October 1951. It left the Southern in June 1958 for the LMR and after serving from seven different depots settled at Carlisle Kingmoor in June 1967, from where it was withdrawn when Kingmoor closed to steam on 31 December 1967.   *G. W. Sharpe*

Below: 4-6-2 No 71000 *Duke of Gloucester*, now well known in preservation, approaches Shrewsbury on the line from Crewe in August 1956. It was released to traffic from Crewe Works during the week ended 22 May 1954 and put to work at Crewe North. At the beginning of 1955 it was on loan to Swindon Works for tests and on 19 April it commenced running tests on the line to Reading and Westbury with the dynamometer car and up to 20 coaches. In June, when the tests were completed, it returned to Crewe North until withdrawal during the week ended 24 November 1962.   *G. W. Sharpe*

No.	Shed	No.	Shed	No.	Shed	No.	Shed	No.	Shed
73005	63A	73070	6A	76006	71C	78002	89C	80020	61A
73006	63A	73071	6A	76007	71A	78003	89C	80021	61A
73007	63A	73072	6A	76008	71A	78004	85A	80022	66A
73008	63A	73073	10C	76009	71A	78005	89C	80023	66A
73009	63A	73074	10C	76010	71A	78006	89C	80024	67A
73010	20A			76011	71A	78007	89C	80025	67A
73011	19B	**Standard 4-6-0 4MT**		76012	71A	78008	85A	80026	66A
73012	84G	75000	82C	76013	71A	78009	85A	80027	66A
73013	84G	75001	81F	76014	71A	78010	51F	80028	61A
73014	84G	75002	82C	76015	71A	78011	51F	80029	61A
73015	84G	75003	82C	76016	71A	78012	51F	80030	67A
73016	19B	75004	81F	76017	71A	78013	51F	80031	75A
73017	84G	75005	89A	76018	71A	78014	51F	80032	75A
73018	84G	75006	89A	76019	71A	78015	51F	80033	75A
73019	82B	75007	86C	76020	51A	78016	51H	80034	1C
73020	84G	75008	86C	76021	50C	78017	51H	80035	1C
73021	84K	75009	86C	76022	53A	78018	51H	80036	1C
73022	82C	75010	6G	76023	54A	78019	51H	80037	1C
73023	84K	75011	6G	76024	52C	78020	15B	80038	1C
73024	84G	75012	6G	76025	71A	78021	15B	80039	9A
73025	86C	75013	6G	76026	71A	78022	19B	80040	1E
73026	86C	75014	6G	76027	71A	78023	19B	80041	1E
73027	82C	75015	27C	76028	71A	78024	19B	80042	1E
73028	82B	75016	27C	76029	71A	78025	19B	80043	1E
73029	82B	75017	27C	76030	30A	78026	19C	80044	15D
73030	17A	75018	27C	76031	30A	78027	19C	80045	15D
73031	17A	75019	27C	76032	30A	78028	15C	80046	15D
73032	82B	75020	89A	76033	30A	78029	15C	80047	14B
73033	84G	75021	86C	76034	30A	78030	10B	80048	14B
73034	84G	75022	86C	76035	34E	78031	11E	80049	26A
73035	84G	75023	89A	76036	34E	78032	6K	80050	26A
73036	84G	75024	89A	76037	34E	78033	6K	80051	26A
73037	84G	75025	83D	76038	34E	78034	6K	80052	26A
73038	84K	75026	83D	76039	34E	78035	6K	80053	26A
73039	82B	75027	81F	76040	34E	78036	10B	80054	66A
73040	6A	75028	83D	76041	34E	78037	10B	80055	66A
73041	6A	75029	81F	76042	34E	78038	3A	80056	66A
73042	6A	75030	6G	76043	34E	78039	6K	80057	66A
73043	10C	75031	1E	76044	34E	78040	27A	80059	14B
73044	10C	75032	1E			78041	27A	80060	15D
73045	20A	75033	1E	**Standard 2-6-0 3MT**		78042	27A	80061	15D
73046	15C	75034	1E	77000	51F	78043	27A	80062	14B
73047	19B	75035	1E	77001	51F	78044	27A	80063	14B
73048	19B	75036	1E	77002	51F			80064	1C
73049	15C	75037	1E	77003	51F	**Standard 2-6-4T 4MT**		80065	1C
73050	71G	75038	1E	77004	51F	80000	67A	80066	1C
73051	71G	75039	1E	77005	66C	80001	66A	80067	1C
73052	71G	75040	24A	77006	66C	80002	66A	80068	1C
73053	20A	75041	24A	77007	66C	80003	66A	80069	33B
73054	20A	75042	24A	77008	66A	80004	61A	80070	33B
73055	66A	75043	24A	77009	66A	80005	61A	80071	33B
73056	66A	75044	24A	77010	51F	80006	66A	80072	33B
73057	66A	75045	24A	77011	51F	80007	66A	80073	33B
73058	66A	75046	24A	77012	51A	80008	67A	80074	33A
73059	66A	75047	24A	77013	51A	80009	67A	80075	33A
73060	66A	75048	24A	77014	51A	80010	75F	80076	33A
73061	66A	75049	24A	77015	67B	80011	75F	80077	33A
73062	66A			77016	67B	80012	75F	80078	33A
73063	66A	**Standard 2-6-0 4MT**		77017	67B	80013	75F	80079	33B
73064	66A	76000	66B	77018	67B	80014	75F	80080	33B
73065	19B	76001	66B	77019	67B	80015	75F	80081	1E
73066	20A	76002	66B			80016	75A	80082	1E
73067	16A	76003	66B	**Standard 2-6-0 2MT**		80017	75F	80083	1E
73068	17A	76004	66B	78000	89C	80018	75F	80084	1E
73069	17A	76005	71C	78001	85A	80019	75A	80085	1E

Above: Standard 'Clan' class 4-6-2 No 72007 *Clan Mackintosh* is a visitor to Shrewsbury shed in 1955 after a visit to Crewe Works. Built at Crewe, 4 March 1952 was its first day in traffic, going to Carlisle Kingmoor, where it remained allocated until withdrawal during the week ended 4 December 1965. *G. W. Sharpe*

Below: Beautifully maintained by Perth, Standard 5MT 4-6-0 No 73009 is captured on film at Carlisle Kingmoor shed in July 1954. New to Perth from Derby Works during the week ended 21 July 1951, it stayed at 63A until December 1962 when it was reallocated to Glasgow Corkerhill. This was its home until it was withdrawn on 14 July 1966. *G. W. Sharpe*

Released from Swindon Works in May 1954 and allocated to Plymouth Laira, Standard 4MT 4-6-0 No 75027 is at Bristol Bath Road shed on Monday 14 June 1954. At the beginning of October 1954 it moved to Reading and in the following December went to Oxford. Here it remained until March 1959 when Swindon became its home. Subsequent moves included Templecombe, Machynlleth, Liverpool Bank Hall, Aintree, Tebay and, finally, Carnforth, where it stayed on the active list until the end of steam in August 1968. It can still be seen in preservation on the Bluebell Railway.

G. W. Sharpe

Eastleigh shed in June 1956 sees Standard 4MT 2-6-0 No 76019 keeping company with 'E4' class 0-6-2T No 32557 and ' Battle of Britain' 4-6-2 No 34070 *Manston*. Delivered new to Eastleigh from Horwich Works in July 1953, it remained at 71A until March 1960 when Salisbury added it to its roster. It then moved on to Bournemouth in July 1961 and back to Eastleigh in September 1964 for its final years until withdrawal on 20 February 1966. Cohens at Morriston carried out the scrapping in June 1966. *Photomatic/RAS Marketing*

Standard 3MT 2-6-0 No 77019 shelters from the cold in its home shed Hurlford in January 1956, where it had entered service when new from Swindon Works on 3 September 1954. This was the last of the type to be built and remained at 67B until February 1963 when it transferred to Glasgow Polmadie. Perhaps its new owners didn't welcome it, for eight months later No 77019 returned to Hurlford, to be withdrawn on 29 November 1966.

R. H. G. Simpson

Above: Standard 2MT 2-6-0 No 78002 is seen at Borth on the Cambrian line in April 1955 when allocated to Machynlleth. This was a straightforward adoption of the Ivatt design for the LMS with minor alterations to the boiler mountings to conform with other Standard types. No 78002 was built at Darlington Works and was first allocated to Oswestry in December 1952, moving to Machynlleth in June 1953, where it remained until a move to Liverpool Bank Hall in September 1963. A move to Lostock Hall in June 1964 was its last, with withdrawal coming during the week ended 11 June 1966. *G. W. Sharpe*

Below: The Standard 4MT 2-6-4T was based on the Fairburn design and was a very successful engine. No 80032 is at Brighton shed in June 1954. Built at Brighton Works, it was allocated new to Brighton in February 1952 and remained there until December 1963 when it was transferred to Redhill. The last move was to Bournemouth in May 1965 until withdrawal on 29 January 1967; it then went on to Cashmore's at Newport for scrap. *Photomatic/RAS Marketing*

80086	26D	84006	17B	90049	65A	90114	65D	90179	86A
80087	26D	84007	17B	90050	38A	90115	38D	90180	35A
80088	26D	84008	17B	90051	40E	90116	53C	90181	24B
80089	26D	84009	20C	90052	38A	90117	62C	90182	62A
80090	26D	84010	26F	90053	36B	90118	36B	90183	24B
80091	14B	84011	25F	90054	54D	90119	36B	90184	51E
80092	14B	84012	26F	90055	40B	90120	36B	90185	38A
80093	15D	84013	25F	90056	50A	90121	27D	90186	25C
80094	14B	84014	25F	90057	53A	90122	26G	90187	6B
80095	14C	84015	26F	90058	62A	90123	26D	90188	86C
80096	33A	84016	24F	90059	36C	90124	25D	90189	36B
80097	33A	84017	24F	90060	36A	90125	86C	90190	36B
80098	33A	84018	24F	90061	53C	90126	26G	90191	35A
80106	61A	84019	24F	90062	35A	90127	27B	90192	86G
80107	61A			90063	35C	90128	62A	90193	65D
80108	61A	**Austerity 2-8-0 8F**		90064	36A	90129	31B	90194	26D
80109	61A	90000	38A	90065	38E	90130	36B	90195	36B
80110	61A	90001	38A	90066	36B	90131	40B	90196	36B
80111	66A	90002	38A	90067	51E	90132	51B	90197	26G
80112	66A	90003	40B	90068	51B	90133	36C	90198	62B
80113	66A	90004	62A	90069	86A	90134	66A	90199	62A
80114	66A	90005	36B	90070	36C	90135	25C	90200	50A
80115	66A	90006	53A	90071	66B	90136	38A	90201	86E
		90007	38A	90072	53A	90137	38E	90202	38A
Standard 2-6-2T 3MT		90008	53A	90073	38A	90138	24B	90203	40B
82000	88F	90009	53A	90074	51B	90139	38A	90204	27B
82001	88C	90010	84D	90075	38A	90140	26G	90205	26D
82002	88C	90011	53C	90076	51B	90141	27B	90206	26C
82003	88C	90012	51E	90077	62B	90142	27B	90207	81C
82004	88C	90013	36C	90078	53A	90143	24B	90208	38A
82005	88C	90014	51B	90079	31B	90144	36B	90209	36B
82006	88C	90015	36B	90080	38E	90145	40B	90210	53A
82007	88C	90016	51B	90081	51B	90146	36B	90211	36B
82008	88C	90017	62C	90082	53C	90147	6B	90212	6B
82009	88C	90018	31B	90083	40B	90148	86C	90213	25C
82010	72A	90019	62A	90084	38A	90149	85B	90214	84K
82011	72A	90020	62A	90085	36B	90150	36B	90215	38A
82012	71A	90021	53A	90086	51E	90151	35A	90216	27B
82013	72A	90022	53A	90087	40B	90152	81C	90217	53C
82014	71A	90023	31B	90088	35A	90153	36B	90218	38E
82015	71A	90024	36A	90089	53A	90154	38A	90219	26D
82016	71A	90025	38A	90090	51B	90155	51E	90220	36B
82017	72A	90026	54B	90091	51B	90156	35C	90221	40B
82018	72A	90027	51B	90092	51E	90157	6B	90222	26A
82019	72A	90028	35A	90093	35A	90158	35A	90223	40B
82020	2B	90029	40B	90094	53C	90159	24B	90224	40B
82021	2B	90030	53A	90095	38E	90160	53A	90225	86A
82022	72A	90031	36C	90096	35A	90161	36B	90226	26D
82023	72A	90032	36C	90097	61B	90162	35A	90227	6B
82024	72A	90033	38E	90098	51B	90163	26G	90228	25C
82025	72A	90034	35A	90099	53A	90164	27B	90229	36B
82026	51H	90035	40B	90100	50A	90165	35A	90230	51B
82027	51H	90036	38A	90101	27B	90166	36B	90231	24B
82028	51A	90037	36A	90102	26B	90167	86G	90232	36C
82029	51A	90038	38A	90103	38A	90168	62A	90233	53C
82030	88C	90039	38E	90104	36B	90169	35A	90234	25A
82031	88C	90040	38E	90105	26A	90170	68A	90235	38A
		90041	61B	90106	35A	90171	24B	90236	25A
Standard 2-6-2T 2MT		90042	36A	90107	27B	90172	51E	90237	6B
84000	6E	90043	40E	90108	36A	90173	6B	90238	86C
84001	6E	90044	50A	90109	24B	90174	81C	90239	35A
84002	6E	90045	54D	90110	26C	90175	40B	90240	51E
84003	6E	90046	38E	90111	36C	90176	82B	90241	24B
84004	6E	90047	50A	90112	24A	90177	62C	90242	6B
84005	15D	90048	51E	90113	26A	90178	6B	90243	25A

Standard 3MT 2-6-2T No 82029 is seen on a semi-fast at Darlington in October 1956. The design was an amalgam of GWR and LMS features and earlier designs of engines, built to satisfy the need for a modern tank engine with an axle load of 16 tons. Delivered new to Darlington shed from Swindon Works and added to stock on 13 December 1954, it operated from 51A until October 1958 when Malton shed received it. The next reallocation was in June 1960 to Scarborough; it then went back to Malton in 1961. York was the next allocation in April 1963, followed by a regional transfer to the Southern to Guildford five months later. Bournemouth acquired the engine at the end of 1963 and in October 1964 Nine Elms received it, where it remained until the end of steam on the Southern and with No 82019 was the last of the class to remain serviceable. Its last working was on 8 July 1967, the last Saturday of steam, when unusually it powered the 7.18am Waterloo to Salisbury as the rostered engine failed on shed and Nine Elms had nothing else to spare. It retired to Salisbury shed and was withdrawn. It remained there, along with 57 other withdrawn engines, until November 1967 when it left for Bird's yard at Risca for scrapping.

Photomatic/RAS Marketing

90244	35A	90271	26C	90298	40B	90325	25B	90352	53A
90245	26A	90272	53A	90299	38D	90326	25D	90353	25A
90246	35A	90273	51B	90300	25C	90327	26A	90354	26B
90247	25A	90274	24B	90301	36A	90328	24C	90355	86E
90248	26A	90275	40B	90302	40B	90329	25A	90356	84G
90249	25A	90276	38A	90303	38A	90330	36B	90357	25A
90250	36B	90277	25A	90304	36B	90331	24C	90358	36B
90251	82B	90278	27B	90305	36A	90332	25B	90359	26D
90252	36B	90279	35A	90306	26B	90333	25A	90360	26A
90253	35A	90280	40B	90307	26B	90334	25A	90361	25A
90254	26B	90281	25C	90308	25G	90335	24C	90362	25A
90255	36B	90282	27B	90309	54B	90336	25G	90363	25A
90256	35A	90283	26A	90310	25A	90337	25A	90364	26D
90257	6B	90284	81C	90311	36B	90338	26A	90365	38E
90258	24C	90285	40B	90312	81F	90339	25A	90366	26A
90259	35A	90286	36B	90313	81C	90340	36B	90367	24C
90260	25A	90287	40E	90314	24B	90341	25A	90368	38A
90261	84G	90288	38A	90315	86G	90342	25A	90369	2E
90262	25C	90289	26A	90316	26C	90343	26C	90370	25A
90263	38A	90290	36B	90317	6B	90344	51E	90371	24B
90264	24B	90291	26A	90318	25G	90345	25B	90372	25G
90265	25A	90292	25A	90319	67C	90346	38A	90373	51B
90266	24D	90293	31B	90320	24C	90347	25B	90374	24D
90267	26C	90294	40B	90321	25D	90348	24A	90375	27B
90268	81C	90295	24C	90322	25G	90349	35A	90376	26A
90269	38A	90296	38A	90323	86E	90350	62A	90377	51E
90270	36A	90297	26C	90324	26B	90351	25G	90378	53A

Standard 2MT 2-6-2T No 84005, is seen at Bedford St Johns on Monday 11 April 1955 after working the push-pull from Bletchley. Virtually identical to the earlier Ivatt LMS type, No 84005 was built at Crewe Works and entered service at Bedford shed during the week ended 29 August 1953. It later spent time at Neasden, Kentish Town, Wellingborough and finally Leicester Midland, where it was withdrawn during the week ended 30 October 1965.

G. W. Sharpe

90379	25A	90406	25A	90433	38A	90460	38D	90487	51B
90380	25A	90407	25G	90434	51B	90461	51B	90488	51B
90381	25A	90408	26D	90435	51B	90462	51B	90489	65A
90382	53A	90409	53A	90436	65D	90463	62B	90490	36C
90383	36A	90410	36B	90437	38A	90464	68A	90491	38A
90384	38A	90411	40E	90438	35A	90465	51B	90492	40B
90385	25A	90412	25A	90439	35A	90466	84G	90493	65D
90386	66C	90413	26B	90440	65D	90467	53C	90494	35A
90387	24B	90414	25A	90441	62A	90468	66C	90495	36B
90388	26A	90415	25A	90442	40B	90469	36A	90496	38A
90389	26A	90416	27B	90443	31B	90470	53C	90497	53C
90390	26A	90417	25A	90444	62B	90471	40B	90498	36B
90391	38A	90418	38D	90445	54B	90472	62A	90499	38A
90392	2E	90419	26D	90446	51B	90473	38A	90500	50A
90393	40B	90420	24B	90447	35C	90474	38E	90501	35C
90394	38D	90421	36B	90448	38E	90475	51B	90502	35A
90395	25G	90422	36C	90449	40E	90476	38A	90503	51B
90396	25A	90423	2E	90450	53A	90477	40B	90504	38E
90397	24C	90424	50A	90451	51B	90478	53C	90505	67C
90398	24A	90425	36C	90452	51B	90479	53A	90506	36B
90399	36B	90426	51B	90453	40B	90480	31B	90507	38E
90400	36B	90427	53C	90454	35A	90481	51B	90508	40B
90401	26C	90428	35A	90455	61B	90482	53A	90509	38E
90402	38D	90429	53C	90456	36C	90483	84D	90510	40B
90403	25A	90430	53A	90457	51B	90484	38E	90511	53C
90404	51E	90431	40B	90458	53A	90485	81C	90512	36C
90405		90432	38A	90459	51B	90486	38E	90513	62C

90514	35A	90542	62C	90570	27D	90598	36B	90626	26D
90515	62B	90543	25D	90571	53C	90599	27D	90627	53A
90516	38E	90544	86A	90572	86C	90600	62B	90628	66B
90517	50A	90545	40E	90573	85B	90601	31B	90629	38A
90518	50A	90546	26B	90574	38E	90602	31B	90630	86C
90519	38A	90547	62C	90575	62C	90603	50A	90631	25A
90520	38E	90548	26A	90576	26A	90604	25A	90632	26B
90521	36B	90549	65D	90577	35A	90605	51B	90633	25A
90522	31B	90550	31B	90578	25D	90606	6B	90634	38A
90523	26A	90551	35A	90579	84C	90607	25A	90635	25A
90524	86C	90552	26G	90580	36B	90608	31B	90636	36A
90525	26A	90553	62C	90581	25A	90609	53A	90637	25A
90526	35A	90554	35A	90582	36B	90610	25A	90638	38E
90527	25G	90555	26D	90583	40B	90611	54B	90639	25A
90528	35A	90556	25A	90584	27D	90612	36B	90640	24C
90529	81F	90557	24B	90585	86A	90613	35A	90641	26C
90530	26A	90558	26A	90586	53C	90614	62A	90642	25D
90531	25C	90559	35A	90587	36B	90615	25A	90643	27B
90532	2E	90560	62C	90588	25G	90616	66A	90644	25A
90533	26A	90561	26A	90589	26A	90617	25A	90645	25G
90534	62A	90562	25G	90590	36B	90618	38A	90646	36C
90535	26A	90563	82B	90591	25G	90619	25B	90647	36C
90536	66A	90564	26B	90592	24B	90620	25A	90648	38A
90537	36A	90565	86C	90593	25D	90621	25B	90649	25G
90538	36A	90566	6B	90594	40B	90622	25D	90650	25G
90539	62A	90567	40E	90595	24C	90623	53C	90651	25A
90540	36C	90568	26D	90596	36C	90624	25A	90652	25A
90541	24C	90569	31B	90597	36B	90625	51B	90653	36B

A clean Austerity 2-8-0, No 90564, is seen at Shrewsbury after works attention at Crewe in April 1954. It was allocated to Manchester Agecroft after transfer from London's Bricklayers Arms shed during the week ended 16 June 1951, a time when the Southern was transferring away all its 2-8-0s. Built by Vulcan Foundry in 1943, it remained working from Agecroft until June 1960 when it transferred to Lostock Hall, then went back to Agecroft in October of the next year. May 1963 saw it on Gorton's roster, and later in the year it went to Lees Oldham. Return to Gorton in February 1964 was the prelude to its withdrawal three months later, during the week ended 25 April.

G. W. Sharpe

90654	25A	90682	25A	90710	25A	90753	64D	92004	86A
90655	25B	90683	35A	90711	25G	90754	66B	92005	86A
90656	25A	90684	25G	90712	26C	90755	65F	92006	86A
90657	35A	90685	85B	90713	26B	90756	66B	92007	86A
90658	24C	90686	84K	90714	36C	90757	65F	92008	15A
90659	35A	90687	27B	90715	26A	90758	66B	92009	15A
90660	40B	90688	53C	90716	84G	90759	65F	92010	31B
90661	53C	90689	24C	90717	38A	90760	66B	92011	31B
90662	38A	90690	62A	90718	26D	90761	66B	92012	31B
90663	53C	90691	85B	90719	25A	90762	66B	92013	31B
90664	25G	90692	25A	90720	24C	90763	68A	92014	30A
90665	35A	90693	86C	90721	25D	90764	66B	92015	15A
90666	25G	90694	25B	90722	25A	90765	65F	92016	15A
90667	6B	90695	53A	90723	25D	90766	66B	92017	15A
90668	31B	90696	36A	90724	25A	90767	66A	92018	15A
90669	26A	90697	38E	90725	26C	90768	64D	92019	15A
90670	50C	90698	25G	90726	25G	90769	68A	92030	35A
90671	27D	90699	25G	90727	62C	90770	66B	92031	31B
90672	38E	90700	36B	90728	25G	90771	66B	92032	35A
90673	25A	90701	84G	90729	26C	90772	66B	92033	35A
90674	36A	90702	6B	90730	35A	90773	65F	92034	35A
90675	26A	90703	38A	90731	25D	90774	68A	92035	35A
90676	86A	90704	53A	90732*	31B			92036	35A
90677	53C	90705	62C			**Standard 2-10-0 9F**		92037	35A
90678	25D	90706	26A	**Austerity 2-10-0 8F**		92000	86A	92038	35A
90679	25A	90707	25D	90750	66B	92001	86A	92039	35A
90680	25B	90708	26A	90751	66A	92002	86A	92040	35A
90681	24C	90709	35A	90752	66B	92003	86A	92041	35A

Built by the North British Locomotive Co in 1945, Austerity 2-10-0 No 90756 is at Motherwell shed in September 1955. Based at 66B throughout its entire time on British Railways, it was withdrawn along with the remaining members of the class on 29 December 1962. *Photomatic/RAS Marketing*

Above: The pioneer Co-Co diesel, No 10000, was built at Derby by the LMS and allocated to Camden on 13 December 1947. From March 1953 to April 1955 it worked on the Southern Region from Nine Elms, and this view in August 1954 shows the engine at Bournemouth station. Returning to the LMR it was again allocated to Camden and moved on to Willesden in November 1959. Placed in store at Derby Works in December 1962, it was withdrawn on 7 December 1963 and remained in store until February 1968 when it was sent to Cashmore's yard at Great Bridge for scrap.

R. H. G. Simpson

Below: Not introduced until 1955 were the 10 2-10-0s fitted with Crosti boilers, and this was the first, No 92020, seen at Shrewsbury in 1956. All were allocated to Wellingborough, this one being received on 21 May. Not entirely a success, the boilers were later converted to conventional form. No 92020 stayed at Wellingborough until October 1963 when it was sent to Kirkby in Ashfield, and to Speke Junction in September 1964, to finally settle at Birkenhead in January 1965. Withdrawal came during the week ended 21 October 1967.

G. W. Sharpe

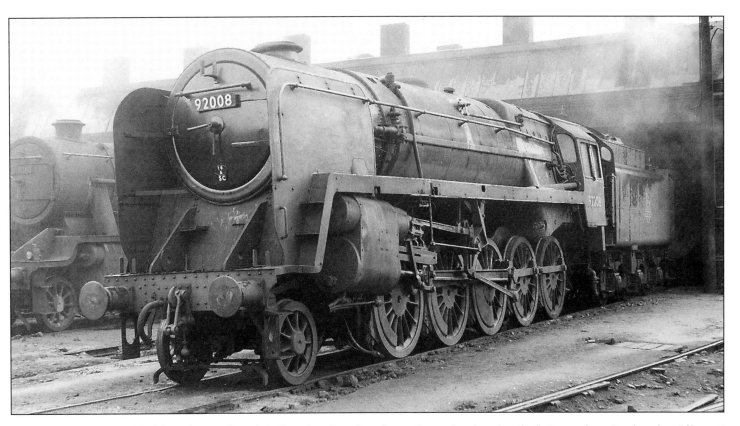

Above: The Standard 2-10-0 freight engine was the culmination of modern steam locomotive engineering when the first examples entered service at Newport Ebbw Junction in January 1954. After teething troubles, they settled down to be a resounding success. The first to go new to Wellingborough from Crewe Works during the week ended 6 March 1954 was No 92008, seen here at Shrewsbury shed in March 1955. It stayed at Wellingborough until June 1957 when it was moved to Saltley. From November 1959 it operated from Rowsley and from June 1962 changed between Saltley, Rowsley, and Kirkby in Ashfield, going to Liverpool Speke Junction for a longer spell in December 1964. Warrington Dallam added it to its operating stock in August 1967 until withdrawal two months later, during the week ended 7 October. *G. W. Sharpe*

Below: Another 'one-off', the 2-D-2 Paxman/Fell diesel No 10100 is seen at Derby shed in April 1955. Powered by four Paxman 500hp 12-cylinder engines, it was built at Derby Works in conjunction with Fell Developments Ltd to the designs of Lt-Col L. F. R. Fell and was completed in December 1950. Trials then started, and it was allocated to Derby shed on 19 February 1952. It remained the property of the makers until bought by BR in 1955. Withdrawal came in November 1958 and after the removal of the power equipment, it remained stored at Derby Works until February 1960 and by the 11th of that month had been completely cut up. *P. H. Groom*

Above: Birmingham New Street station on Saturday 2 July 1955 sees the 1.55pm from Wolverhampton to Euston calling at Platform 3 with 1 Co-Co 1 diesel No 10202 in charge. Built at Ashford Works in October 1951, it worked on the Southern Region until April 1955 when it was transferred to Camden. In November 1959 Willesden became its base and in January 1963 it entered Derby Works for storage, withdrawal coming on 7 December the same year. Storage at Derby continued until February 1968 when it was cut up at Cashmore's, Great Bridge.

Michael Mensing

Below: Derby Works in March 1956 sees Bo-Bo diesel No 10800 awaiting attention. Built by the North British Locomotive Co, it started trials on the LMR in June 1950 and operated from Willesden, then Bletchley from December 1950 to July 1952. Norwood Junction then had it to try and in December 1954 until February 1955 it was operating from Plaistow. Rugby subsequently had it on allocation until withdrawal on 8 August 1959. It was sold to Brush Traction at Loughborough in 1961 who rebuilt the engine as a research locomotive.

P. H. Groom

Diesel and Gas Turbine Locomotives

LMS/English Electric Co-Co

10000	70A
10001	70A

LMR/Fell diesel mechanical 4-8-4

10100	17A

SR/BR/English Electric 1 Co-Co 1

10201	70A
10202	70A
10203	70A

North British prototype Bo-Bo

10800	33A

BR diesel mechanical 0-6-0 shunter

11001	20B

Drewry class 04 diesel mechanical 0-6-0 shunter

11100	32B
11101	31B
11102	31B
11103	32E
11105	51C
11106	51C
11107	51C
11108	34A
11109	34A
11110	30F
11111	30F
11112	32B
11113	30F
11114	34A
11115	30F

Hunslet diesel mechanical 0-4-0 shunter

11500	32B
11501	32B

North British diesel hydraulic 0-4-0 shunter

11700	51C
11701	51C
11702	51C

LMS/Hawthorn Leslie 0-6-0 shunter

12000	5B
12001	5B
12002	5B

LMS/English Electric 0-6-0 shunter

12003	8C
12004	5B
12005	5B

12006	18A
12007	8C
12008	8C
12009	5B
12010	5B
12011	8C
12012	5B
12013	1A
12014	8C
12015	8C
12016	8C
12017	8C
12018	8C
12019	5B
12020	5B
12021	5B
12022	5B
12023	5B
12024	8C
12025	8C
12026	8C
12027	8C
12028	8C
12029	1A
12030	5B
12031	5B
12032	5B

LMS/English Electric class 11 0-6-0 shunter

12033	1A
12034	1A
12035	1A
12036	1A
12037	1A
12038	18A
12039	21A
12040	21A
12041	21A
12042	21A
12043	21A
12044	21A
12045	18A
12046	18A
12047	18A
12048	18A
12049	1A
12050	1A
12051	1A
12052	1A
12053	1A
12054	1A
12055	1A
12056	18A
12057	18A
12058	16A
12059	21A
12060	21A
12061	21A
12062	21A
12063	14A
12064	14A
12065	14A

12066	14A
12067	14A
12068	14A
12069	16A
12070	18A
12071	18A
12072	18A
12073	9D
12074	21A
12075	21A
12076	21A
12077	21A
12078	1A
12079	68A
12080	68A
12081	12A
12082	12A
12083	12A
12084	68E
12085	68E
12086	68E
12087	12A
12088	3D
12089	3D
12090	3D
12091	3A
12092	3A
12093	3B
12094	3B
12095	3D
12096	16A
12097	16A
12098	16A
12099	16A
12100	16A
12101	16A
12102	16A
12103	30A
12104	30A
12105	30A
12106	30A
12107	30A
12108	30A
12109	30A
12110	30A
12111	30A
12112	34B
12113	53C
12114	53C
12115	53C
12116	53C
12117	53C
12118	53C
12119	53C
12120	53C
12121	53A
12122	53A
12123	34B
12124	34B
12125	34A
12126	34A
12127	40B
12128	31B

12129	34A
12130	31B
12131	34A
12132	31B
12133	40B
12134	40B
12135	30A
12136	30A
12137	34B
12138	34A

BR diesel electric class 08 0-6-0 shunter

13000	82B
13001	82B
13002	82B
13003	82B
13004	84E
13005	67C
13006	67C
13007	67B
13008	67B
13009	67B
13010	71A
13011	71A
13012	71A
13013	71A
13014	71A
13015	1A
13016	1A
13017	1A
13018	1A
13019	1A
13020	3D
13021	3C
13022	14A
13023	14A
13024	14A
13025	84E
13026	84E
13027	84E
13028	84E
13029	84E
13030	81A
13031	81A
13032	81A
13033	81A
13034	84B
13035	84B
13036	84B
13037	84B
13038	84B
13039	84B
13040	70B
13041	70B
13042	70B
13043	73C
13044	73C
13045	73C
13046	73C
13047	73C
13048	75C
13049	73C

13050	1A
13051	1E
13052	1E
13053	2A
13054	2A
13055	2A
13056	18A
13057	15A
13058	15A
13059	15A
13060	36B
13061	36B
13062	36B
13063	36B
13064	36B
13065	38E
13066	38E
13067	38E
13068	38E
13069	38E
13070	53A
13071	53C
13072	53C
13073	53A
13074	53A
13075	53A
13076	53A
13077	53A
13078	53A
13079	53A
13080	53A
13081	53A
13082	21A
13083	16A
13084	16A
13085	16A
13086	16A
13087	8C
13088	8C
13089	8C
13090	3B
13091	3C
13092	75C
13093	75C
13094	75C
13095	75C
13096	75C
13127	35A
13128	35A
13129	35A
13130	35A
13131	35A
13132	65F
13133	65F
13134	65F
13135	65F
13136	65F

LNER/English Electric 0-6-0 diesel shunter

15000	31B
15001	31B
15002	31B

Above: Class 04 0-6-0 diesel shunter No 11131 is at Stratford shed in 1956. Entering traffic on 18 October 1955, it was renumbered D2225 in September 1959 and transferred to Manchester Newton Heath in July 1964, then on to Wigan Springs Branch in May 1968. Withdrawn on 15 March 1969, it was sold to the NCB and operated at Manvers Main Colliery, Wath, until finally being withdrawn in July 1985.   *R. H. G. Simpson*

Below: Added to stock on 2 January 1955, 0-4-0 diesel shunter No 11502 was allocated to Ipswich where it was photographed in 1956. It was used in the docks which required street running, hence the motion being covered and front and rear iron grids. Renumbered D2952 in May 1958, it remained at Ipswich until withdrawn on 25 December 1966. Scrapping was carried out at the Slag Reduction Plant at Ickles, South Yorkshire, in August 1967.   *R. H. G. Simpson*

Above: Another addition to stock during 1955 on 29 August was this North British Loco Co-built 0-4-0 diesel shunter No 11703, seen here at Dundee in 1956. Renumbered D2703 on 20 February 1960, further allocations were Polmont in October 1957 and Grangemouth in May 1964. Withdrawn on 3 February 1968, it was scrapped at the Shipbreaking Industries yard at Faslane in May 1968.

R. H. G. Simpson

Below: Ex-works at Derby in 1954 is LMS-built 0-6-0 diesel shunter No 12038. Built at Derby in December 1945 and numbered 7125, it was first allocated to Crewe South. Renumbered in April 1951, it was allocated to Toton in October 1946, Speke Junction in November 1966, Lostock Hall in May 1967 and Wigan Springs Branch in December 1967. It was withdrawn on 11 January 1969, but records show it was used after this date at Liverpool Edge Hill due to a locomotive shortage. It was withdrawn permanently the following November and after storage at Allerton was cut up at Cohens yard at Kettering in July 1971.

Initial Photographics/R. J. Buckley

Above: Later to become Class 08, 0-6-0 diesel shunter No 13030 is at Old Oak Common shed in June 1955. Built at Derby Works, it entered traffic at 81A in October 1953 and was renumbered D3030 in October 1958 and 08022 in February 1974. Reallocations were as follows: Reading, August 1964; Old Oak Common, November 1964; Shirebrook, July 1967; Knottingley, May 1973; and Tinsley, August 1977. It was withdrawn in March 1985. *R. H. G. Simpson*

Below: Based on an earlier Southern Railway design and built at Ashford Works, the Class 12 diesel shunter is represented by No 15220 at Bricklayers Arms shed in July 1953. New in July 1949, it was first allocated to Hither Green. In March 1952 it moved to Norwood Junction, then back to Hither Green in July 1953. It went on to Ashford in February 1958 and once again back to Hither Green in October 1964 until withdrawal in October 1971. *G. W. Sharpe*

Above: The Brown-Boveri Gas Turbine A1A-A1A No 18000 is seen near Old Oak Common in March 1957. This had been built in Switzerland and delivered to Swindon Works on 4 February 1950, being added to stock at Old Oak Common in May 1950, where it stayed until withdrawal on 16 December 1960. It remained in a derelict condition at Swindon until sold in January 1965 to the International Union of Railways for use by its research department. Until 1968 it was stored in Bellinzona Works of the Swiss Federal Railways, with the gas turbine engine removed. By June 1969 it was at the Vienna Arsenal European Testing Station for experimental tests, and remained there until returned to the UK for preservation in 1985. *P. H. Groom*

Below: This scene is at Penistone in April 1954 with a line of electric locomotives headed by No 26047 stabled for the weekend. Later to become Class 76, this engine had been built at Gorton Works and entered traffic on 22 August 1952 for working the Woodhead route. Named *Diomedes* in September 1960 and renumbered 76047 in February 1974, it was withdrawn in November 1980 and cut up after storage at Booth's yard at Rotherham in May 1983. *G. W. Sharpe*

Above: Later to become Class 77, electric locomotive No 27001 is at Wath shed on the day it was released to traffic: 22 March 1954. Built at Gorton Works, it was named *Ariadne* in October 1959 and withdrawn along with the six other members of the class on 5 October 1968. It was exported to the Netherlands in September 1969 and renumbered 1505, returning to this country for preservation at the Greater Manchester Museum of Science and Industry.

Photomatic/RAS Marketing

Below: The shape of things to come. The prototype Deltic descends Camden Bank in October 1956 on the 'Merseyside Express'. Built by English Electric at its own expense, it started trials on 24 October 1955 from Liverpool Speke Junction. Allocated to Camden in October 1956 and Hornsey in January 1959, it was withdrawn in March 1961 after it had failed. It returned to Vulcan Foundry and was stored until moved by road to the London Science Museum, arriving on 28 April 1963.

P. H. Groom

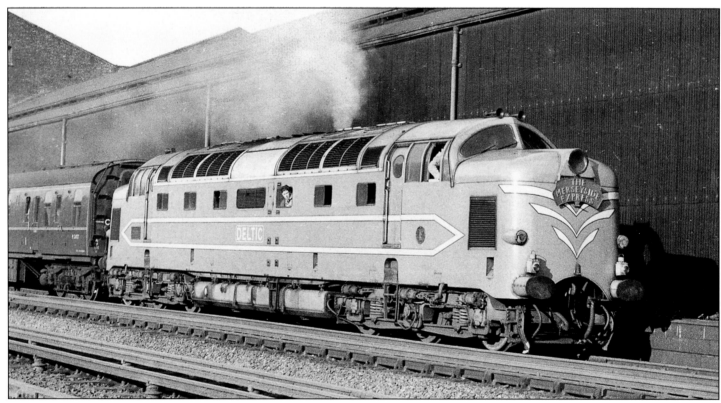

15003	31B	15102	81A	15202	75C	15219	75C	15232	71A
15004	31B	15103	81A	15203	75C	15220	73C	15233	71A
		15104	81A			15221	73C	15234	73C
Class Y11 petrol 0-4-0		15105	81A	**BR/English Electric class**		15222	73C	15235	73C
shunter		15106	81A	**12 0-6-0 shunter**		15223	73C	15236	73C
15098	30A			15211	75C	15224	73C		
15099	30A	**BR/Petter/Brush**		15212	75C	15225	73C	**Brown-Bovery Gas**	
		0-6-0 shunter		15213	75C	15226	73C	**Turbine A1A-A1A**	
GWR/Hawthorn-		15107	82B	15214	75C	15227	73C	18000	81A
Leslie/English Electric				15215	75C	15228	73C		
0-6-0 diesel shunter		**SR/English Electric**		15216	75C	15229	73C	**Metropolitan-Vickers gas**	
15100	82B	**0-6-0 shunter**		15217	75C	15230	71A	**turbine Co-Co**	
15101	81A	15201	75C	15218	75C	15231	71A	18100	81A

Electric Locomotives

`SR/English Electric class		26010	Reddish	26028	Reddish	26046	Reddish	**LNER/English class EB1**	
CC Co-Co		26011	Reddish	26029	Reddish	26047	Reddish	**Bo-Bo**	
20001	Selhurst	26012	Reddish	26030	Reddish	26048	Reddish	26510	Ilford
20002	Selhurst	26013	Reddish	26031	Reddish	26049	Reddish		
20003	Selhurst	26014	Reddish	26032	Reddish	26050	Reddish	**BR/EMI class EM2 Co-Co**	
		26015	Reddish	26033	Reddish	26051	Reddish	27000	Reddish
LNER/BR Metropolitan-		26016	Reddish	26034	Reddish	26052	Reddish	27001	Reddish
Vickers class EM1 Bo-Bo		26017	Reddish	26035	Reddish	26053	Reddish	27002	Reddish
26000*	Reddish	26018	Reddish	26036	Reddish	26054	Reddish	27003	Reddish
26001	Reddish	26019	Reddish	26037	Reddish	26055	Reddish	27004	Reddish
26002	Reddish	26020	Reddish	26038	Reddish	26056	Reddish	27005	Reddish
26003	Reddish	26021	Reddish	26039	Reddish	26057	Reddish	27006	Reddish
26004	Reddish	26022	Reddish	26040	Reddish				
26005	Reddish	26023	Reddish	26041	Reddish	**NER/Brush and**			
26006	Reddish	26024	Reddish	26042	Reddish	**Thomson-Houston class**			
26007	Reddish	26025	Reddish	26043	Reddish	**ES1 Bo-Bo**			
26008	Reddish	26026	Reddish	26044	Reddish	26500	52B		
26009	Reddish	26027	Reddish	26045	Reddish	26501	52B		

Service Locomotives

Service No	BR No	Locomotive Type	Allocation
1	68845	J52 class 0-6-0ST	Doncaster Works
2	68816	J52 class 0-6-0ST	Doncaster Works
3	68181	Y3 class Sentinel 0-4-0T	Ranskill Wagon Works
4	68132	Y1 class Sentinel 0-4-0T	Ranskill Wagon Works
5	68165	Y3 class Sentinel 0-4-0T	Doncaster Wagon Works
6	68133	Y1 class Sentinel 0-4-0T	Peterborough Engineer's Yard
7	68166	Y3 class Sentinel 0-4-0T	Boston Sleeper Depot
23		0-4-0 Petrol Shunter	Didcot Stores
24		0-4-0 Petrol Shunter	Taunton Engineer's Department
26		0-4-0 Petrol Shunter	Didcot Stores
27		0-4-0 Petrol Shunter	Reading Signal Works
31	68382	J66 class 0-6-0T	Stratford Works London
32	68370	J66 class 0-6-0T	Stratford Works London
33	68129	Y4 class 0-4-0T	Stratford Works London
36	68378	J66 class 0-6-0T	Stratford Works London
37	68130	Y1 class Sentinel 0-4-0T	Lowestoft Engineer's Department
38	68168	Y3 class Sentinel 0-4-0T	Lowestoft Engineer's Department
39	68131	Y1 class Sentinel 0-4-0T	Lowestoft Engineer's Department
40	68173	Y3 class Sentinel 0-4-0T	Lowestoft Engineer's Department
41	68177	Y3 class Sentinel 0-4-0T	Lowestoft Engineer's Department
42	68178	Y3 class Sentinel 0-4-0T	Cambridge Engineer's Department

Service No	BR No	Locomotive Type	Allocation
51	68136	Y1 class Sentinel 0-4-0T	Faverdale Works Darlington
52	11104	Drewry 0-6-0 Diesel Shunter	West Hartlepool Permanent Way Depot
53	68152	Y1 class Sentinel 0-4-0T	York Engineer's Yard
55	68091	Y8 class 0-4-0T	York Motive Power Depot
11304		Aspinall Rebuilt 0-6-0ST	Horwich Works
11305		Aspinall Rebuilt 0-6-0ST	Horwich Works
11324		Aspinall Rebuilt 0-6-0ST	Horwich Works
11368		Aspinall Rebuilt 0-6-0ST	Horwich Works
11394		Aspinall Rebuilt 0-6-0ST	Horwich Works
68153		Y1 class Sentinel 0-4-0T	Darlington Permanent Way Depot
CD3		LNWR 0-6-0ST	Wolverton Carriage Works
CD6		LNWR 0-6-0ST	Wolverton Carriage Works
CD7		LNWR 0-6-0ST	Wolverton Carriage Works
CD8		LNWR 0-6-0ST	Wolverton Carriage Works
DS74		Bo-Bo Electric	Durnsford Road Power Station
DS75		Bo Electric	Waterloo & City Line
DS77		C14 class 0-4-0T	Redbridge Sleeper Depot
DS377		AIX class Terrier 0-6-0T	Brighton Works
DS600		Fowler 0-4-0 Diesel Shunter	Eastleigh Carriage Works
DS680		A1 class 0-6-0T	Lancing Carriage Works
DS681		A1X class 0-6-0T	Lancing Carriage Works
DS1173		Drewry 0-6-0 Diesel Shunter	Hither Green Engineer's Depot London
DS3152	30272	G6 class 0-6-0T	Meldon Quarry
ED1		Fowler 0-4-0 Diesel Shunter	Beeston Creosote Works
ED2		Fowler 0-4-0 Diesel Shunter	Beeston Creosote Works
ED3		Fowler 0-4-0 Diesel Shunter	Castleton Permanent Way Depot
ED4		Fowler 0-4-0 Diesel Shunter	Northampton Engineers
ED5		Fowler 0-4-0 Diesel Shunter	Castleton Permanent Way Depot
ED6		Fowler 0-4-0 Diesel Shunter	Beeston Creosote Works

Narrow Gauge Locomotives

No	Gauge	Locomotive Type	Allocation
7	1' 11½"	Davies and Metcalfe 2-6-2T	Vale of Rheidol Railway Aberystwyth
8	1' 11½"	Davies and Metcalfe 2-6-2T	Vale of Rheidol Railway Aberystwyth
9	1' 11½"	Davies and Metcalfe 2-6-2T	Vale of Rheidol Railway Aberystwyth
822	2' 6"	Beyer Peacock 0-6-0T	Welshpool & Llanfair Railway
823	2' 6"	Beyer Peacock 0-6-0T	Welshpool & Llanfair Railway
Wren	0' 18"	Beyer Peacock 0-4-0ST	Horwich Works

Locomotives Withdrawn During 1955

No	Month Withdrawn	Last Allocation	No	Month Withdrawn	Last Allocation
39	August	Cardiff East Dock	79	July	Cardiff Cathays
59	July	Cardiff East Dock	83	May	Cardiff East Dock
66	July	Cardiff East Dock	204	July	Cardiff East Dock
69	July	Duffryn Yard	208	July	Cardiff East Dock
70	July	Duffryn Yard	210	March	Cardiff East Dock
78	August	Cardiff East Dock	211	May	Cardiff East Dock

No	Month Withdrawn	Last Allocation
215	July	Cardiff East Dock
216	January	Cardiff East Dock
290	July	Cardiff East Dock
308	December	Cardiff East Dock
343	October	Cardiff Cathays
345	September	Cardiff Cathays
346	October	Cardiff Cathays
352	March	Treherbert
356	January	Abercynon
360	February	Cardiff Cathays
365	October	Abercynon
366	October	Treherbert
371	January	Cardiff East Dock
372	February	Barry
374	September	Cardiff East Dock
666	April	Newport Pill
681	February	Cardiff East Dock
1153	October	Swansea Danygraig
2034	September	Kidderminster
2035	March	Newport Ebbw Junction
2043	January	Birkenhead
2061	April	Wellington
2070	August	Bristol St Philips Marsh
2082	June	Birkenhead
2088	August	Taunton
2090	March	Newport Ebbw Junction
2092	August	Birkenhead
2097	March	Plymouth Laira
2136	April	Birkenhead
2144	May	Worcester
2162	March	Llanelly
2165	March	Llanelly
2166	May	Swansea East Dock
2176	March	Llanelly
2182	August	St Blazey
2183	May	Wrexham Croes Newydd
2186	April	Wrexham Croes Newydd
2474	April	Reading
2513	July	Brecon
3014	October	Carmarthen
3023	October	Birmingham Tyseley
3032	October	Bristol St Philips Marsh
4405	September	Newton Abbot
4406	September	Newton Abbot
4410	September	Plymouth Laira
4506	March	Neyland
4521	December	Gloucester Horton Road
4522	February	Aberbeeg
4523	October	Truro
4530	March	Plymouth Laira
4532	February	Bristol Bath Road
4533	March	Pontypool Road
4534	February	Plymouth Laira
4535	February	Bristol Bath Road
4537	February	Penzance
4539	October	Bristol Bath Road
4541	October	Neyland
4542	September	Plymouth Laira
5112	October	Stafford Road
5113	October	Newton Abbot
5395	October	Machynlleth
9000	March	Machynlleth
9003	October	Machynlleth
30203	December	Wadebridge
30434	February	Guildford
30467	September	Nine Elms
30485	April	Nine Elms
30490	June	Nine Elms
30740	December	Bournemouth
30743	October	Bournemouth
30746	October	Eastleigh
30752	December	Nine Elms
31154	August	Folkestone
31158	April	Gillingham
31166	May	Tonbridge
31225	June	Bricklayers Arms
31277	August	Tonbridge
31294	September	Bricklayers Arms
31309	May	Redhill
31320	December	Gillingham
31335	July	St Leonards
31496	August	Guildford
31513	January	Ashford
31531	March	Dover
31555	February	Stewarts Lane
31586	September	Guildford
31591	May	Guildford
31661	August	Ashford
31666	December	Tonbridge
31687	April	Hither Green
31698	October	Tonbridge
31713	April	Gillingham
31718	September	Stewarts Lane
31734	October	Tonbridge
32094	April	Plymouth Friary
32167	October	Brighton
32169	July	Brighton
32328	January	Basingstoke
32330	August	Basingstoke
32390	October	Brighton
32453	July	Bricklayers Arms
32465	March	Horsham
32482	October	Brighton
32489	May	Norwood Junction
32490	December	Guildford
32496	October	Brighton
32501	July	Reading
32516	October	Brighton
32518	June	Brighton
32568	February	Basingstoke
32576	July	Brighton
32586	March	Brighton
W19	November	Ryde IoW
W23	August	Ryde IoW
W34	August	Newport I.O.W.
40377	August	Llandudno Junction
40405	March	Manchester Longsight
40419	September	Crewe North
40448	November	Carlisle Upperby
40472	September	Skipton
40522	October	Crewe North
40535	August	Nottingham
40562	December	Bradford Manningham
40903	August	Carstairs
40906	January	Glasgow Corkerhill
40908	July	Glasgow Corkerhill

No	Month Withdrawn	Last Allocation	No	Month Withdrawn	Last Allocation
40912	April	Dumfries	43581	July	Shrewsbury
40913	August	Glasgow Corkerhill	43600	May	Shrewsbury
40915	November	Hurlford	43636	November	Carlisle Kingmoor
40916	July	Glasgow Polmadie	43676	October	Leicester Midland
40921	November	Perth	43686	December	Bradford Manningham
40924	March	Perth	43723	September	Toton
41059	November	Bedford	43755	November	Sheffield Grimesthorpe
41061	May	Bradford Manningham	43775	November	Sheffield Grimesthorpe
41067	February	Bradford Manningham	43781	November	Sheffield Grimesthorpe
41069	November	Gloucester Barnwood	43791	November	Birmingham Saltley
41070	November	Sheffield Millhouses	43803	September	Birmingham Saltley
41072	October	Sheffield Millhouses	43810	April	Toton
41076	May	Rugby	43817	September	Birmingham Saltley
41081	November	Lancaster	43835	October	Coalville
41091	April	Leicester Midland	43867	October	Westhouses
41104	August	Leeds Holbeck	43894	September	Coalville
41107	September	Lancaster	43909	August	Birmingham Saltley
41117	April	Gloucester Barnwood	44006	October	Westhouses
41124	January	Holyhead	46604	August	Warwick
41127	August	Stranraer	46616	September	Swansea Victoria
41129	May	Stranraer	47183	September	Shrewsbury
41130	August	Carstairs	47184	December	Crewe South
41135	August	Stranraer	47232	April	Swansea Victoria
41136	October	Lancaster	47237	April	Gloucester Barnwood
41149	August	Greenock	47252	January	Bedford
41154	August	Manchester Trafford Park	47253	June	Burton-on-Trent
41161	November	Manchester Trafford Park	47970	July	Toton
41169	July	Manchester Trafford Park	47975	July	Toton
41175	April	Dumfries	47985	June	Toton
41176	January	Glasgow Corkerhill	47989	November	Toton
41177	November	Stranraer	47990	May	Toton
41183	February	Ayr	47991	December	Toton
41188	November	Lower Darwen	47993	December	Hasland
41198	November	Leicester Midland	49140	September	Crewe Works
41516	October	Burton-on-Trent	49554	August	Sowerby Bridge
41523	March	Burton-on-Trent	49557	November	Newton Heath
41671	November	Kentish Town	49570	August	Newton Heath
41672	December	St Albans	50648	November	Rose Grove
41682	January	Nottingham	50651	December	Rose Grove
41713	August	Kentish Town	50656	March	Bolton
41725	August	Shrewsbury	50686	August	Bradford Manningham
41749	June	Staveley Barrow Hill	50715	February	Sowerby Bridge
41859	December	Leeds Stourton	50731	November	Bolton
41865	June	Burton-on-Trent	50807	April	Bradford Low Moor
41889	April	Derby	50869	November	Bradford Low Moor
41938	February	Leicester Midland	51376	April	Bolton
41971	February	Skipton	51379	April	Goole
41972	February	Skipton	51436	March	Newton Heath
41973	February	Skipton	51470	October	Newton Heath
41974	February	Skipton	51472	April	Newton Heath
43252	June	Sheffield Grimesthorpe	51477	August	Fleetwood
43273	October	Rowsley	51510	November	Manchester Belle Vue
43298	November	Staveley Barrow Hill	51511	October	Bolton
43310	December	Staveley Barrow Hill	51530	November	Liverpool Aintree
43317	October	Westhouses	52021	August	Wigan Springs Branch
43331	December	Westhouses	52045	August	Manchester Patricroft
43351	December	Carlisle Kingmoor	52053	March	Wakefield
43454	February	Bedford	52150	March	Bradford Low Moor
43494	November	Burton-on-Trent	52164	June	Bury
43497	December	Normanton	52194	August	Lower Darwen
43524	November	Staveley Barrow Hill	52215	March	Blackpool
43544	December	Birmingham Saltley	52220	February	Lower Darwen
43568	May	Birmingham Saltley	52272	April	Lostock Hall

216

No	Month Withdrawn	Last Allocation	No	Month Withdrawn	Last Allocation
52317	June	Newton Heath	58851	February	Devons Road, Bow
52331	August	Goole	58852	June	Devons Road, Bow
52397	June	Sutton Oak	58887	April	Bletchley
52408	August	Sowerby Bridge	58891	September	Abergavenny
52416	July	Liverpool Aintree	58904	September	Shrewsbury
52447	December	Lower Darwen	58925	September	Abergavenny
52465	July	Nuneaton	61523	March	Stratford
52522	March	Lower Darwen	61562	August	Ipswich
52561	February	Bradford Low Moor	61722	September	Glasgow Parkhead
52569	April	Lees, Oldham	62262	October	Keith Junction
52575	December	Bolton	62269	September	Keith Junction
52582	May	Southport	62272	March	Keith Junction
52608	February	Rhyl	62273	January	Keith Junction
54438	May	Dumfries	62274	September	Aberdeen Kittybrewster
54443	October	Dumfries	62275	December	Keith Junction
54446	August	Carstairs	62276	August	Aberdeen Kittybrewster
54448	February	Perth	62278	July	Aberdeen Kittybrewster
54450	October	Forfar	62279	May	Aberdeen Kittybrewster
54451	September	Edinburgh Dalry Road	62355	November	Alnmouth
54454	October	Forfar	62359	October	Leeds Neville Hill
54457	February	Motherwell	62384	August	Selby
54460	October	Motherwell	62525	September	Cambridge
55145	April	Stirling	62531	March	Cambridge
55177	June	Edinburgh Dalry Road	62536	July	Peterborough Spital
55187	February	Glasgow Corkerhill	62541	October	Cambridge
55193	April	Forfar	62549	December	Cambridge
55194	March	Perth	62552	October	Ipswich
55196	December	Oban	62554	November	Norwich
56020	March	Bromsgrove	62557	October	Cambridge
56248	January	Glasgow Polmadie	62559	December	King's Lynn
56263	December	Glasgow Polmadie	62573	October	King's Lynn
57235	October	Ayr	62574	December	Cambridge
57260	October	Hamilton	62579	March	King's Lynn
57282	November	Ardrossan	62585	April	Cambridge
57315	December	Ayr	62607	November	Cambridge
58040	March	Wellingborough	62620	October	Melton Constable
58054	November	Plaistow	62653	October	Northwich
58077	September	Retford	62656	January	Northwich
58084	February	Buxton	62658	August	Northwich
58087	June	Plaistow	62780	September	Cambridge
58125	November	Walsall	62784	May	Cambridge
58127	November	Canklow	62791	April	Cambridge
58129	February	Plaistow	62793	February	Norwich
58133	December	Nottingham	62794	August	Cambridge
58152	November	Wolverhampton Bushbury	62795	March	Cambridge
58162	September	Shrewsbury	64194	November	Colwick
58164	April	Leicester Midland	64212	December	Colwick
58207	September	Shrewsbury	64242	August	Hornsey
58230	December	Birmingham Saltley	64282	April	Retford
58236	November	Burton-on-Trent	64286	October	Sheffield Darnall
58241	June	Shrewsbury	64289	June	Langwith Junction
58257	November	Barrow	64291	November	Sheffield Darnall
58273	October	Barrow	64299	November	Tuxford
58277	November	Bescot	64301	May	Colwick
58286	October	Monument Lane	64307	July	Immingham
58300	April	Leicester Midland	64323	October	Immingham
58375	February	Widnes	64326	August	Manchester Gorton
58376	March	Widnes	64334	November	Doncaster
58394	August	Bangor	64342	March	Manchester Gorton
58409	December	Penrith	64347	March	Retford
58412	December	Carlisle Upperby	64350	August	Lincoln
58427	December	Widnes	64356	August	Mexborough
58430	March	Widnes	64358	October	Langwith Junction

No	Month Withdrawn	Last Allocation	No	Month Withdrawn	Last Allocation
64360	July	Sheffield Darnall	67300	December	Sunderland
64369	October	Colwick	67301	March	Hull Botanic Gardens
64370	June	Annesley	67304	February	Blaydon
64374	July	Mexborough	67307	May	Sunderland
64390	May	Colwick	67308	November	Pickering sub-shed
64391	January	Barnsley	67309	March	Hexham sub-shed
64400	November	Mexborough	67310	September	Sunderland
64413	November	Manchester Gorton	67314	December	West Hartlepool
64415	October	Manchester Gorton	67316	December	Sunderland
64436	November	Barnsley	67327	February	Aberdeen Kittybrewster
65082	January	Tweedmouth	67328	November	Sunderland
65088	November	Hexham sub-shed	67336	March	Sunderland
65090	December	Blaydon	67345	December	Sunderland
65314	August	Bathgate	67350	April	Hull Botanic Gardens
65359	December	King's Lynn	67353	April	Hull Botanic Gardens
65384	March	Stratford	67360	January	King's Lynn
65422	July	March	67361	April	Hull Botanic Gardens
65483	December	Colwick	67368	October	Peterborough Spital
65494	January	Colwick	67371	April	Hull Botanic Gardens
65498	December	Colwick	67375	April	Hull Botanic Gardens
65510	March	Ipswich	67382	April	Hull Botanic Gardens
65516	March	Norwich	67383	February	Louth
65517	May	South Lynn	67385	April	Hull Botanic Gardens
65524	March	Norwich	67387	February	Yarmouth South Town
65543	May	Stratford	67389	April	Hull Botanic Gardens
65552	January	Stratford	67401	December	Manchester Gorton
65569	February	Norwich	67403	April	Manchester Gorton
65574	April	Norwich	67405	May	Manchester Gorton
65723	March	York	67411	May	Barnsley
67162	August	Yarmouth Vauxhall	67414	June	Wrexham Rhosddu
67187	August	Lowestoft	67455	February	Aberdeen Kittybrewster
67188	December	Colchester	67457	June	Hawick
67190	November	Lowestoft	67459	October	Polmont
67191	November	Colchester	67463	September	Polmont
67196	March	Colchester	67467	March	Glasgow Kipps
67197	March	Stratford	67498	August	Dundee Tay Bridge
67198	August	Stratford	67499	November	Dundee Tay Bridge
67204	September	Lowestoft	68093	May	Edinburgh St. Margarets
67205	November	Stratford	68094	April	Glasgow Kipps
67206	September	Lowestoft	68105	April	Edinburgh St Margarets
67207	December	Lowestoft	68112	January	Glasgow Yoker
67210	July	Stratford	68120	August	Glasgow Kipps
67213	February	Stratford	68121	July	Glasgow Kipps
67215	September	Stratford	68122	August	Edinburgh St. Margarets
67217	November	Colchester	68125	September	Stratford
67220	July	Ipswich	68148	December	Hull Dairycoates
67222	August	Bury St Edmunds	68155	August	Bridlington
67223	December	Lowestoft	68158	September	Selby
67226	November	Lowestoft	68169	July	Immingham
67232	November	Lowestoft	68183*	September	Hull Dairycoates
67233	December	Lowestoft	*Transferred to Departmental Stock as Dept 8		
67236	August	Bury St Edmunds	68185	April	Immingham
67237	August	Bury St Edmunds	68206	March	Immingham
67238	November	Cambridge	68209	February	Wrexham Rhosddu
67239	December	Stratford	68222	February	Ipswich
67241	March	Blaydon	68223	July	Yarmouth Vauxhall
67243	September	Sunderland	68225	March	Ipswich
67249	March	Hexham sub-shed	68226	August	Colchester
67266	December	Leeds Neville Hill	68236	November	Darlington
67268	April	Tweedmouth	68238	September	Normanton
67271	February	Stockton	68259	September	Darlington
67293	April	Malton	68270	November	Gateshead
67296	March	South Blyth	68284	October	Hull Dairycoates

No	Month Withdrawn	Last Allocation
68289	June	Borough Gardens
68300	March	Darlington
68303	June	Middlesbrough
68307	June	Middlesbrough
68337	November	Thornton Junction
68358	March	West Hartlepool
68383	October	Staveley Great Central
68393	July	Starbeck
68420	April	Stockton
68428	February	Heaton
68432	May	Darlington
68514	July	Norwich
68523	December	Norwich
68531	October	Wrexham Rhosddu
68544	January	Polmont
68584	August	Wrexham Rhosddu
68590	September	Stratford
68592	July	Norwich
68594	November	Ipswich
68597	October	Norwich
68606	March	Ipswich
68611	July	Lowestoft
68758	November	Colwick
68765	December	Colwick
68769	September	Doncaster
68771	October	New England
68783	October	New England
68787	October	Colwick
68790	July	Ardsley
68795	November	Doncaster
68796	November	Doncaster
68797	November	Peterborough Spital
68804	October	Doncaster
68805	October	London King's Cross
68806	December	Doncaster
68807	September	Colwick
68810	November	Colwick
68812	September	Colwick
68814	November	Colwick
68818	November	London King's Cross
68820	December	New England
68852	December	Colwick
68856	November	Doncaster
68858	December	Doncaster
68861	October	London King's Cross
68864	October	London King's Cross
68865	October	Doncaster
68868	October	Ardsley
68873	September	Colwick
68879	September	New England
68881	December	London King's Cross
68883	September	Hornsey
68884	September	New England
68889	May	Peterborough Spital
69050	March	Woodford Halse
69064	January	Frodingham
69069	July	Woodford Halse
69095	October	Gateshead
69115	May	Leeds Neville Hill
69117	July	Leeds Neville Hill
69119	July	Leeds Neville Hill
69253	November	Sheffield Darnall
69256	November	Boston
69264	February	Mexborough
69273	June	London Neasden
69275	November	Lincoln
69278	November	Barnsley
69279	June	Staveley Great Central
69280	November	Mexborough
69282	July	Retford
69285	November	Sheffield Darnall
69287	July	Sheffield Darnall
69288	April	Wrexham Rhosddu
69291	November	Barnsley
69301	December	Staveley Great Central
69303	November	Barnsley
69304	March	Manchester Trafford Park
69306	November	Mexborough
69310	November	Colwick
69313	March	Retford
69330	February	Wrexham Rhosddu
69338	March	Manchester Gorton
69352	June	Wrexham Rhosddu
69353	November	Manchester Gorton
69357	November	Mexborough
69364	August	Manchester Trafford Park
69367	November	Barnsley
69368	May	Barnsley
69377	June	Heaton
69378	September	Bridlington
69381	June	Hull Dairycoates
69386	February	Hull Dairycoates
69392	May	Sunderland
69394	October	Tyne Dock
69424	June	Tyne Dock
69427	June	Tyne Dock
69429	July	Tyne Dock
69431	March	Ardsley
69435	March	Hornsey
69436	July	Hammerton Street
69439	November	Hammerton Street
69441	May	Hammerton Street
69445	January	Hornsey
69449	April	Hammerton Street
69451	October	Hammerton Street
69454	February	Hammerton Street
69455	May	Hammerton Street
69458	November	Hornsey
69459	March	Hammerton Street
69460	August	Hornsey
69463	October	Ardsley
69464	August	Hammerton Street
69465	December	Hornsey
69466	July	Hornsey
69475	April	Hammerton Street
69476	March	Colwick
69483	March	Leeds Copley Hill
69514	September	Glasgow Parkhead
69773	March	Hull Dairycoates
69778	May	Hull Springhead
69785	November	Hull Springhead
69788	November	Hull Springhead
69914	August	Stockton
69919	February	Stockton
69999	December	Manchester Gorton
Dept 6	November	P'borough Engineers Depot

Locomotives Added to Stock During 1955

No	Month to Traffic	First Allocation
From Swindon Works		
1600 class 0-6-0PT 2F		
1655	January	Llanelly
1656	January	Newport Ebbw Junction
1657	January	Hereford
1658	February	Swindon
1659	February	Carmarthen
1660	February	Wrexham Croes Newydd
1661	March	Kidderminster
1662	March	Worcester
1663	March	Wellington
1664	March	St Blazey
1665	April	Llanelly
1666	April	Llanelly
1667	May	Hereford
1668	May	Taunton
1669	May	Bristol St Philips Marsh
From Yorkshire Engine Company		
9400 class 0-6-0PT 4F		
3400	December	Cardiff East Dock
9498	March	Birmingham Tyseley
9499	July	Newport Ebbw Junction
From Derby Works		
Standard 4-6-0 5MT		
73075	April	Glasgow Polmadie
73076	April	Glasgow Polmadie
73077	May	Glasgow Eastfield
73078	May	Glasgow Eastfield
73079	May	Glasgow Corkerhill
73080	June	London Stewarts Lane
73081	June	London Stewarts Lane
73082	June	London Stewarts Lane
73083	July	London Stewarts Lane
73084	July	London Stewarts Lane
73085	August	London Stewarts Lane
73086	August	London Stewarts Lane
73087	August	London Stewarts Lane
73088	September	London Stewarts Lane
73089	September	London Stewarts Lane
73090	October	Manchester Patricroft
73091	October	Manchester Patricroft
73092	October	Manchester Patricroft
73093	November	Manchester Patricroft
73094	November	Manchester Patricroft
73095	November	Manchester Patricroft
73096	November	Manchester Patricroft
73097	December	Manchester Patricroft
73098	December	Manchester Patricroft
73099	December	Manchester Patricroft
From Doncaster Works		
73100	August	Glasgow Corkerhill
73101	September	Glasgow Corkerhill
73102	September	Glasgow Corkerhill
73103	September	Glasgow Corkerhill
73104	September	Glasgow Corkerhill

No	Month to Traffic	First Allocation
73105	December	Glasgow Eastfield
73106	December	Glasgow Eastfield
73107	December	Glasgow Eastfield
73108	December	Glasgow Eastfield
73110	October	London Nine Elms
73111	October	London Nine Elms
73112	October	London Nine Elms
73113	October	London Nine Elms
73114	November	London Nine Elms
73115	November	London Nine Elms
73116	November	London Nine Elms
73117	November	London Nine Elms
73118	December	London Nine Elms
73119	December	London Nine Elms
From Swindon Works		
Standard 4-6-0 4MT		
75065	August	Dover
75066	September	Dover
75067	September	Dover
75068	September	Dover
75069	September	Dover
75070	October	Exmouth Junction
75071	October	Exmouth Junction
75072	November	Exmouth Junction
75073	November	Exmouth Junction
75074	November	Exmouth Junction
75075	November	Exmouth Junction
75076	December	Exmouth Junction
75077	December	Exmouth Junction
From Doncaster Works		
Standard 2-6-0 4MT		
76045	March	Gateshead
76046	March	Gateshead
76047	March	Gateshead
76048	March	Gateshead
76049	April	Gateshead
76053	April	Redhill
76054	April	Redhill
76055	April	Redhill
76056	May	Redhill
76057	May	Redhill
76058	June	Redhill
76059	June	Redhill
76060	July	Redhill
76061	July	Redhill
76062	July	Redhill
From Darlington Works		
Standard 2-6-0 2MT		
78045	October	Aberdeen Kittybrewster
78046	October	Hawick
78047	October	Hawick
78048	October	Edinburgh St Margarets
78049	November	Edinburgh St Margarets
78050	November	Motherwell
78051	November	Motherwell

No	Month to Traffic	First Allocation
78052	November	Motherwell
78053	November	Motherwell
78054	December	Motherwell

From Derby Works
Standard 2-6-4T 4MT

No	Month to Traffic	First Allocation
80058	January	Glasgow Polmadie

From Brighton Works

No	Month to Traffic	First Allocation
80099	January	London Plaistow
80100	January	London Plaistow
80101	February	London Plaistow
80102	March	London Plaistow
80103	March	London Plaistow
80104	March	London Plaistow
80105	April	London Plaistow
80116	May	York
80117	May	Whitby
80118	June	Whitby
80119	June	Whitby
80120	July	Whitby
80121	July	Aberdeen Kittybrewster
80122	August	Aberdeen Kittybrewster
80123	September	Dundee Tay Bridge
80124	September	Dundee Tay Bridge
80125	October	Stirling
80126	October	Perth
80127	November	Glasgow Corkerhill
80128	November	Glasgow Corkerhill
80129	December	Glasgow Polmadie
80130	December	Glasgow Polmadie

From Swindon Works
Standard 2-6-2T 3MT

No	Month to Traffic	First Allocation
82032	January	Barry
82033	January	Newton Abbot
82034	January	Newton Abbot
82035	March	Barry
82036	April	Barry
82037	April	Swansea Victoria
82038	May	Worcester
82039	May	Swansea Victoria
82040	May	Barry
82041	June	Barry

No	Month to Traffic	First Allocation
82042	June	Barry
82043	June	Barry
82044	August	Barry

From Crewe Works
Standard 2-10-0 9F

No	Month to Traffic	First Allocation
92020	May	Wellingborough
92021	May	Wellingborough
92022	May	Wellingborough
92023	May	Wellingborough
92024	June	Wellingborough
92025	June	Wellingborough
92026	June	Wellingborough
92027	June	Wellingborough
92028	July	Wellingborough
92029	July	Wellingborough
92042	January	New England
92043	January	March
92044	January	March
92045	February	Wellingborough
92046	February	Wellingborough
92047	February	Wellingborough
92048	February	Wellingborough
92049	March	Wellingborough
92050	August	Toton
92051	August	Toton
92052	August	Toton
92053	September	Toton
92054	September	Toton
92055	September	Toton
92056	October	Toton
92057	October	Toton
92058	October	Toton
92059	October	Toton
92060	November	Tyne Dock
92061	November	Tyne Dock
92062	November	Tyne Dock
92063	November	Tyne Dock
92064	December	Tyne Dock
92065	December	Tyne Dock
92066	December	Tyne Dock
92067	December	Doncaster
92068	December	Doncaster
92069	December	Doncaster

Diesel Locomotives

No	Month to Traffic	First Allocation
Hudswell Clarke Diesel Mechanical 0-6-0		
11116	December	Birkenhead
Drewry Diesel Mechanical 0-6-0 Class 04		
11121	July	London Stratford
11122	July	London Stratford
11123	July	London Stratford
11124	August	Norwich
11125	August	Norwich
11126	August	Norwich
11127	September	London Stratford
11128	September	London Stratford

No	Month to Traffic	First Allocation
11129	September	London Stratford
11130	September	London Stratford
11131	October	London Stratford
11132	October	London Stratford
11133	November	London Stratford
11134	November	London Stratford
11135	December	London Stratford
Hunslet Diesel Mechanical 0-6-0 Class 05		
11136	October	Ipswich
11137	October	Ipswich

No	Month to Traffic	First Allocation	No	Month to Traffic	First Allocation

Hunslet Diesel Mechanical 0-4-0

No	Month to Traffic	First Allocation
11502	January	Ipswich

North British Loco Co Diesel Hydraulic 0-4-0

No	Month to Traffic	First Allocation
11703	August	Dundee West
11704	September	Edinburgh St Margarets
11705	September	Edinburgh St Margarets
11706	December	Edinburgh St Margarets

Class 08 Diesel Electric 0-6-0
From Derby Works

No	Month to Traffic	First Allocation
13097	January	Norwood Junction
13098	January	Norwood Junction
13099	January	Norwood Junction
13100	January	Norwood Junction
13101	February	Norwood Junction
13102	February	Severn Tunnel Junction
13103	February	Severn Tunnel Junction
13104	February	Severn Tunnel Junction
13105	February	Banbury
13106	March	Banbury
13107	March	Banbury
13108	March	Banbury
13109	March	Banbury
13110	March	Banbury
13111	March	Stourbridge Junction
13112	April	Shrewsbury
13113	April	Shrewsbury
13114	April	Shrewsbury
13115	April	Shrewsbury
13116	April	Shrewsbury

BR/Crossley Diesel Electric 0-6-0
From Derby Works

No	Month to Traffic	First Allocation
13117	June	Toton
13118	June	Toton
13119	June	Toton
13120	July	Toton
13121	August	Toton
13122	September	Toton
13123	September	Toton
13124	September	Toton

BR/Blackstone Diesel Electric 0-6-0 Class 10
From Darlington Works

No	Month to Traffic	First Allocation
13137	March	Hull Dairycoates
13138	March	Hull Dairycoates
13139	March	Hull Dairycoates
13140	April	Hull Alexandra Dock
13141	May	Hull Alexandra Dock
13142	June	Hull Dairycoates
13143	June	Hull Dairycoates
13144	June	Newport
13145	June	Newport
13146	July	Newport
13147	July	Newport
13148	July	Newport
13149	July	Newport
13150	July	Newport
13151	August	Newport

BR/Blackstone Diesel Electric 0-6-0 Unclassified
From Darlington Works

No	Month to Traffic	First Allocation
13152	February	Immingham
13153	February	Immingham
13154	February	Immingham
13155	February	Immingham
13156	March	Immingham
13157	March	Immingham
13158	March	Immingham
13159	August	Immingham
13160	August	Immingham
13161	September	Immingham
13162	September	London King's Cross
13163	September	London King's Cross
13164	September	London King's Cross
13165	October	London King's Cross
13166	October	London King's Cross

Class 08 Diesel Electric 0-6-0
From Derby Works

No	Month to Traffic	First Allocation
13167	August	Birmingham Saltley
13168	August	Birmingham Saltley
13169	September	Rugby
13170	September	Carlisle Upperby
13171	September	Carlisle Upperby
13172	September	Crewe South
13173	September	Crewe South
13174	September	Crewe South
13175	October	Crewe South
13176	October	Crewe South
13177	October	Chester
13178	October	Chester
13179	October	Derby
13180	October	Derby
13181	October	Derby
13182	October	Bristol St Philips Marsh
13183	October	Bristol St Philips Marsh
13184	October	Bristol St Philips Marsh
13185	November	Bristol St Philips Marsh
13186	November	Bristol St Philips Marsh
13187	November	Bristol St Philips Marsh
13188	November	Severn Tunnel Junction
13189	November	Severn Tunnel Junction
13190	November	Severn Tunnel Junction
13191	November	Wolverhampton Oxley
13192	November	Birmingham Tyseley
13193	November	Shrewsbury
13194	November	Shrewsbury
13195	November	Reading
13196	December	Reading
13197	December	Glasgow Polmadie
13198	December	Glasgow Polmadie
13199	December	Glasgow Polmadie
13200	December	Glasgow Polmadie
13201	December	Glasgow Polmadie
13202	December	Glasgow Polmadie
13203	December	Motherwell
13204	December	Motherwell
13205	December	Motherwell
13206	December	Hamilton

No	Month to Traffic	First Allocation	No	Month to Traffic	First Allocation
From Darlington Works			13224	June	Norwood Junction
13217	April	Norwood Junction	13225	June	Norwood Junction
13218	April	Norwood Junction	13226	July	Norwood Junction
13219	April	Norwood Junction	13227	December	Newport
13220	April	Norwood Junction	13228	December	Middlesbrough
13221	April	Norwood Junction	13229	December	Middlesbrough
13222	June	Norwood Junction	13230	December	Hull Dairycoates
13223	July	Norwood Junction	13231	December	Hull Dairycoates

Diesel Multiple-Units Introduced in 1954 and 1955

No	Month to Traffic	First Allocation	No	Month to Traffic	First Allocation
Derby Lightweight Two-Car DMBT			E79042	1955 July	Norwich
E79000	1954 April	Hammerton Street	E79043	1955 July	Norwich
E79001	1954 April	Hammerton Street	E79044	1955 August	Norwich
E79002	1954 May	Hammerton Street	E79045	1955 August	Norwich
E79003	1954 May	Hammerton Street	E79046	1955 August	Norwich
E79004	1954 May	Hammerton Street			
E79005	1954 May	Hammerton Street	**Metropolitan Cammell Two-Car DMBS**		
E79006	1954 August	Hammerton Street	M79076	1955 December	Bury
E79007	1954 Sept	Hammerton Street	M79077	1955 December	Bury
M79008	1955 January	Carlisle Upperby	M79078	1955 December	Bury
M79009	1955 January	Carlisle Upperby	M79079	1955 December	Bury
M79010	1955 January	Carlisle Upperby	M79080	1955 December	Bury
M79011	1955 January	Carlisle Upperby	M79081	1955 December	Bury
M79012	1955 January	Carlisle Upperby	M79082	1955 December	Bury
M79013	1955 January	Carlisle Upperby			
M79014	1955 January	Carlisle Upperby	**Derby Lightweight Two-Car DMBS**		
M79015	1955 January	Carlisle Upperby	M79118	1955 November	Carlisle Upperby
M79016	1955 January	Carlisle Upperby	M79119	1955 December	Carlisle Upperby
M79017	1955 January	Carlisle Upperby	M79120	1955 December	Carlisle Upperby
M79018	1955 January	Carlisle Upperby	M79121	1955 December	Monument Lane
M79019	1955 January	Carlisle Upperby	M79122	1955 December	Monument Lane
M79020	1955 January	Carlisle Upperby	M79123	1955 December	Monument Lane
E79021	1955 January	Lincoln			
E79022	1955 January	Lincoln	**Derby Lightweight Four-Car DMBS**		
E79023	1955 January	Lincoln	E79150	1955 September	South Gosforth
E79024	1955 February	Lincoln	E79151	1955 September	South Gosforth
E79025	1955 February	Lincoln	E79152	1955 September	South Gosforth
E79026	1955 March	Lincoln	E79153	1955 September	South Gosforth
E79027	1955 March	Lincoln	E79154	1955 September	South Gosforth
E79028	1955 April	Lincoln			
E79029	1955 May	Lincoln	**Derby Lightweight Two-Car DTCL**		
E79030	1955 May	Lincoln	E79250	1955 June	Norwich
E79031	1955 May	Lincoln	E79251	1955 June	Norwich
E79032	1955 May	Lincoln	E79252	1955 June	Norwich
E79033	1955 June	Lincoln	E79253	1955 June	Norwich
E79034	1955 June	Norwich	E79254	1955 June	Norwich
E79035	1955 June	Norwich	E79255	1955 June	Norwich
E79036	1955 June	Norwich	E79256	1955 July	Norwich
E79037	1955 June	Norwich	E79257	1955 July	Norwich
E79038	1955 June	Norwich	E79258	1955 July	Norwich
E79039	1955 June	Norwich	E79259	1955 July	Norwich
E79040	1955 July	Norwich	E79260	1955 August	Norwich
E79041	1955 July	Norwich			

No	Month to Traffic	First Allocation
E79261	1955 August	Norwich
E79262	1955 August	Norwich

Derby Lightweight Four-Car TBT

No	Month to Traffic	First Allocation
E79325	1955 September	South Gosforth
E79326	1955 September	South Gosforth
E79327	1955 September	South Gosforth
E79328	1955 September	South Gosforth
E79329	1955 September	South Gosforth

Derby Lightweight Four-Car TT

No	Month to Traffic	First Allocation
E79400	1955 September	South Gosforth
E79401	1955 September	South Gosforth
E79402	1955 September	South Gosforth
E79403	1955 September	South Gosforth
E79404	1955 September	South Gosforth

Derby Lightweight Two-Car DMCL

No	Month to Traffic	First Allocation
E79500	1954 April	Hammerton Street
E79501	1954 April	Hammerton Street
E79502	1954 May	Hammerton Street
E79503	1954 May	Hammerton Street
E79504	1954 May	Hammerton Street
E79505	1954 May	Hammerton Street
E79506	1954 August	Hammerton Street
E79507	1954 September	Hammerton Street

Derby Lightweight Four-Car DMC

No	Month to Traffic	First Allocation
E79508	1955 September	South Gosforth
E79509	1955 September	South Gosforth
E79510	1955 September	South Gosforth
E79511	1955 September	South Gosforth
E79512	1955 September	South Gosforth

Derby Lightweight Two-Car DTCL

No	Month to Traffic	First Allocation
M79600	1955 January	Carlisle Upperby
M79601	1955 January	Carlisle Upperby
M79602	1955 January	Carlisle Upperby
M79603	1955 January	Carlisle Upperby
M79604	1955 January	Carlisle Upperby
M79605	1955 January	Carlisle Upperby
M79606	1955 January	Carlisle Upperby
M79607	1955 January	Carlisle Upperby
M79608	1955 January	Carlisle Upperby
M79609	1955 January	Carlisle Upperby

No	Month to Traffic	First Allocation
M79610	1955 January	Carlisle Upperby
M79611	1955 January	Carlisle Upperby
M79612	1955 January	Carlisle Upperby
E79613	1955 January	Lincoln
E79614	1955 January	Lincoln
E79615	1955 January	Lincoln
E79616	1955 February	Lincoln
E79617	1955 February	Lincoln
E79618	1955 March	Lincoln
E79619	1955 March	Lincoln
E79620	1955 April	Lincoln
E79621	1955 May	Lincoln
E79622	1955 May	Lincoln
E79623	1955 May	Lincoln
E79624	1955 May	Lincoln
E79625	1955 June	Lincoln

Metropolitan Cammell Two-Car DTCL

No	Month to Traffic	First Allocation
M79626	1955 December	Bury
M79627	1955 December	Bury
M79628	1955 December	Bury
M79629	1955 December	Bury
M79630	1955 December	Bury
M79631	1955 December	Bury
M79632	1955 December	Bury

Derby Lightweight Two-Car DTCL

No	Month to Traffic	First Allocation
M79639	1955 November	Carlisle Upperby
M79640	1955 December	Carlisle Upperby
M79641	1955 December	Carlisle Upperby
M79642	1955 December	Monument Lane
M79643	1955 December	Monument Lane
M79644	1955 December	Monument Lane

British United Traction Motor Second Four-Wheel Unit

No	Month to Traffic	First Allocation
M79740	1954 March	Watford

British United Traction Trailer Second Four-Wheel Unit

No	Month to Traffic	First Allocation
M79741	1954 March	Watford

British United Traction Motor Brake Second Four-Wheel Unit

No	Month to Traffic	First Allocation
M79742	1955 January	Watford
M79743	1955 July	Watford
M79744	1955 July	Watford
M79745	1955 July	Watford

Ex-GWR Diesel Railcar Allocations

No		No		No		No		No	
1	81D	10	85A	17	84D	24	82B	31	81C
3	81F	11	87E	18	81D	25	82F	32	85A
4	86A	12	81F	19	85A	26	84D	33	81D
5	85A	13	86A	20	85B	27	81C	34	81C
6	85A	14	84F	21	86A	28	82B	35	82B
7	85A	15	81F	22	84F	29	84D	36	82B
8	84F	16	81D	23	82B	30	86G	38	81D